Fighting Seventeen

Marcus Stewart 04

Fighting Seventeen

A Photographic History of VF-17 in World War II

Lee Cook

Schiffer Military History
Atglen, PA

Author's Note

The author has made every conceivable effort to contact every source possible for information about the squadron. However, he would be extremely interested in hearing from families or relatives of men who served with Fighting 17, or anyone who may have relevant photographs, information, letters, or stories relating to Fighting 17, the Skull and Crossbones Squadron. Any material will be fully credited and referenced to its original source.

Frontispiece: "First Kill for the Jolly Rogers" by Marc Stewart. Lt. Ray Beacham is credited with the first kill for Fighting 17 after an engagement with a Zero on November 1, 1943. Art courtesy Marc Stewart, www.AviationArtbyMarcStewart.com.

Book Design by Ian Robertson.

Library of Congress Control Number: 2011923416

Printed in China.
ISBN: 978-0-7643-3664-5

We are interested in hearing from authors with book ideas on related topics.

Published by Schiffer Publishing Ltd.
4880 Lower Valley Road
Atglen, PA 19310
Phone: (610) 593-1777
FAX: (610) 593-2002
E-mail: Info@schifferbooks.com.
Visit our web site at: www.schifferbooks.com
Please write for a free catalog.
This book may be purchased from the publisher.
Please include $5.00 postage.
Try your bookstore first.

In Europe, Schiffer books are distributed by:
Bushwood Books
6 Marksbury Avenue
Kew Gardens
Surrey TW9 4JF, England
Phone: 44 (0) 20 8392-8585
FAX: 44 (0) 20 8392-9876
E-mail: Info@bushwoodbooks.co.uk.
Visit our website at: www.bushwoodbooks.co.uk
Try your bookstore first.

Contents

Fighting 17 Roster ... 6
Acknowledgments ... 8
Foreword ... 10
Introduction ... 11

Chapter 1: In Memoriam ... 13
Chapter 2: Corpus Christi ... 56
Chapter 3: Chance Vought ... 63
Chapter 4: Fighting 17 in Training ... 71
Chapter 5: Shakedown Cruise ... 88
Chapter 6: Ondongo - Place of Death ... 94
Chapter 7: Carriers and Ships ... 110
Chapter 8: Life in the Islands ... 119
Chapter 9: Ground Crew ... 128
Chapter 10: Carrier Air Service Unit (C.A.S.U.) 12 ... 139
Chapter 11: New Zealand Fighter Wing ... 148
Chapter 12: Bougainville and Rabaul ... 154
Chapter 13: On with the War ... 190
Chapter 14: Life After Combat ... 213
Chapter 15: Fighting 17 in Color ... 252
Chapter 16: The Skull and Crossbones Lives On ... 263

Appendix A: Victory Credits ... 271
Appendix B: War Diary ... 276
Appendix C: Tactical Organization ... 280
Appendix D: Roster of the U.S.S. *Bunker Hill* ... 282

Bibliography ... 283

Fighting 17 Roster

The forty-three pilots who went into combat with Fighting 17 in October 1943 at Ondongo, New Georgia, are as follows:

Name	Nickname or Known as
Robert Sidney Anderson	*Andy*
Bradford Warren Baker	*Brad*
Shelton Ray Beacham	*Ray*
Thaddeus Richard Bell	*Thad, Juggy*
John Thomas Blackburn	*Tom, Tommy*
George Franklin Bowers	*Hap*
Howard McClain Burriss	*Mac, Teeth*
Jack M. Chasnoff	*Jack*
Lemuel Doty Cooke	*Lem*
Paul Cordray	*Paul*
Daniel Gerald Cunningham	*Danny*
Merl William Davenport	*Butch, Mother*
Clyde Howard Dunn	*Clyde*
John Orrin Ellsworth	*Fatso*
Doris Clyde Freeman	*Chico*
Carl Wilson Gilbert	*Gil*
Clement Dexter Gile	*Timmy*
Douglas Hugo Charles Gutenkunst	*Doug*
James Alex Halford, Jr.	*Lucky Jim*
Roger Richards Hedrick	*Rog*
Robert Hugh Hill	*Windy*

Name	Nickname or Known as
Robert Roy Hogan	*Bob*
Donald Allan Innis	*Stinky*
Robert Hal Jackson	*Hal*
Frank Andrew Jagger	*Andy*
John Henry Keith	*John*
Louis Marsden Kelley	*Lou*
Ira Cassius Kepford	*Ike*
Tom Killefer	*Tom, TK*
John Milton Kleinman	*Johnny*
Thomas Frederick Kropf	*Tom*
Melvin Monroe Kurlander	*Mel, Kurly*
William Lee Landreth	*Country*
Donald Thomas Malone	*Don*
Harry Andrew March, Jr.	*Dirty Eddie*
Earl May, Jr.	*Earl*
William Preston Meek	*Bill*
Charles Alfred Pillsbury	*Chuck*
Wilbert Peter Popp	*Beads, Peter*
Mills Schanuel	*Mills*
Walter John Schub	*Wally*
Frederick James Streig	*Big Jim*
Whitfield Carlisle Wharton, Jr.	*Whit*

Fighting 17 Roster

The following replacement pilots reported to Fighting 17 in December 1943 and January 1944 for the second tour:

Kenneth Paul Babkirk	*Ken*
Edward Ellsworth Beeler	*Ed*
Harold James Bitzegaio	*Bitz*
Oscar Ivan Chenoweth, Jr.	*Oc*
Mervin Ward Cole	*Ward, Ace*
Jack Evans Diteman	*Jack*
Percy Eugene Divenney	*Perce*
James Cass Dixon	*Jimmy*
Richard Martin Einar, Jr.	*Dick*
James Warren Farley	*Snark*
Louis Allen Fitzgerald	*Lou*
George Monteith Keller, Jr.	*George, Dumbo*
Harvey Matthews	*Matty*
James Miller	*Jim*
Robert Mims	*Bobby*
Donald Roy McQueen	*Don, Red*
Lionel Thiel McQuiston	*Mac*
Earle Carpenter Peterson, Jr.	*Pete*
Harmond Becker Richardson, Jr.	*Hink*
C. L. Smith	
John Malcolm Smith	*Smitty*
Jack Raby Travers	*Jack*

The following officers served with Fighting 17 during the training period (January 1943 to August 1943):

Robert Wayne Kieffer	*Bob*
Raymond Webster Ferguson	*Ray*
Fred Davies Henderson, Jr.	*Tuffy*
William Edward Maher	*Bill*
William Burnham	*Bill*
Sam Carlton	*Sam*
Marvin Russell Novak	*Russ*
Edward Bennett Turner	
John Hailey Cantrell	
Norman Dale Kellogg	

Non-Flying Officers

Glenn Franklin Hall	*Glenn*
Basil Duke Henning	*Duke*
Lyle Franklyn Herrmann	*Doc*
Lester Raymond Kincaid	*Les*
R. L. Mills	

Acknowledgments

Since I first started researching Fighting 17 in 1993 I have had the continued support, encouragement, and help of a great many people. I would like to acknowledge the magnificent co-operation and assistance of all the members of Fighting Squadron Seventeen and their families who have provided photographs, information, tapes, and other valuable documents to make this book possible. I am indebted to "the Skipper," Tom Blackburn, for encouraging me to pursue my research into his great squadron. His passing drove me on further to fulfil the publication of the squadron history to the best of my ability.

"Country" and "Ginger" Landreth took me under their wing and helped me to press on over the years, and I thank them for their help, support, and faith.

I would like to thank the veterans and families whose contact resulted from Tom's roster in 1993, many of whom I first met at Oshkosh in 1994 and at two further reunions, for their support and continued assistance to this day. This includes the men who served alongside Fighting 17 and who worked with them in training or ground support roles.

"Andy" and Betty Jagger, Wilbert Peter "Beads" and Jean Popp, Wally and Maureen Schub, Rear Admiral Roger Hedrick, Mills and Marilee Schanuel, Mel "Kurly" Kurlander, Hal and Barbara Jackson, Jack and Alice Chasnoff, Dan and Ruthie Cunningham, Robert "Windy" Hill, Tom and Carolyn Killefer, "Hap" and Alice Bowers, Harold and Betty Bitzegaio, "Big Jim" and Vera Streig, Lennard "Red" Edmisten, George and Laurie Mauhar, Everett Lanman, Joy Anderson Schroeder, Boone Guyton, Alison Henning, Kraeg and Tim Kepford, Therese Smith, Joyce Wharton, Jim and Jan Dixon, "Hap" and Marje Harlow, Don McQueen, Charles E. Dixon, Ray and Milly DeLeva, and Marvin "Russ" Novak.

The family members and others associated with Fighting Seventeen have made a huge contribution, providing records, letters, anecdotes, and photographs, many of which have not been published before. So many have helped, and I would like to extend my sincere thanks to Alexandra Bowers, John Chasnoff, Katie Cole, Del and Pat May, Ned Beeler, Rick and Cathy Einar, Dora Taylor, Lloyd Taylor, Alida Christinaz, Mike DeBorde, Steve Smith, Barney Smith and the Smith family, Joni Logsdon Baker, Dale Logsdon, Mike Rowland, Frances Kleinman Rowland, Sally and Del Reeves, Phil Schanuel, Toni and Rob Sennott, John and Mary Deveney, Mark Blackburn, Paul Blackburn, Randolph Soggs, Jack Burriss, Kelly Burriss, Bob Burriss, Jay Burriss, Mac and Dorothy Burriss, Judy Chasnoff Smith, John and Adele Chenoweth, Chip Chenoweth, John M. Cordray, Sr., John M. Cordray, Jr., Don and Sue Arvin, Joanie Diteman, Carol Lifton, Ken Edmisten, Gwen Ferguson, Patrick and Lori Kirk, Larry Gilbert, Ralph Gilbert, Ann Phillip, Phillip Gutenkunst, Rick Hedrick, Cameron Henning, Morgan Henning Stebbins, William Peake Henning, Jerry Halford, Bill and Bobbie Askew and the Keith family, Robert W. Kieffer, Jr., Pat Kieffer, Wade Killefer, Keith Kurlander, Barby Neary, Earl and Josie Malone, Betsy Bryant, Katherine Ritter, Susan Ritter, Bob Peterson, Earle Peterson III, Deanna Beacham, Jamie Blackburn, John Pillsbury, George S. Pillsbury, Greg Winterrowd, Dave and Janice Streig, Mark and Janece Streig, Robin Litwin, Bill Birk, Dolores Fina, John P. Kepchia, Forrest Bean, John Hussey, Robert P. Cooke III and Nancy Cooke, Harmond Richardson IV and the Richardson family, Donna Kerr, Michael Shaw, Della McQuiston, Ray Fitzgerald, Jeanne Anne Fitzgerald, Kevin Fitzgerald, Yatidi Fitzgerald, Sarah Bradshaw Lewis, Paul Matthews, Cindy Spriggs, Kimberley Cunningham, George R. Edwards, Lyle Herrmann, Jr., Roger and Mary Stehman, John Kincaid, Linda Landreth Phelps, Mary Kelley, Ellen Babkirk Kelley Ray, Kenneth John Kelley, Sidney Buff, Jim Bitzegaio, Greg Pruis, Peter S. Guyton, Henry Sakaida, Bill Owens, Kay and Larry Fechter, Andrew Layton, Martin Kauper, Keith Hoey, Phyllis Garrett, Joseph G. Nason, Christine Silengo, Barbara Cantrell Spalding, and Lisa Turner Maddox. All have helped me above and beyond the call of duty.

Great assistance was provided to me by Robert Lawson, whose photograph collection is at the National Museum of Naval Aviation, Pensacola, Roger Mott, Bob Pisz, Curt Lawson, and Bill Addison at NMNA. Jan Jacobs Managing Editor, the Hook magazine, and Doug Siegfried at Tailhook Association, Frank Olynyk for his victory credit information, and the staff at the National Personnel Records Center in St. Louis, Missouri, and National Archives and Records Administration, Ariana Jacob at the Department of the Navy, Naval History and Heritage Command, Archives Branch and the Naval Academy Annapolis, Maryland.

My research covered the globe, and with a strong input from New Zealand. My thanks to Heidi Kuglin, Archivist and Access Services, Archives New Zealand, Matthew O'Sullivan, Keeper of Photographs at Air Force Museum of New Zealand, Wellington Library, New Zealand, Jenni Chrisstoffels Research Librarian, Turnbull Library Pictures, Alexander Turnbull Library, Wellington, New Zealand.

Neill Atkinson Acting Chief Historian, Ministry for Culture and Heritage New Zealand – Te Manatu Taonga and Jason Darwin Project Manager and Director (Acting), New Zealand Electronic Text Centre.

A number of museums and associations have provided assistance. Pete Elizondo and Dick Atkins at Vought Heritage, John Ratzenburger and Harry Bridges at Dare County Regional Airport Museum, Al Hiegel and John Lambert, *U.S.S. Independence* Reunion Group and Harold Rubin at the American Fighter Aces Association, Roger Mansell Director, Center For Research, Allied POWS under the Japanese.

A number of aviation artists have contributed their excellent work for this book, including: Marc Stewart, Steven Heyen, Domenic DeNardo, Wade Meyers, Sam and Mindy Lyons, and Len Krenzler. Paul Bowen provided some of his wonderful photos of Corsairs that still fly in Fighting 17 colors.

My thanks to Brad Hood of Vintage Fighters and Jerry Yagen of the Fighter Factory, award winning restorers of vintage aircraft, including "Bent-Wing Birds."

Cdr. B. M. "BG" Garrison Commanding Officer, Strike Fighter Squadron 103 for the present day "Skull and Crossbones" photographs.

Bob Biondi and Ian Robertson at Schiffer publishing for encouraging my first book, and also their support for this latest one.

My thanks also to my family, Martin and Millie Cook, Audrey and Derek Barnett, and to my wife Jackie, a constant source of inspiration and support during what has been a long, arduous process getting the book completed. To my daughters Charli, Natalie, and Lani for putting up with the "Dad's on the laptop again" moments - lots of them!

To my brother Howard and his wife Peta for their constant support, inspiration, advice, and meticulous attention to detail with this project.

I hope I have managed to include everyone who has helped, but to anyone who has assisted me and I have missed a profound thank you.

Foreword

When Lee Cook invited me to contribute the foreword to *Fighting 17: A Pictorial History*, I was pleased and honored to accept the opportunity to do so. I have been in correspondence with Lee for seventeen years since he started researching Fighting Seventeen's history.

Following on from his excellent book *The Skull and Crossbones Squadron - VF-17 in World War II*, Lee has managed to compile the most extensive collection of photographs of Fighting 17 yet seen, to tell the story in photographs.

A likable group of pros from the beach towns of California to the Carolina coast and spots in-between.

Ably led by Commanders Tom Blackburn and Roger Hedrick, and supported by a highly trained cadre of enlisted personnel, my comrades performed their duties with murderous intensity. But through it all, they maintained an irreverent (if somewhat mordant) sense of humor.

Looking back over the years, that which still resonates:

"*Approaching Target: Charge guns; bandits sighted: red brown shapes slice through our formations: full rpm throttle: radio comes alive; blue grey sky abruptly mottled with black puffs and crimson fires; Tally Ho!*"

Mills Schanuel

Mills Schanuel
Fighting Seventeen

Introduction

After the publication of my first book in 1998, *The Skull and Crossbones Squadron - VF-17 in World War II*, I received some photographs which unfortunately were too late to include in the book. I had talked about the possibility of a pictorial history with Schiffer Publishing in 1997 and they supported the concept. I continued my research for many years, and in the end it became a full time occupation. With the improved access provided in current times by the internet the focus of my research was locating families of Fighting 17 veterans. This continues to this day.

I managed to locate many family members who have since contributed greatly to this project and given me their full support. As with my previous book, my primary sources are the squadron members and their families, and official sources, such as personnel and archival records.

With access to some unique original material I was able to find out what happened to every original member of the squadron and all of the replacement pilots who went into combat with Fighting 17.

In my seventeen years of research I have located hundreds of previously unpublished photographs and information from the families of men who served with Fighting 17.

I particularly wanted to honor the men who died in training, combat, or shortly after their service with Fighting 17.

One of the most time consuming tasks was to verify photographs coming from a range of different sources and credit them correctly. Every endeavour has been made to ensure that this is the case.

I have had the great pleasure of access to the collection that Chance Vought sent to every member of Fighting 17 in June 1944 after they came back from overseas; this was as a thank you from Vought for their considerable efforts.

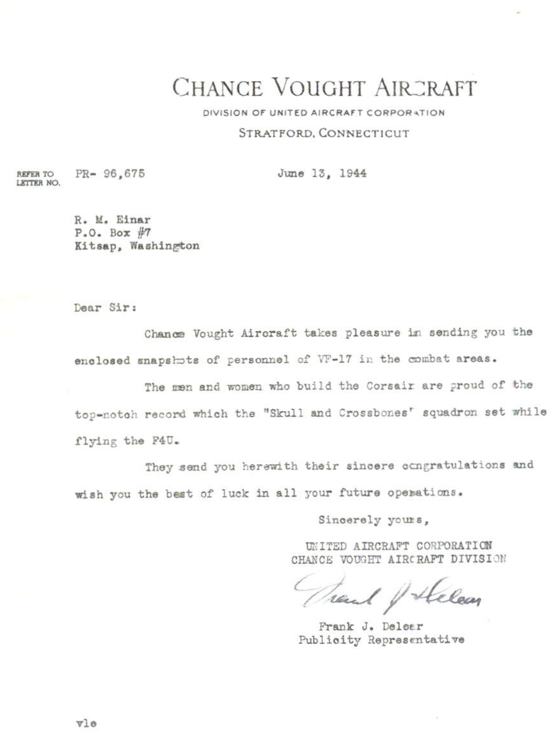

CHANCE VOUGHT AIRCRAFT
DIVISION OF UNITED AIRCRAFT CORPORATION
STRATFORD, CONNECTICUT

REFER TO LETTER NO. PR- 96,675

June 13, 1944

R. M. Einar
P.O. Box #7
Kitsap, Washington

Dear Sir:

Chance Vought Aircraft takes pleasure in sending you the enclosed snapshots of personnel of VF-17 in the combat areas.

The men and women who build the Corsair are proud of the top-notch record which the "Skull and Crossbones" squadron set while flying the F4U.

They send you herewith their sincere congratulations and wish you the best of luck in all your future operations.

Sincerely yours,

UNITED AIRCRAFT CORPORATION
CHANCE VOUGHT AIRCRAFT DIVISION

Frank J. Deleer
Publicity Representative

vle

The collection included numerous "*snap shots*" taken in the Solomon Islands, although many have passed into private collectors' hands over the years. Chance Vought were delighted with Fighting 17's efforts, which had proved the Corsair to the U.S. Navy. I have credited the photos to Chance Vought as the correct source for these photos; however, they often appear in other publications elsewhere credited to other collections.

Due to Fighting 17's record breaking success in the Solomon Islands in 1943 and 1944 they were besieged by photographers and reporters, and many photos in this book date from this time. All the other photos in this book are from original sources, such as relatives of Fighting 17 pilots and their families, and from official archive and U.S. Navy sources.

I take great pride in the accuracy of these photos, none of which have been bought on auction sites, but were sought through diligent investigation.

With considerable attention to detail I have researched social security records, marriage records, and national census records, all of which are in the public domain, to try and locate as many of the men who served with Fighting 17 and their families as possible. I have had the approval, support, and help from more than fifty families of the men who served with Fighting 17, with over one hundred contributors in total.

Following contact with family members, I was then able to contact the National Personnel Records Center and National Archives and Records Administration for the service information of the men who served, which gave me as complete a picture of their service and achievements with Fighting 17 as was possible to achieve. I then added this information to the extensive collection of photographs I had accumulated for this book.

This work is the culmination of seventeen years of dedicated and meticulous research, and a goal I have had to honor the men of Fighting 17, from the moment of my first contact with "the Skipper," Tom Blackburn, and since I first saw a Fighting 17 marked F4U Corsair taxi in front of me all those years ago.

1

In Memoriam

I was not born when World War II broke out in 1939, and I often wonder what sort of world it would have been had Germany and Japan been allowed to do as they pleased. Thankfully young men all over the free world took up arms against this tyranny and fought for their countries to remain free. As is the nature of warfare, many men die not only in combat, but also in training or in accidents. Although they were young and inexperienced they were brave and courageous.

This chapter is dedicated to the men of Fighting 17 who died in combat, training, or accidents during or just after the war.

I have been blessed with a loving wife, three lovely daughters, a fulfilling life, and several careers. Many young men died before their time and never had the chance to live a long life or achieve what they would have liked to. They had dreams unfulfilled and so much to live for. I can relate to what it feels like to lose a brother aged twenty-one, and although my brother did not die in combat or the service of his country, his tragic loss was felt by all the members of our family just as the men, who in the pages that follow, were missed by their loved ones. For the families who were informed of pilots missing in action, they could face an agonizing wait of years until they had confirmation of what happened to their loved ones.

Doug Gutenkunst, "Big Jim" Streig and "Tuffy" Henderson in the spring of 1943 on the beach at Nags Head, North Carolina. *Courtesy the Chasnoff Family.*

Ensign Fred Davies "Tuffy" Henderson, Jr.
Plane Crash August 24, 1943

Ensign Henderson's call sign was "Tuffy," and this was how he was known by the squadron. He had been with Fighting 17 since it was formed in January 1943. He was born on August 26, 1915, in Beeville, Texas, and prior to joining the Navy in 1942 was studying for a Bachelor of Science Degree in Petroleum Engineering.

Fred Davies "Tuffy" Henderson, Jr., pictured in January 1942. "Tuffy" was a founder member or "Plank Owner" of the squadron when it was first commissioned on January 1, 1943. *Courtesy U.S. Navy photo.*

He trained at N.A.S. Corpus Christi, Texas, and accepted his appointment as an Ensign in October 1942. He was a popular member of the squadron and had become very much part of the team.

On August 24, 1943, shortly before the squadron departed for combat, "Tuffy" and five shipmates were practicing gunnery runs on a towed sleeve. He and Ensign Bill Maher made an approach, both focusing on the target sleeve at the same time, unaware of each other's presence, neither seeing the other and continuing on until they collided. When the aircraft came apart neither pilot left their aircraft, but crashed into the sea about twenty miles west of

Oceana, Virginia. After an extensive search by boats at the scene of the accident, carried out immediately after the crash, neither pilot nor aircraft could be recovered.

Ensign Henderson was awarded the American Campaign Medal and WWII Victory Medal.

William Edward Maher from Brooklyn, New York, who joined Fighting 17 in the spring of 1943. He died in a mid - air collision with "Tuffy" Henderson on August 24, 1943. *Courtesy U.S. Navy photo.*

Ensign William Edward Maher
Plane Crash August 24, 1943

Ensign Bill Maher was involved in the same accident as "Tuffy" Henderson. Born on December 1, 1920, in Brooklyn, New York, he was educated at N.Y.U. School of Commerce. He enlisted in the Navy in March 1942 and was accepted as an Aviation Cadet in July 1942. In January 1943 he accepted his appointment as an Ensign and reported to Fighting 17 in April 1943. Ensigns Henderson and Maher were flying F4U-1s as part of a practice gunnery flight on August 24, 1943, and were making high side and overhead gunnery runs on a target sleeve towed at 9000 feet. At 11:30, on a simultaneous gunnery run at the target, he collided at 8500 feet with "Tuffy" Henderson. One aircraft exploded on impact, the other shearing off its starboard wing, and crashed into the sea twenty miles west of Oceana, Virginia.

Aviators at N.A.S. Melbourne, April 12, 1943. Back Row L – R, standing: Ens. Baker, Ens. Maher, Ens. Jagger, and Ens. Ellsworth. Front Row L-R: Ens. Hill, Lt. Hoffman, and Ens. Wharton, Jr. From this training class only the instructor Lt. Hoffman did not serve with Fighting 17. *Courtesy Tailhook Collection / National Archives.*

The surrounding area was searched by aircraft and boats, but neither pilots nor aircraft were recovered.

Ensign Maher was awarded the American Campaign Medal and WWII Victory Medal.

John Henry Keith from Bronson, Kansas, in January 1942. *Courtesy U.S. Navy photo.*

Lt. (jg) John Henry
Keith Missing in Action November 1, 1943

Johnny Keith was a founder member or "Plank Owner" of the squadron when it was formed on January 1, 1943. He was born on October 30, 1921, in Bourbon County, Kansas, and educated at Fort Scott Junior College and High School. His scholastic record was excellent, and he was regarded as an excellent school citizen. On April 16, 1942, he entered flight training at N.A.S. Corpus Christi, and completed his training at N.A.S. Miami. In October 1943 he accepted his appointment as an Ensign.

On November 1, 1943, John's aircraft was hit by anti-aircraft fire over Kulitunai Harbor, Shortland Island. As a result of the damage he sustained he was forced to make a water landing about fifteen miles S.E. of Faisi Island. He was seen to get out of his plane, but was not seen with his raft. By the time the pilots had landed and reported that Keith had ditched his plane it was too dark to attempt a rescue mission. Jim Halford, with the attack flight at Kulitunai Harbor, had called Eskimo Base (Barakoma) five times, to request that a Dumbo (flying boat) be sent out on a rescue. The pilots were told that there would be an attempt to rescue Lt. (jg) Keith with a Dumbo in the morning. The next morning Operations said that all available fighters were being used for cover, and that they could not send a rescue Dumbo unescorted. It was left to Fighting 17 to initiate searches, and on November 2, 1943, Lt. Bell's division carefully searched from 09:15 to 11:15 in the area around the spot where Keith went down. However, despite excellent search weather they could find no trace of him. Further searches were carried out over the next two days but they were unsuccessful, and Lt. (jg) Keith was never seen again.

John Keith in early 1942 during his flight training. He was one of many Fighting 17 pilots who trained at N.A.S. Corpus Christi, Texas. *Courtesy the Keith Family Collection.*

John Keith in winter of 1942 as a young Ensign. *Courtesy the Keith Family Collection.*

John Keith with family members taken on the farm where John's parents lived, L – R: Sister Dottie, Brother James, Mother Leola and John in his uniform. *Courtesy the Keith Family Collection.*

Ensign John Keith with his girlfriend Betty, who was a school teacher. *Courtesy the Keith Family Collection.*

John Keith graduated as an Ensign in October 1942. *Courtesy the Keith Family Collection.*

In one of the last letters he wrote home, dated October 10, 1943, he said:

"Today the squadron had the day off. Probably our last for several long months. We're leaving sometime soon for a station in the combat zone. Where I don't know and don't care.

We've been waiting so long that most of us are eager to get started. You know that I'm not a sailor any longer and haven't been for awhile. It has its advantages and disadvantages.

I finally made lieutenant (jg) as of the first of October - that is if I pass my physical. It means about $25 a month more pay so I think I'll increase my allotment. If I were married there would be $96 more. Think a country gal from Kansas could live on that? Dottie, when you write hereafter alternate your letters with V-mail & air mail. V-mail is a little slower sometimes but more dependable. Be sure you write often. Mail is almost priceless even where I am now. Love, John."

The country gal from Kansas he was referring to was his girlfriend Betty, who was a teacher. Lt. (jg) John Keith was the first member of Fighting 17 to be posted missing in action. Lt. (jg) Keith was awarded the Navy Unit Commendation, Purple Heart, Asiatic - Pacific Campaign Medal, and World War II Victory Medal.

Ensign Bradford Warren Baker
Missing in Action November 17, 1943

Brad Baker was born July 3, 1918, in Los Angeles, California. He was educated at Eastern Washington College of Education in Cheney, Washington, and the University of Idaho from September 1938 to February 1941, where he was a member of the Reserve Officers Training Corps military band. He also attended East Nash College of Education for one year. Whilst at school Brad played in dance bands, and during summer vacations he worked in service stations and as a carpenter and foreman for his father. During the summer of 1940, he built a small home under his father's supervision for Mr Fred Miller at 1020 East 26th Street, Spokane, Washington.

On leaving college in the spring of 1941 he worked for the Spokane Sash and Door Co. of Spokane, Washington, and for a month after worked for Standard Stations Inc. in Spokane, followed by Baker, Oregon, and La Grande, Oregon. He resigned at La Grande and went to work as a mechanic for Boeing Aircraft Co. in Seattle, Washington. From there he went to Portland to enlist in the U.S. Navy.

On March 2, 1942, Brad applied to be a Naval Aviation Cadet, but he was short of three credits for the minimum educational requirements. After careful consideration he was selected due to many other aspects of his application. He became an Aviation Cadet on July 1, 1942, at N.A.S. Jacksonville, and an Ensign on January 1, 1943. He was designated a Naval Aviator on January 5, 1943, and reported to Fighting 17 on May 12, 1943.

He was listed missing in action on November 17, 1943. He was in a flight of eight aircraft attacking a large formation of Japanese fighters over Empress Augusta Bay, Bougainville.

In the letter that follows to Ensign Baker's parents Lt. Cdr. Tom Blackburn wrote about the action from which he went missing:

"My dear Mr and Mrs Baker,

It is my painful duty to confirm the report you have received that your son, Bradford, is missing in action since 17 November when he was out in a flight of eight planes which attacked a large formation of Japanese fighters off Empress Augusta Bay. The battle degenerated into a melee as they always do when a small group pitches into a large one but Brad stayed with section leader Lt. Paul Cordray as long as he could, was last reported by Cordray as being in his proper position covering Cordray as the latter attacked a group of three Jap fighters. As Cordray recovered from the attack Brad was not to be found. When he failed to return to our base we sent out searches which covered the area where the battle had taken place minutely. After three days of searching we were forced to the reluctant conclusion that he was not to be found.

We all miss Brad very deeply, his charm, his unfailing cheerfulness and his humor played a big part in making this a happy squadron. Although he always professed to be frightened out of his wits his actions invariably showed the contrary, when the chips were down we all knew that Brad would be right in there, turning in a brilliant performance. On the 11th November in the face of

Ensign Bradford Warren Baker n October 1943. *Courtesy the Tom Blackburn Collection.*

Back Row L – R: Earl May, Thad Bell, Duke Henning, Tom Killefer, Walter Schub and Lyle Herrmann. Front Row L – R: "Timmy" Gile, Tom Blackburn, Brad Baker, Hal Jackson and "Andy" Anderson. Brad Baker third from left, front row. Taken at Ondongo in November 1943. *Courtesy U.S. Naval Historical Center / M. W. "Butch" Davenport Collection.*

intense anti-aircraft fire from our own forces, without regard for his own safety, he pressed home his attack on a Japanese torpedo plane attacking our forces and shot it down in flames.

The squadron lost a brilliant, gallant pilot and I personally, share in your tremendous loss for Brad was one of my 'sons' as well as yours. If there is anything I can do to help, please let me know.

Sincerely
Tom Blackburn."

Paul Cordray wrote home about the loss of Brad Baker and was devastated by it, quoting "*One minute he was there the next he was not!*"

Ensign Baker was an accomplished musician who played the accordion whenever the squadron got together for a party and to sing songs, and was sorely missed by everyone.

Leading Japanese fighter ace Lt. (jg) Tetsuo Iwamoto took part in the action at Empress Augusta Bay on this day, although it has not been possible to confirm beyond doubt that he was in combat with Ensign Baker.

Ensign Baker was awarded the Air Medal, Purple Heart, American Campaign Medal, Navy Unit Commendation, Asiatic - Pacific Area Campaign Medal with one Bronze Star, and World War II Victory Medal.

Lt. Charles Alfred "Chuck" Pillsbury
Missing in Action November 21, 1943

Charles Alfred "Chuck" Pillsbury was named after his grandfather, who was one of the three founders of what ultimately became The Pillsbury Company (that was purchased by Grand Met in 1989).

His father John S. Pillsbury was one of the Chief Executives of Pillsbury Flour Mills and Director of Northwestern National Bank and Trust Company.

"Chuck" Pillsbury was born on April 4, 1917, in Minneapolis, Minnesota, and educated at St. Paul's School, Concord, NH, and Yale University, graduating in the class of 1939 with a Bachelor of Arts Degree. He quoted "*My college courses included two years of calculus, and one year of advanced algebra, chemistry, physics and engineering drawing.*"

After graduation from Yale in 1939, he worked briefly for a bank and then joined the Navy, becoming an Aviation Cadet on December 2, 1940. He became an Ensign on May 31, 1941, reporting to N.A.S. Pensacola for flight training. He reported on August 10, 1942, to N.A.S. New York for duty with the Aircraft Delivery Unit, and on October 8, 1942, to Naval Proving Grounds, Dahlgren, Virginia.

Charles Alfred "Chuck" Pillsbury was appointed an Ensign on May 31, 1941. He was from the famous flour milling family and was named after the founder of the company. *Courtesy George S. Pillsbury.*

He had converted to fly torpedo bombers and fighters at N.A.S. Corpus Christi before flying a research torpedo bomber that was dropping sea mines in the Bay of Fundy. From there on December 31, 1942, he went to Norfolk to join Fighting 17. On March 1, 1943, he was promoted to Lieutenant.

Lt. Pillsbury's life and exploits are well described in the official records of his school, St. Paul's in Minneapolis:

"*Charles Pillsbury was the third of four brothers who, one or more at a time were continually at the school from 1927 to 1939. He entered the second form in 1930 and graduated in 1935. He won his S.P.S. in football, hockey and rowing, and was awarded the Gordon Medal. In his Sixth Form year he was three times elected to the Council, and he 'supervised' in the Lower. On graduation from Yale, where he played three years on the Varsity hockey team and rowed two years on the Junior Varsity crew, he worked for about a year in the Investment Department of the Northwestern National Bank in Minneapolis.*

In the summer of 1940 he enlisted in the Navy. He received his wings and was commissioned Ensign in June 1941, after training at Pensacola. Assigned to multi-engined patrol bombers, he received additional training at Pensacola and at Corpus Christi, and then was selected as specialized instructor in the use of flying instruments. In July, 1942, he was transferred to Floyd Bennett Field to ferry new types of Navy fighters to the Pacific Coast. That October he was assigned to the Naval Station at Dahlgren, Virginia; thence detached to Debert, Nova Scotia, for experimental work in association with civilian scientists and technicians from the U. S. Naval Ordnance Bureau.

After two months in Nova Scotia, Pillsbury was ordered back to Dahlgren, and shortly thereafter assigned to Fighting Squadron Seventeen, then fitting out in Norfolk, Virginia. This squadron of which Pillsbury became operational officer.

Between 27 October and 21 November, 1943, Lt. Pillsbury made 37 combat sorties, flying 114.8 combat hours. He led 5 strafing missions in the face of intense anti – aircraft fire. His leadership and skill in handling less experienced pilots was a vital factor in squadron efficiency. He has been missing since 21 November when he disappeared while on a strafing mission in the Kahili area."

In his letter home to his friends Connie and Guy on November 17, 1943, Lt. Pillsbury describes some of Fighting 17's movements in the Pacific. This was one of the last letters "Chuck" Pillsbury wrote, as he was listed missing in action on November 21, 1943.

"*Dear Connie and Guy,*

As you might have heard I finally got to Honolulu for a few days. We were stationed at Ford Island but I managed to get to Waikiki usually in time for dinner and spent a few nights first at the Moana and then the Halekilani Hotel which was really a pleasant place.

Tom Killefer and I had two adjoining rooms there and gave a small party which the hotel did not appreciate.

Girls are difficult to get hold of there as you may imagine but I met a few and really had a wonderful time during my short stay.

I was hoping that Hawaii would be our resting place as it is for many aviators but now if we get any rest at all it will probably be either in Sydney or Auckland.

We were attached to one of the new carriers and left Norfolk on one but then after getting to Pearl Harbor via Panama and San Diego we were taken off this ship. After about 6 days in Honolulu we got on a small carrier and were carried south. Now we are on a small island about which no one has ever heard. We are doing a lot of flying but have a hard time finding the Japs. I've only seen them once so far and then did not get close enough for a shot. Some members of the squadron have been lucky and gotten in some scraps. In one flight they got 18 planes and in three others 13. Two days ago some AA gunner put two pretty big holes in my left wing but the plane flew okay. We are lucky in having the best fighter in this area so have not much to worry about and are eager to find some Zeros. We are quartered and fed pretty well but seem to be getting up between 3 & 4 in the morning and fly often 8½ hours per day. On two days I flew over 10 hours which is a little tiring in a single seat fighter.

I do not know what is in store for me but I would just as soon stay out here until the Japs give up.

Give my best to all your family, Connie, and hope to see you and Guy after this conflict is finished.

As ever Chuck."

This is a portrait that his family commissioned in honor of "Chuck" Pillsbury's memory after he was listed missing in action on November 21, 1943. *Courtesy George S. Pillsbury*

On December 21, 1943, Lt. Cdr. Tom Blackburn wrote the following letter to "Chuck's" parents:

"Dear Mr and Mrs Pillsbury,

It is with a deep feeling of personal loss and sorrow that I write to you to confirm the report that your son Charles is missing in action. He and Ensign Hogan were strafing Japanese positions on the southeast end of Bougainville Island on November 21st; they split to avoid a particularly heavy concentration of anti-aircraft guns and when Hogan turned back to re-join he couldn't find Charles. He searched as long as he had sufficient fuel and the squadron subsequently made extensive careful searches for a period of three days. Unfortunately the jungle growth in that area is extremely thick and it is virtually impossible to see even a house even if directly over it.

Charles and I got to be very good friends in the eleven months we worked together, in spite of quite divergent temperaments, and I know I speak for the whole squadron when I say that we could have spared anyone else better. Charles was careful and painstaking in his instructing of the younger pilots who, to a man, worshipped him. We always teased him about his inquisitive mind and love for figuring out and testing the solution of difficult problems but respected, the while, the results and the knowledge obtained.

Charles was a gallant, excellent officer and a 'good shipmate' and I am proud to have had him under my command.

Sincerely

Tom Blackburn."

After the war, during the period January 21 to 23, 1949, a team searched Kangu Hill and adjoining areas in an effort to locate Lt. Pillsbury's aircraft or his remains. Despite their best efforts they were unable to locate Lt. Pillsbury or his Corsair.

Nothing further happened until May 7, 1968, when the Royal Australian Air Force visited the Buin area and located the wreckage of a Corsair which was identified as Lt. Pillsbury's. It was concluded that his death probably occurred upon impact of the aircraft or as a result of anti-aircraft fire prior to impact. His remains were returned to his family, and he is buried in the Pillsbury family plot in Minneapolis.

Lt. Pillsbury was third in command of Fighting 17 and was awarded the Air Medal, Purple Heart, Navy Unit Commendation, American Defense Service Medal, Asiatic - Pacific Area Campaign Medal with one Bronze Star, American Campaign Medal, and World War II Victory Medal.

Kenneth Paul Babkirk at Junior High School. *Courtesy the Babkirk and Bean Family.*

Ensign Kenneth Paul Babkirk
Missing in Action January 17, 1944

Kenneth Paul Babkirk was born in Nashua, New Hampshire, on August 26, 1923. After graduating from the John Bartram High School in January 1941 he took a job as a private chauffeur for an elderly lady. This was his first employment. About three months later, because his services were no longer needed, he became em-

Ensign Kenneth Paul Babkirk in 1943. *Courtesy the Babkirk and Bean Family*

L – R: Ellen Babkirk (Sister), Ida Babkirk (Mother), Kenneth Paul Babkirk and James Babkirk (Father). *Courtesy the Babkirk and Bean Family.*

Ensign Kenneth Paul Babkirk as a young Ensign in 1943. *Courtesy the Babkirk and Bean Family.*

ployed as a slate roofer for a period of about two months. He quit this job in July 1941 and went to work with the United States Engineering Department. In October he was promoted to lineman (Marine), and further promoted in March 1942 to oiler.

He enlisted in the U.S.N.R. on June 16, 1942, and his rating was changed from Seaman Second Class to Aviation Cadet on August 7, 1942. His enlistment was terminated to accept his appointment as an Ensign on June 21, 1943. He then reported to N.A.S. Pensacola and N.A.S. Jacksonville. He reported to Carrier Qualification Training Unit, Glenview, Illinois, on September 20, 1943, and from there was assigned to N.A.S. Quonset Point, Rhode Island, flying with VF (N) 76. He then reported to Fleet Air West Coast, San Diego, and then C.A.S.U. Five on December 6, 1943.

He departed the States on December 7, 1943, and reported to Fighting 17 on December 21, 1943. He was detached from Fighting 17 on January 8, 1944, and assigned to VF-40, at which time he had 360 hours total service flying time. His previous fighter time was approximately 50 hours in the F4F and 180 hours in the F4U, including 20 hours with Fighting 17.

After joining VF-40 on January 8, 1944, Ensign Babkirk had 12.8 hours in familiarization training in the F6F Hellcat. On January 17, 1944, his first combat mission, Ensign Babkirk was

Ensign Kenneth Paul Babkirk on June 25, 1943. *Courtesy the Babkirk and Bean Family.*

flying his Hellcat as close fighter cover for an SBD - TBF strike on Rabaul, New Britain. He failed to return from the mission and was last seen apparently uninjured by Ensign Robert Carlson, on whose wing he was flying, about three - quarters of the way from Simpson Harbor to Cape Gazelle, New Britain, at about 3000 feet. This was after the bombers with their fighter cover had made their run and were on the way to their rally point. At this approximate location, two Kawasaki Ki 61 "Tony's" attacked Carlson and Babkirk; Carlson maneuvered violently, and in evading them did not see Ensign Babkirk after that time. Many TBFs and fighters were in the rear of the position, which Carlson and Babkirk held. Two TBFs were reported as seen to go into the water; however, on the flight's return to base only one TBF was found to be missing. It must therefore be presumed that Babkirk's F6F was mistaken as a downed TBF. No trace of Ensign Babkirk or his aircraft was reported from subsequent flights over the area. The following letter was sent by his squadron mate and good friend Jack Travers to Kenneth Babkirk's parents.

"*Dear Mr Babkirk,*

Since your son Kenneth and I had been such good friends and had been together for so long, I was instructed to take an inventory of his personal effects.

All of us are hoping that there is still some chance that he may be safe. He was certainly a good friend of mine, and I deeply regret his loss. If I may help you in any way he is concerned, I will be glad to do all that is possible.

Sincerely yours

Jack R. Travers
Ensign U.S.N.R."

Just eight days after being detached from Fighting 17, Ensign Kenneth Babkirk was listed as missing in action. He was 20 years old. Ensign Babkirk was awarded the Purple Heart, American Area Campaign Medal, Asiatic - Pacific Area Campaign Medal, Navy Unit Commendation, and World War II Victory Medal.

Ensign Kenneth P. Babkirk at N.A.S. Pensacola, Florida, in 1943. *Courtesy the Babkirk and Bean Family.*

Another view of Ensign Kenneth P. Babkirk at N.A.S. Pensacola, Florida, in 1943. *Courtesy the Babkirk and Bean Family.*

Lt. (jg) James Warren "Snark" Farley
Missing in Action January 26, 1944

James Warren Farley was born in Horton, Kansas, on October 13, 1919. Immediately after graduating from Horton (Kansas) High School he obtained work in the employ of the International Harvester Company at East Moline, Illinois. Later he worked for the Electro-Motive Corporation, a subsidiary of General Motors. He worked for these two companies for a total of two years. He attended St. Ambrose College at Davenport, Iowa, for two years from 1939 to 1941. He then worked as a bus boy in a tavern while attending college.

He became interested in flying and wanted to enlist in the Naval Air Corps, and for this reason took the primary C.A.A. Course at St. Ambrose College in Davenport, Iowa.

On June 13, 1941, Reverend E. J. Kinnavey, Co-ordinator of the Civilian Pilot Training Program at St. Ambrose College, wrote the following recommendation to the Navy for James Farley.

"*This letter is written to recommend to you, James Warren Farley, a student who has completed primary CPT training here at St. Ambrose College.*

James Warren Farley has acquitted himself with an enviable record here in his primary training. Throughout this course he has constantly manifested an enthusiasm about his flying. He is punctual about attendance, responsive to instructions, attentive to corrections. Aviation became an absorbing interest for him and he has devoted his time and ability in mastering this art.

You will find him manly and self-reliant, dependable in any situation and clear in his thinking and judgement. He makes friends easily and will adjust himself to new surroundings with an easy grace. In character he is earnest, sincere and morally upright. His character is beyond reproach.

I can recommend him to you most cordially and without qualification for further consideration in advancing his aviation career. I am confident that he will aquit himself in his advanced training with the same credit with which he has already completed his primary work."

On February 2, 1942, he became an Aviation Cadet, and on 5 February reported to N.A.S. Corpus Christi for training. On July 13, 1942, he was appointed as an Ensign and reported to the Carrier Qualification Training Unit at N.A.S. Glenview. On November 30, 1942, he reported to Escort Scouting Squadron Twenty, which on March 1, 1943 was changed to Composite Squadron Twenty. On 5 March he reported to Fighting Squadron Three, and then on March 29, 1943, reported to Composite Squadron Thirty One. On July 1, 1943, he was promoted to Lt. (jg), and he reported to Composite Squadron Sixteen on July 13, 1943. He was then assigned on September 11, 1943, to Fighting Squadron Eleven, where his Commanding Officer stated "*He has an excellent mental attitude for a combat pilot and his personal character is excellent.*"

James Warren Farley in August 1941 *Courtesy U.S. Navy.*

Lt. (jg) James Warren Farley reported to Fighting 17 on December 10, 1943. He was reported missing in action on January 26, 1944, on his first combat mission with Fighting 17. *Courtesy U.S. Navy.*

On November 21, 1943, he reported to Fighting Squadron Ten, and was assigned to Fighting 17 on December 10, 1943.

Lt. (jg) James Farley was listed missing in action on January 26, 1944, when he made a crash landing in the sea during an attack on Lakunai Airfield, New Britain. It was his first combat mission with Fighting 17.

Lt. (jg) Farley was awarded the Purple Heart, Navy Unit Commendation, Asiatic - Pacific Area Campaign Medal with two Bronze Stars, American Defense Service Medal, and World War II Victory Medal.

Lt. (jg) Robert Roy Hogan
Missing in Action January 26, 1944

Bob Hogan was born on February 10, 1920, in Atlanta, Georgia. He was educated at the University of Denver, Colorado, and was captain of the football team in 1942.

On December 1, 1941, John E. Lawson, Dean of Men at the University of Denver, wrote to the U.S. Navy to support Bob Hogan's application to join:

"*Mr. Hogan has been an outstanding student leader during his three and one half years on the campus. He has participated in intercollegiate athletics, earning his letter in both football and basketball on several occasions, and has also held high office in the various student government organizations. His record is excellent insofar as behaviour is concerned and is satisfactory from an academic standpoint. His qualities of leadership are such that there is no question as to his making an excellent officer.*"

Bob Hogan was accepted as an Aviation Cadet in April 1942 and reported to N.A.S. Corpus Christi for training. He was designated as a Naval Aviator on November 5, 1942. *Courtesy U.S. Navy.*

Bob Hogan in October 1943 at Pearl Harbor. *Courtesy the Tom Blackburn Collection.*

Bob Hogan entered flight training on April 30, 1942, at N.A.S. Corpus Christi, and completed his training at N.A.S. Miami. He was appointed as an Ensign on October 16, 1942, and reported to N.A.S. Miami on November 12, 1942. On December 16, 1942, he was detached from N.A.S. Miami and reported to N.A.S. Jacksonville. On February 10, 1943, he was detached from N.A.S. Jacksonville and reported to the Carrier Qualification Training Unit, Norfolk, and then to Fighting 17.

Bob Hogan was listed missing in action on January 26, 1944, on his first mission of the second tour after a strike on Lakunai Airfield, New Britain. He was never seen again and left a young wife, Verna.

He completed one combat tour with Fighting 17 and is credited with ¼ of a Betty bomber on November 6, 1943, and is also credited with shooting down a Zeke on November 11, 1943.

Lt. (jg) Hogan was awarded the Air Medal, Purple Heart, Asiatic - Pacific Campaign Medal with two Bronze Stars, Navy Unit Commendation, and World War II Victory Medal.

Lt. Thaddeus Richard "Juggy" Bell
Missing in Action January 27, 1944

Thad Bell was born on June 8, 1918, in Montreal, Canada. He was Educated at Stanford University and graduated with an A.B. Degree in Social Science. He applied to join the Navy and had the following to say on his application in September 1940:

"My occupational experience has been limited to two summers work in a lumber camp in British Colombia. I was offered a job by the same camp in the summer of 1939, but refused as I planned an automobile trip around the United States.

I also did traffic work for the Stanford Board of Athletic Control at football games in 1937 and 1938, but I do not think this would be termed occupational."

Bob Hogan coming out of a shelter at Bougainville in January 1944. *Courtesy Vought.*

Bob Hogan in front of a Corsair probably in Norfolk early in 1943. *Courtesy U.S Naval Historical Center / M.W. "Butch" Davenport Collection.*

Thad "Juggy" Bell in 1940. *Courtesy U.S. Navy photo.*

Thad Bell accepted his appointment as an Ensign on July 16, 1941. *Courtesy U.S. Navy photo.*

Thad Bell in the summer of 1941. *Courtesy U.S. Navy photo.*

On September 4, 1940, Frank McLaughlin, President of the Puget Sound Power and Light Company endorsed Thad Bell's application to join the Navy:

"I have been advised that Thaddeus Richard Bell, son of Mr. and Mrs. E. H. Bell, has made application to go to Pensacola for training as a flying cadet. I heartily endorse this young man, whom I have known for some time, and have been intimately associated with his splendid mother and father. As to his character, education and ability I cannot speak too highly. He seems to me to be just the type of young man you would want and be glad to have.

Lt. Thaddeus Richard "Juggy" Bell. He was listed missing in action on January 27, 1944. *Courtesy the Tom Blackburn Collection.*

As State Chairman for Navy Day and as a Director of the Navy League of the United States I have come in contact with a great many officers and personnel of the Navy and have an exceptionally high regard for them and I am always desirous of seeing that the young men they take in are "tops;" therefore I strongly recommend to you the application of Thad Bell."

Thad Bell was successful with his application and joined the U.S. Navy on February 1, 1941, as an Aviation Cadet. On February 10, 1941, he reported to N.A.S. Pensacola for training, where he stood First in a class of 82.

November 1943, Ondongo. Back Row L – R: Paul Cordray, "Ike" Kepford, Thad Bell and "Butch" Davenport. Front Row L – R: Hal Jackson, "Chico" Freeman. *Courtesy Robert Lawson Photograph Collection, National Museum of Naval Aviation / U.S. Navy photo.*

He reported to N.A.S. Miami on July 4, 1941, and accepted his appointment as an Ensign on July 16, 1941. On July 23, 1941, he was designated a Naval Aviator, and on September 2, 1941, he reported to N.A.S. Jacksonville and was promoted to Lt. (jg) on October 1, 1942. On February 4, 1943, he reported to the Carrier Qualification Training Unit, and on completion to Fighting 17. On October 1, 1943, he was promoted to Lieutenant.

Lt. Bell was awarded the Air Medal for "*Outstanding airmanship and gallant devotion to duty.*" Part of the citation stated:

"Lt. Bell was flying cover with his squadron when attacked by more than one hundred Japanese aircraft threatening the security of American surface forces. Fighting against tremendous odds, Lt. Bell held tenaciously on to his targets, flying through intense anti-aircraft fire of his own ships to press home his attack. He succeeded in shooting down two Japanese bombers out of a formation of thirty during the action."

Lt. Bell was listed as missing in action on January 27, 1944, when he failed to return from a combat mission over Rabaul, New Britain.

In addition to the Air Medal, Lt. Bell was awarded the Purple Heart, Navy Unit Commendation, American Defense Service Medal, Asiatic - Pacific Area Campaign Medal with two Bronze Stars, and World War II Victory Medal.

Thad's father, Edward Bell, was the President of the American Can Company, a very large manufacturer of cans. After the war, he invited Mills Schanuel and his wife Marilee out for dinner. Mills and Thad were very close, having completed basic and fighter training together.

When Mills left his job at the San Francisco Examiner, Edward Bell offered Mills a position with the American Can Company, presumably the job that had been saved for his son. Mills declined for personal reasons, but Ed Bell recommended him for a job at Wilbur Ellis, a brokerage firm, which is where Mills worked for the rest of his working life, eventually forming his own firm in Chicago. Ed Bell never recovered from his son's death, and sadly died from the results of alcohol addiction in 1956. Mills named one of his sons Robert Bell Schanuel in honour of his friend.

Lt. (jg) Thomas Frederick Kropf
Missing in Action January 30, 1944

Tom Kropf was born in Wamego, Kansas, on January 26, 1919. His military experience consisted of four semesters of basic Reserve Officers Training Corps training taken at Kansas State College during his Freshman and Sophomore years at that school. His occupational experience was at the Wamego Seed and Elevator Company of Wamego, Kansas, during five summers and during his spare time during the school terms. During this time he drove a truck, worked in the grain elevator, in the ice plant, and in the office as a clerk and bookkeeper. He thus earned his own way through school and college and graduated with a Bachelor of Science Degree in Mechanical Engineering.

Tom was a member of the Flying Tigers of Kansas State, having taken 37 hours flying and received his pilot's license with the Civilian Pilot Training Program. He was a member of the student branch of the Mechanical Engineering Society.

Thomas Frederick Kropf in May 1942. Tom studied at Kansas State College and graduated with a Bachelor of Science Degree in Mechanical Engineering. *Courtesy the Kropf Family.*

Tom joined the Navy on May 4, 1942, as an Aviation Cadet, and on May 14, 1942, he reported to N.A.S. Corpus Christi for training. He was appointed an Ensign on October 16, 1942, and on November 5, 1942, was designated a Naval Aviator. On November 12, 1942, he reported to N.A.S. Miami, and then to N.A.S. Jacksonville for further training. He reported to the Carrier Qualification Training Unit, Norfolk, Virginia, and then Fighting 17 on March 8, 1943. He was promoted to Lt. (jg) on January 1, 1944.

Lt. (jg) Tom Kropf was listed as missing in action on January 30, 1944, when he failed to return from an attack on enemy shipping in Simpson Harbor, Rabaul. *Courtesy the Kropf Family.*

Tom Kropf pictured on October 12, 1943, at Pearl Harbor. *Courtesy the Tom Blackburn Collection.*

L – R: Phillip Gutenkunst, Mother Gertrude and Doug Gutenkunst in 1942. When their father Hugo drowned in 1927 their mother Gertrude raised the two boys alone. *Courtesy the Gutenkunst Family.*

He was reported as missing in action on January 30, 1944, when he failed to return from an attack on enemy shipping in Rabaul Harbor.

On February 1, 1944, Lt. Cdr. Tom Blackburn wrote the following letter to Tom's parents:

"*Dear Mr and Mrs Kropf,*

I write sorrowfully to elaborate on the report that your son Thomas is missing in action since an attack we made on a well defended Japanese stronghold on January 30th. We encountered bad weather and strong fighter opposition and in the fierce battle that raged as they tried to break through us to get at our bombers Tom and his section leader Lt. Mills Schanuel got separated and Tom failed to return to the home base.

It is possible that he is cruising in his life raft or is hiding out in the jungle but, frankly the chances are against it.

Tom is a fine courageous officer whose work in the squadron has been excellent and we miss him keenly. We join you in praying that he'll return and soon. You may be sure that any word of him will be sent on to you immediately. If I can be of any assistance please do not hesitate to write.

Very sincerely
J. T. Blackburn."

Lt. (jg) Kropf was awarded the Navy Unit Commendation, Purple Heart, Asiatic - Pacific Campaign Medal with two Bronze Stars, and World War II Victory Medal.

In Wamego City Cemetery today can be found the Kropf family plot, including graves of his parents and two brothers and Tom's memorial stone. His sister is also buried near that plot with her husband.

Lt. (jg) Douglas Hugo Charles Gutenkunst
Plane Crash January 30, 1944

Douglas was born on January 17, 1919, in Owen Sound, Canada. The name Douglas came from his mother's maiden name, Hugo from his father, and Charles from his grandfather. Douglas attended Hartford Grade School and University School of Milwaukee,

DEPARTMENT OF THE NAVY
Date 8 Oct., 1942
NAVAL AVIATOR No. C-60
This Certifies that
Douglas H.C. GUTENKUNST
Ensign, A-V(N), USNR
born 17 *day of* Jan., 1919
having fulfilled the conditions prescribed by the United States Navy Department, was appointed a
NAVAL AVIATOR
on 8 October, 1942
A.E. MONTGOMERY, Captain
USN, Commandant
Chief of Naval Personnel.
U. S. GOVERNMENT PRINTING OFFICE

Doug Gutenkunst's Naval Aviator's Certificate. *Courtesy the Gutenkunst Family.*

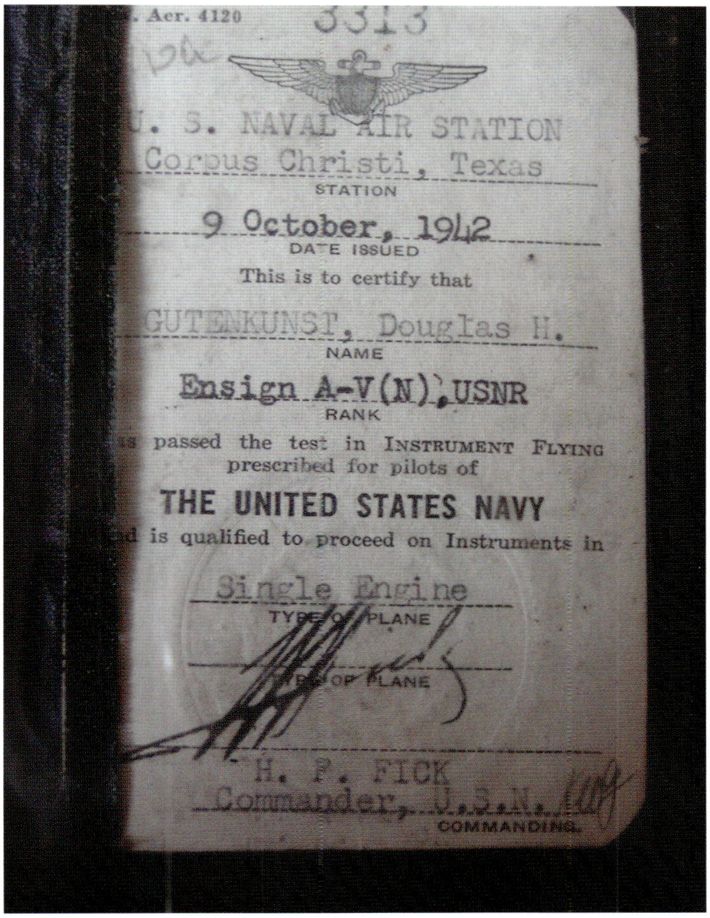

. Aer. 4120 3313

U. S. NAVAL AIR STATION
Corpus Christi, Texas
STATION
9 October, 1942
DATE ISSUED
This is to certify that
GUTENKUNST, Douglas H.
NAME
Ensign A-V(N), USNR
RANK
has passed the test in INSTRUMENT FLYING
prescribed for pilots of
THE UNITED STATES NAVY
and is qualified to proceed on Instruments in
Single Engine
TYPE OF PLANE
TYPE OF PLANE
H. F. FICK
Commander, U.S.N.
COMMANDING

Another view of Doug Gutenkunst's Naval Aviator's Certificate. Like many other Fighting 17 pilots he trained at N.A.S. Corpus Christi. *Courtesy the Gutenkunst Family.*

Doug Gutenkunst in October 1943. He was Tom Blackburn's wingman and scored four confirmed victories with Fighting 17. *Courtesy the Tom Blackburn Collection.*

graduating in 1937. He was a very good student and excelled in athletics. He was the Captain of the basketball team and also Captain of the tennis team.

His father Hugo died in 1927 by drowning when fishing in Pine Lake. His mother Gertrude raised her two boys with Douglas, continuing his education at Brown University in Providence, Rhode Island, and graduating in 1941.

He joined the R.O.T.C. Navy Air Division and was called into the Naval Air Corps, starting his training in Glenview, Illinois. On April 27, 1942, he became an Aviation Cadet, and on April 30, 1942, reported to N.A.S. Corpus Christi, and then to Pensacola for final training. He was commissioned an Ensign on October 1, 1942, and designated Naval Aviator on October 8, 1942. He reported to N.A.S. Miami on October 15, 1942, for further training, and then to the Carrier Qualification Training Unit on November 22, 1942, and on completion to Fighting 17. At some stage during his leave Doug went home and got engaged, and was planning to marry his fiancée, Mary Cudahy, on one of his leaves, although not knowing when. He was promoted to Lt. (jg) on October 1, 1943, and between October 27 and December 1, 1943, Lt. (jg) Gutenkunst flew 44 sorties with a total of 131.1 hours of combat flying. He saw action against the enemy twice on November 1, 1943, and November 11, 1943, and on eight strafing missions encountered heavy anti-aircraft fire six times. On one of these strafing missions on November 28, 1943, he was hit by anti-aircraft fire and forced to ditch.

On his second tour between January 26 and January 30, 1944, he flew five missions over Rabaul and made contact with the enemy each time. On January 26, 1944, he shot down two Zekes, and on January 28, 1944, shot down two more Zekes. Just four days later on January 30, 1944, he was killed in a mid - air collision as he was coming in to land, as described in the following letter

Doug Gutenkunst as a young Ensign in 1942. *Courtesy the Gutenkunst Family.*

Lt. (jg) Doug Gutenkunst on Bougainville in January 1944. *Courtesy U.S. Naval Historical Center / M. W. "Butch" Davenport Collection.*

A view of the cemetery on Bougainville where Doug Gutenkunst was buried. *Courtesy Alexandra Bowers.*

Doug Gutenkunst's grave on Bougainville. He died in a mid - air collision when coming into land after a combat mission on January 30, 1944. *Courtesy Alexandra Bowers.*

Doug Gutenkunst's grave on Bougainville. His remains were returned to the U.S. on June 3, 1948, for final burial as requested by next of kin to be buried at Forest Home Cemetery, Milwaukee. *Courtesy Robert Lawson Photograph Collection, National Museum of Naval Aviation / U.S. Navy photo.*

written on February 1, 1944, by Lt. Cdr. Tom Blackburn to Doug's mother:

"*My Dear Mrs Gutenkunst,*

It is with intense shock and pain that I have to inform you that Douglas was killed on the night of January 30th. We were coming in to land after dark, after an attack on Japanese shipping, and as he swung in to land, another plane, whose pilot had been apparently shot up by Japanese fighters, collided with him in mid - air killing them both instantly.

Doug was recovered from the wreckage and after positive identification had been made by our Doctor, was buried in a simple, impressive Military funeral conducted by a Catholic Navy Chaplain at Army Cemetery, Number One, Bougainville Island.

As you know Doug had flown brilliantly as my wingman for many months and we had become very close friends. His cheerful ways and quick mind made him a valued member of the squadron and we all feel his loss keenly, no one more so than I.

On the 26th January we had gone together as always, on an attack on a Japanese stronghold and to my (and his) delight he shot down four Japanese planes for sure, for which action he will be recommended for decoration, and which action finally gave him the chance to show what an expert pilot he really was. On the afternoon of the 30th we had a hurry up call for fighters and Doug volunteered to go with me to help foray the escort for the bombers, although he had already completed one dangerous mission that day. We were safely home and all but ready for supper when the tragedy struck.

Doug had been going to Church regularly, attending Mass and Confession last Sunday.

He was a gallant, courageous officer, and an outstanding officer in all respects, as well as a fine shipmate and friend.

Please accept my sincere sympathy for you in your great loss, which I share. If I can furnish any information, or be of any assistance, please do not fail to communicate with me.

Yours very truly

J. T. Blackburn."

Howard McLain Burriss as a young boy. *Courtesy the Burriss Family.*

Lt. (jg) Gutenkunst was awarded the Distinguished Flying Cross posthumously for "*heroism and extraordinary achievement.*"

His body was returned to the U.S. on June 3, 1948, as requested by his family, and he was buried at Forest Home Cemetery, Milwaukee.

In addition to the DFC he was awarded the Navy Unit Commendation, Asiatic - Pacific Area Campaign Medal, and the World War II Victory Medal.

Lt. (jg) Howard McClain "Teeth" Burriss
Missing in Action January 31, 1944

Howard McClain Burriss had two nicknames: "Mac" from his middle name, and by which he signed squadron photos; and "Teeth,"

Howard McClain Burriss. "Mac - all boy," as his mother used to say. *Courtesy the Burriss Family.*

Christmas 1931 at Granville, Ohio. The Burriss boys, "Mac," Charles and Bob. *Courtesy the Burriss Family.*

"Mac" Burriss, as he was known by family and friends, grew up in Granville, Ohio. *Courtesy the Burriss Family.*

which was his call sign in the squadron. His family remember "Mac" having the nickname "Teeth" even before his military service, as he had "Pearly Choppers" and a disarming smile that made him popular with the ladies.

Howard McClain Burriss was the son of Oliver Howard Burriss and Shirley (Slack) Burriss. His mother was a descendant of Charles Swan (1749-1832), who was a private in Capt. William Crawford's company 5th Battalion, Washington County, Pennsylvania Militia and fought in the American Revolution. McClain comes from his grandmother's name Dora McClain, and his other Grandmother was Carrie Wright, first cousin to Wilbur and Orville.

"Mac" was born in Washington, D.C. on March 28, 1921, but grew up in Granville, Ohio. He was the middle son and a twin of a girl who died at birth. When his father died on February 18, 1932, the remaining family moved back in with his mother's family on Cedar Street in Granville, Ohio. Burriss was educated at Denison University and Butler University. He had a very good singing voice and played the trumpet in his band. He was adventurous and travelled abroad to youth hostels before the war. Burriss enlisted in the United States Naval Reserve as a Seaman Second Class on January 2, 1942, whilst a student at Denison University.

He reported to Naval Reserve Aviation Base, Chicago (Glenview), IL, on January 29, 1942, for elimination flight training. On March 15, 1942, he successfully completed his training and was recommended for appointment as an Aviation Cadet. On March 19, 1942, he reported to N.R.A.B. Dallas, Texas, and on April 11, 1942, he transferred to Naval Air Station, Corpus Christi, Texas, to accept his appointment as an Aviation Cadet. "Mac" was designated a Naval Aviator on October 8, 1942, and on October 9, 1942, was commissioned as an Ensign. He then reported to N.A.S. Miami, Florida, for temporary duty involving flying under instruction on October 16, 1942. He completed carrier qualification training at N.A.S. Norfolk, Virginia, and "Mac" was then assigned to

"Mac" Burriss as a young man. He was educated at Denison University, Granville, Ohio. *Courtesy the Burriss Family.*

"Mac" Burriss during flight training in 1942. *Courtesy the Burriss Family.*

Fighting 17 when it was commissioned on January 1, 1943. He was promoted to Lt. (jg) on October 1, 1943, just prior to going into combat.

Lt. (jg) Burriss soon proved himself an exceptional fighter pilot when on November 11, 1943, he shot down a Betty bomber, a Kate torpedo bomber, and another Kate shared with another pilot. This was achieved while flying close to a U.S. task force and during intense anti - aircraft fire.

His next score was on January 27, 1944, and despite being hit and badly damaged he managed to shoot down a Zeke before having to ditch into the sea. He was picked up shortly after and taken back to base.

On January 29, 1944, twenty Corsairs were assigned as cover for SBD Dauntlesses in a joint SBD - TBF strike on Tobera Airfield, New Britain. As the formation was coming in the Roving High Cover, Burriss and "Ike" Kepford, spotted twelve Zekes below them at about 24,000 ft. over Cape Gazelle. With utter disre-

Howard McClain "Mac" Burriss at Ondongo in November 1943. *Courtesy the Burriss Family.*

gard for their own personal safety and with no heed for the numerical superiority of the enemy they pressed home their attacks to the limit, working as a pair, first one, then the other, protecting the other's tail they succeeded in shooting down four Zekes each, with the whole action lasting about ten minutes.

Both Burriss and Kepford were recommended for the Navy Cross. Kepford was awarded the Navy Cross and Burriss the Silver Star. The citation for Burriss stated:

"With utter disregard for his own personal safety and with no heed for the numerical superiority of the enemy he pressed home his attacks to the limit and by superb marksmanship succeeded in shooting down four (4) Zekes. His tireless devotion to duty, his extraordinary heroism in the face of numerically superior enemy forces, and his audacious airmanship were in keeping with the highest traditions of the United States Naval Service."

On his final mission on an attack on Tobera Airfield, near Rabaul, on January 31, 1944, Burriss was hit by Zekes over Kabanga Bay and his aircraft was seen to be smoking heavily and had to make a water landing. When last seen he had his plane well under control, landing in St. George's Channel. However, he was never seen again and was listed as missing in action. In addition to the Silver Star, Burriss was also awarded the Distinguished Flying Cross, Purple Heart, Air Medal, Navy Unit Commendation, Asiatic - Pacific Area Campaign Medal with two Bronze Stars, and the World War II Victory Medal.

Burriss named all his aircraft "Barb" after his girlfriend Barbara Bjelke, who was devastated by his loss.

Lt. (jg) Donald Thomas Malone
Missing in Action February 4, 1944

Don Malone was born on April 16, 1920, in Eureka, California, and studied at Arcata Union High School in California from September 1933 and graduated in June 1937.

Skull and Crossbones ace "Teeth" Burriss, who scored 7.5 Japanese aircraft whilst flying with Fighting 17. "Teeth" was his radio call sign. This photo is of Burriss in Bobby Mims' aircraft at Bougainville in January 1944, and not his own aircraft as stated in my book *The Skull and Crossbones Squadron. Courtesy U.S. Naval Historical Center / M. W. "Butch" Davenport Collection.*

Howard "Mac" Burriss had been dating Barbara Bjelke, whom he met while attending Denison University. She was a beauty queen, and was devastated when she heard he had been shot down. He named all his aircraft "Barb." She is pictured with the family dog, Ferdie. *Courtesy the Burriss Family*

Donald Thomas Malone in January 1942. *Courtesy U.S. Navy.*

Don Malone was appointed an Ensign on December 1, 1942. *Courtesy Earl Malone.*

He attended Fresno State College, where he sang in the college choir and was an accomplished musician on the violin, clarinet, and saxophone. He led a dance band until 1941, playing for Saturday night dances at scattered farm halls.

Whilst at Fresno he enrolled in the Secondary Civilian Flight Program. He became hooked on flying and completed his primary training at Humboldt State College on December 22, 1941, and after finishing the course he became an aerobatic flyer.

Becoming a Navy pilot was his main goal, and after some trouble passing the eye test he became an Aviation Cadet and started training in Oakland, California, where he flew Stearman trainers at the Livermore Airport.

On his application to the Navy Don Malone had the following to say:

"I have had no military experience of any kind. Occupationally my experiences are few. I worked on ranches around my home doing various kinds of ranch work, mainly in the summer, with the

Aviation Cadet Don Malone with a group of other cadets taken at N.A.S. Corpus Christi in the summer of 1942. Don 3rd from left back row. *Courtesy Earl Malone.*

Don Malone in flight gear during his training in 1942. *Courtesy Earl Malone.*

haying crews. I pitched, shocked, and mowed hay. Some of these jobs required the driving of a team of horses.

When I graduated from high school I applied for and received a job as high school bus driver. After two years of college I quit and got a job in the California Barrel Company, Arcata, California. I worked at numerous jobs in this factory, but the one I held the longest was running a slicer machine."

Don became an Aviation Cadet on June 1, 1942, and reported to N.A.S. Corpus Christi for training and was commissioned as an Ensign on December 1, 1942. On 17 December he was designated a Naval Aviator, and on December 24, 1942, he reported to N.A.S. Miami for further training and then to N.A.S Jacksonville. On April 11, 1943, he reported to the Carrier Qualification Training Unit in Norfolk, Virginia, and then on to Fighting 17. He was promoted to Lt. (jg) on January 1, 1944.

He served two tours of duty in the combat zone, which for Don ran from October 27, 1943, through to December 1, 1943, during which period he was based at Ondongo, and from January 26, 1944, through to February 4, 1944, at which time he was based at Piva Yoke, Bougainville.

He flew thirty-eight combat sorties and participated in four strafing missions against enemy shipping and shore installations on Bougainville and the Shortlands, meeting heavy concentrations of enemy anti-aircraft fire on each mission. He encountered enemy aircraft on five occasions: on November 1, 1943, over Empress Augusta Bay, Bougainville, and on January 26, 28, and 30 and February 4, 1944, over Rabaul. While accounting for no enemy aircraft himself, he ably supported his section and division leaders while they shot down nine Japanese aircraft.

On February 4, 1944, he was shot down by a Japanese Zeke following an attack against Tobera Airfield, near Rabaul. He was forced to bail out and was never seen again. He was listed as missing in action.

Lt. (jg) Malone was awarded the Air Medal, Purple Heart, Navy Unit Commendation, Asiatic - Pacific Area Campaign Medal, and World War II Victory Medal.

Ensign Percy Eugene Divenney
Missing in Action February 4, 1944

Percy Divenney was born January 1, 1924, in Cherryville, North Carolina. His occupational experience was four years of farm working, delivering papers for two years, and working in a clothing store for about two years. He graduated from Claremont High School on May 25, 1941, and then studied at Lenoir Rhyne College. He enrolled in the Civilian Pilot Training Program spring course at Lenoir Rhyne College and completed it on June 10, 1942.

Percy applied to the U.S. Navy in May 1942 and became an Aviation Cadet on August 7, 1942. He was commissioned as an Ensign on June 16, 1943, and was designated a Naval Aviator on

Ensign Don Malone pictured at the end of 1942 or early 1943. Becoming a Navy pilot had become Don's main goal, and after some trouble passing the eye test he became an Aviation Cadet on June 1, 1942. *Courtesy Earl Malone.*

Don Malone at the end of 1942 or early 1943. He was listed as missing in action on February 4, 1944, when he was shot down by a Japanese Zeke on retirement from an attack against Tobera Airfield near Rabaul. *Courtesy Earl Malone.*

Percy Eugene Divenney's graduation from Claremont High School on May 25, 1941. Percy Divenney far right back row. *Courtesy the Deveney Family Collection.*

Lenoir Rhyne's College Basketball team. Percy Divenney on back row (middle 4th from right). *Courtesy the Deveney Family Collection.*

Percy Divenney as a young man. *Courtesy the Deveney Family Collection.*

Percy Divenney graduated from Claremont High School on May 25, 1941, and then attended Lenoir Rhyne College. *Courtesy the Deveney Family Collection.*

July 2, 1943, at N.A.S. Pensacola. He received further training at N.A.S. Jacksonville and then reported to the Carrier Qualification Training Unit, Glenview, Illinois, and to Fighting Squadron Twenty One on November 12, 1943. On December 7, 1943, he reported to Carrier Aircraft Service Unit Five, and from there reported to Fleet Air West Coast for transportation to the Pacific on December 23, 1943. Ensign Divenney reported to Fighting 17 on January 11, 1944.

Between January 28, 1944, and February 4, 1944, Divenney flew four missions over Rabaul, meeting enemy aircraft on each sortie. On 28 January he was part of the low cover on an SBD - TBF strike on Tobera Airfield. The formation was attacked by fifty to sixty Zekes and Hamps. Despite being his first combat mission Divenney shot down two Zekes.

On February 4, 1944, while escorting B-24s in a strike on Tobera his undercarriage wheels came down, thus drastically slowing his aircraft. He was jumped by eight Zekes, and despite the protection given him by his section leader and his own evasive action he was shot down and listed as missing in action. He was just 20 years old.

Percy Divenney received his wings at N.A.S. Pensacola, Florida, on July 2, 1943. *Courtesy the Deveney Family Collection.*

On his C.A.A. airman's certificate you will notice Percy Divenney's name was spelt Deveney. On all Naval records his name is listed as Divenney, but his family have spelt it Deveney for the last 45 years. *Courtesy the Deveney Family Collection.*

Percy Divenney as a young Ensign at N.A.S. Pensacola in 1943. *Courtesy the Deveney Family Collection.*

One of a few snapshots that Percy Divenney sent home to his mother during training at N.A.S. Pensacola in 1943. *Courtesy the Deveney Family Collection.*

N. Aer. 4120 9860

U.S. NAVAL AIR STATION
PENSACOLA, FLORIDA
STATION
2 July 1943
DATE ISSUED
This is to certify that
PERCY E. DIVENNEY
NAME
Ens., A-V(N) USNR
RANK
has passed the test in INSTRUMENT FLYING
prescribed for pilots of
THE UNITED STATES NAVY
and is qualified to proceed on Instruments in
Single Engine
TYPE OF PLANE

TYPE OF PLANE
G. D. MURRAY
COMMANDING

(Seal)

Received

(Rank and Service)

Percy Divenney was designated a Naval Aviator on July 2, 1943, as stated on his Naval Aviator's Certificate. *Courtesy the Deveney Family Collection.*

Ensign Percy Divenney was listed as missing in action February 4, 1944. He was shot down by a Japanese Zeke during an attack against Tobera Airfield. He was just 20 years old. *Courtesy the Deveney Family Collection.*

Ensign Percy Divenney at N.A.S. Pensacola in 1943. Divenney started his Navy flight training as an Aviation Cadet on August 7, 1942. *Courtesy the Deveney Family Collection.*

Ensign Divenney was recommended for the Distinguished Flying Cross but was awarded the Air Medal instead.

In addition to the Air Medal he also received the Navy Unit Commendation, Asiatic - Pacific Campaign medal and Bronze Star, American Campaign Medal, Purple Heart, and World War II Victory Medal.

Note: The Divenney name has been spelt in various ways by the family, which is why you see his documents with different spelling of his name.

Ensign Clyde Howard Dunn
Missing in Action February 17, 1944

Clyde Dunn was born in Pawnee Station, Kansas, on December 17, 1922. He spent the first seventeen years of his life on a large farm, and became familiar and skilled with farm work. He was educated at Fort Scott Junior College, Fort Scott, Kansas, entered high school at Fort Scott, Kansas, in September 1936 and graduated on May 29, 1936. He was an excellent student with all A's and B's on his report card. During his second year of college he worked afternoons in a large chain grocery store (Safeway) in Fort Scott, Kansas. Upon graduation he accepted a position with the Western Insurance Companies of Fort Scott, where he worked in the statistical department. There he became acquainted with accounting and the casualty insurance business in general.

He applied to the U.S. Navy in March 1942 and was given the following recommendation by Robert J Morrison, Examiner - Auto Department, Western Casualty and Surety Company:

Clyde Howard Dunn in March 1942. *Courtesy U.S. Navy.*

"I have known this young man since he was a child and know him to be of high moral character, excellent intelligence and a hard, reliable and dependable worker.

I was one of his teachers in school and have been associated with him in commercial life. He has my unqualified recommendation."

Clyde was trained at N.A.S. Corpus Christi, commissioned as an Ensign on June 1, 1943, and designated a Naval Aviator on June 9, 1943. On June 15, 1943, he reported to N.A.S. Melbourne, Florida, for further training. He then reported to the Carrier Qualification Unit, Glenview, Illinois, and then N.A.S. Norfolk.

His fitness report on August 14, 1943, showed a Mark of 3.6 as an aviator, which was excellent. It stated:

"This officer has a high personal and military character. He is industrious, deliberate and conscientious at all tasks performed."

Percy Divenney and a couple of buddies during flight training at N.A.S. Pensacola in 1943. *Courtesy the Deveney Family Collection.*

Ensign Clyde Dunn in October 1943. He was listed missing in action on February 17, 1944, in the vicinity of Rabaul, New Britain. His aircraft failed to return from the attack against enemy shipping. *Courtesy the Tom Blackburn Collection.*

On September 1, 1943, he reported to Carrier Aircraft Service Unit Twenty One, and on September 6, 1943, was one of the last pilots to be assigned to Fighting 17 just before they left for the Pacific. Despite Ensign Dunn and his close friend Ensign "Beads" Popp having no flying hours in the F4U Corsair they were taken along.

He served two tours of duty in the combat zone from November 21, 1943, until December 2, 1943, during which period he was based at Ondongo, and from January 26, 1944, until February 17, 1944, at which time he was based at Piva Yoke, Bougainville.

Ensign Dunn flew twenty-five combat sorties and was over Rabaul eleven times on escort missions or fighter sweeps. He encountered enemy aircraft over Rabaul on ten occasions: on January 26, 27, and 31, 1944, and on February 3, 5, 6, 7, 10, 11, and 17, 1944. On January 26, 1944, the SBD Dauntlesses which he was escorting in a strike on Lakunai Airfield were intercepted by fifty or sixty Japanese fighters. During the action he and his section leader attacked four Zekes, which were on the tail of a Corsair and probably destroyed one of them. On his fitness report on February 4, 1944, he was given a 3.7 score rating as pilot. The report Stated:

"*Ensign Dunn is of excellent character and has a pleasant personality. He has done a good job flying as a wingman on daily combat missions.*"

During escort duty for an Avenger strike on Vunakanau Airfield on February 7, 1944, thirty or forty enemy fighters attempted to intercept them. Dunn probably destroyed two Zekes and damaged a third. On February 17, 1944, the SBDs which he was escorting on a shipping strike in Simpson Harbor were intercepted by thirty or forty enemy fighters. Dunn was seen to shoot down one Zeke. However, during the combat he became separated from his division and was never seen again. He was listed as missing in action. Lt. (jg) Clyde Dunn was awarded the Air Medal for his service with Fighting 17. The citation stated.

"*His daring skill and marksmanship, his tireless devotion to duty, and his courage in the face of numerically superior enemy forces were in keeping with the highest traditions of the U.S. Naval Service.*"

In addition to the Air Medal he was also awarded the Purple Heart, Navy Unit Commendation, Asiatic - Pacific Area Campaign Medal with two Bronze Stars, American Campaign Medal, and World War II Victory Medal.

Lt. (jg) James Miller
Missing in Action February 17, 1944

James Miller was born on August 7, 1921, in Kansas City, Kansas. He attended Rosedale High School and graduated on May 23, 1939. He was an honor student, active in school affairs and Student Council President in 1939. He ranked 15th in scholarship in a class of 108 seniors and his grade average was 2.08.

From Rosedale he entered Kansas City, Kansas Junior College from September 11, 1939, and graduated on May 26, 1941.

According to C. W. Harvey, the Assistant Dean, on September 22, 1941.

"*James was one of our outstanding athletes while here in Junior College. He took part in many extra - curricular activities, was president of the K Club, an athletic organization, and in other ways showed excellent qualities of leadership.*"

He entered the Navy immediately after leaving college, and on March 16, 1942, he became an Aviation Cadet and trained at N.A.S. Pensacola.

He was commissioned as an Ensign on August 5, 1942, and reported to Scouting Squadron Twenty in October 1942. Scouting Squadron Twenty was then changed to Composite Squadron Twenty. On March 5, 1943, he reported to Fighting Squadron Three and then Composite Squadron Thirty One on March 29. His fitness report dated September 11, 1943, whilst with the Composite Squadron showed his rating as a pilot was 3.7, which was excellent, and stated: "*In spite of this officers short time in the service he is considered outstanding. His personel and military character are excellent.*"

He was promoted to Lt. (jg) on July 1, 1943, and on July 13, 1943, reported to Composite Squadron Sixteen. The squadron designation was changed to Fighting Squadron Thirty Three, and

James Miller in 1941. Miller was listed as missing in action on February 17, 1944. He was seen to parachute from his aircraft when it was damaged by anti-aircraft fire during an attack against enemy shipping in the vicinity of Rabaul. *Courtesy U.S. Navy.*

from there he was assigned to Fighting Squadron Eleven on September 26, 1943.

On November 12, 1943, he reported to Fighting Squadron Ten and then ordered to Fleet Air South Pacific, where he arrived on December 5, 1943. On December 8, 1943, he reported to Fighting 17.

Between January 25, 1944, and February 17, 1944, during which time he was based at Piva Yoke, Bougainville, Miller flew fifteen combat sorties, of which eleven were escort missions or fighter sweeps over the Rabaul area. He encountered enemy aircraft on nine occasions: on 26, 28, and January 30, 1944, and on 4, 7, 9, 10, 13, and February 17, 1944. On January 26, 1944, the SBD Dauntlesses which he was escorting in a strike on Lakunai Airfield were intercepted by fifty or sixty Japanese fighters. Although his aircraft was badly hit and he himself was wounded in the initial enemy attack, Miller remained over the bombers, and in fighting off an attack by eight Zekes succeeded in shooting down one of them and damaged another. On January 28, 1944, while escorting a TBF Avenger strike on Tobera Airfield, between fifty and seventy Japanese fighters were encountered. In the resulting combat Miller probably destroyed a Zeke which was attacking his wingman and shot down another immediately afterwards. On January 30, 1944, while escorting B-25 Mitchell bombers in a strike on Lakunai Airfield he probably destroyed a Zeke which was attacking another Corsair. On February 17, 1944, whilst he was providing cover for an SBD strike over Simpson Harbor his aircraft was hit by anti-aircraft fire that blew half of his wing off, and he was seen to bail out.

James Miller was the only Fighting 17 pilot shot down who survived to be a prisoner of war, only to face the living hell of being captured by the Japanese on Rabaul. He died in captivity of Beriberi, dysentery, and starvation on May 7, 1945. Of approximately 75-80 POWs at Rabaul only six survived.

Lt. (jg) Miller was credited with two confirmed and two probable victories in his short time with Fighting 17. He was awarded the Distinguished Flying Cross and part of the citation stated:

"His consistent devotion to duty, his excellent marksmanship and his heroic conduct were in keeping with the highest traditions of the United States Naval Service."

In addition to the DFC, Lt. (jg) Miller was awarded the Purple Heart, Navy Unit Commendation, Asiatic - Pacific Area Campaign Medal with one Bronze Star and the World War II Victory Medal.

Just prior to his overseas deployment to Fighting 17 he married Betty Jeanne Sharp, who did not receive positive confirmation until May 1946 that her husband died as a prisoner of war at Rabaul.

Lt. John Milton Kleinman
Plane Crash February 18, 1944

John Kleinman was born on October 3, 1919, in Kissimmee, Florida. He attended Osceola High School, and whilst there he worked through the summer months at the Broadway Pharmacy preceding his first year at the University of Florida. During the two years that

John Milton Kleinman aged two or three. *Courtesy Dale P. Logsdon and Frances Kleinman Rowland.*

John Kleinman as a High School Senior in 1938. *Courtesy Dale P. Logsdon and Frances Kleinman Rowland.*

John Kleinman trained as a Naval Aviator at N.A.S. Pensacola in 1941. *Courtesy Dale P. Logsdon and Frances Kleinman Rowland.*

he attended the University of Florida he received an Associate of Arts Certificate. He also completed three semesters of Military science in field artillery.

In June he commenced a C.A.A. flying school course in Orlando, Florida, which he completed in 35 hours of flying time, the average for the course being over 90. He was a Junior when he enlisted in the Navy.

He became an Aviation Cadet on May 1, 1941, at N.A.S. Pensacola, and then on October 13, 1941, was ordered to N.A.S. Miami. He was designated a Naval Aviator on November 6, 1941 and commissioned as an Ensign on October 8, 1941. He reported on January 2, 1942, to the Advanced Carrier Training Group, and on February 26, 1942, to Fighting Squadron Five. Ensign John Kleinman was recommended for the Navy Cross for his actions on August 24, 1942, in the Solomon Islands area:

"*For extraordinary heroism and distinguished service in the line of his profession as a pilot in the sixth division, Fighting Squadron Five (U.S.S. Saratoga), during the air attack by the Japanese on the U.S.S. Enterprise on August 24, 1942, in the Solomon Islands Area. Ensign Kleinman, flying as wingman on Lt. Hayden M. Jensen, leading the Sixth Division intercepted the second enemy division of nine dive-bombers as they entered their dives upon the Enterprise, following them down and personally destroying two of them before they could release their bombs, thereby saving the Enterprise from possible bomb hits and contributing greatly towards demoralizing the entire enemy attack. His unyielding devotion to duty, maintained with complete disregard for his personal safety, was in keeping with the highest traditions of the United States Naval Service.*"

In letters Johnny wrote home, he couldn't give out any details of where he was or what he was doing, so he would say things like, "*We went hunting yesterday and I shot two turkeys.*"

He was awarded the Distinguished Flying Cross instead of the Navy Cross and Presidential Unit Citation for VF-5 attached to the First Marine Division (August 7, 1942, to December 9, 1942).

He was promoted to Lt. (jg) on October 1, 1942, and reported to Fighting 17 on January 1, 1943, at N.A.S. Norfolk.

John Kleinman married Frances Greene Gainey on August 14, 1943, in Norfolk, Virginia, and on October 1, 1943, he was promoted to Lieutenant. He was one of the few experienced combat

Ensign John Kleinman in 1941. He took his flight training at N.A.S. Pensacola. *Courtesy Dale P. Logsdon and Frances Kleinman Rowland.*

John Kleinman was commissioned as an Ensign on October 8, 1941. *Courtesy Dale P. Logsdon and Frances Kleinman Rowland.*

John Kleinman married Frances Greene Gainey on August 14, 1943. *Courtesy Dale P. Logsdon and Frances Kleinman Rowland.*

John and Frances Kleinman on August 14, 1943, their wedding day. "Veils do get in the way." *Courtesy Dale P. Logsdon and Frances Kleinman Rowland.*

John and Frances Kleinman on August 14, 1943, their wedding day. On the end right is Jim Halford. *Courtesy Dale P. Logsdon and Frances Kleinman Rowland.*

John Kleinman with his mother Jessie Padgett Kleinman in 1942. *Courtesy Dale P. Logsdon and Frances Kleinman Rowland.*

Mr. and Mrs. John Kleinman prior to going on honeymoon to New York on August 14, 1943. *Courtesy Dale P. Logsdon and Frances Kleinman Rowland.*

John and Frances Kleinman just before going to New York for their honeymoon on August 14, 1943. *Courtesy Dale P. Logsdon and Frances Kleinman Rowland.*

veterans that Fighting 17 relied on when they first saw action in the Solomon Islands. On November 11, 1943, operating off the carriers U.S.S. *Bunker Hill* and U.S.S. *Essex*, Fighting 17's mission was to provide cover for the carriers while their squadrons escorted bombers to Rabaul.

When the Japanese attacked Lt. Kleinman saw about eight Kate torpedo bombers at 500 ft. heading for the Task Force. He made one unsuccessful attack on the leading aircraft, recovered with a quick wing over, got on his tail, fired, and the Kate caught fire and crashed into the water. This took place just inside the destroyer screen, and the Kate had not dropped her torpedo. Kleinman continued in over the screen, saw another Kate to his left, and made a beam run from four o'clock. As he was recovering for a second pass he was hit by a 40mm shell from one of the ships. The shell exploded and blew up his instrument panel, wounding him in the face. Kleinman turned to get out of the screen and was jumped by two F6F Hellcats. They made head on runs and hit his wing. Since he had no instruments, Kleinman navigated by the sun back to Barakoma, landing at 04:45. He was awarded the Purple Heart for this mission and had credit for one Kate shot down and one Kate damaged.

He was detached from Fighting 17 on December 17, 1943, and reported on December 27, 1943, to Fleet Air Coast, Jacksonville and then N.A.A.S. Melbourne, reporting on January 30, 1944.

Lt. Kleinman was killed in a crash after take off for a gunnery flight on February 18, 1944, two miles southwest of Naval Auxiliary Air Station, Melbourne, Florida. It is considered that shortly after takeoff he ran into a fog bank moving toward the station, which developed a ceiling of 100 to 150 feet. On investigation the condition of the wreckage of the aeroplane indicated that his aircraft had tried to fly at very low level below the cloud and had hit the ground at a very shallow nose down attitude. Lt. Kleinman had been married for less than six months at the time of his death.

In addition to the Distinguished Flying Cross and Presidential Unit Citation he was awarded the American Defense Service Medal, Asiatic - Pacific Area Campaign Medal, Purple Heart and Navy Unit Commendation.

Lt. (jg) John Orrin "Fatso" Ellsworth
Plane Crash June 3, 1944

John Ellsworth was born on September 22, 1923, in Kingston, New York. He enlisted in the U.S.N.R. on January 31, 1942. He terminated this to accept an appointment as an Aviation Cadet on July 1, 1942, and reported to N.A.S. Jacksonville for training.

He was commissioned as an Ensign on January 16, 1943, and designated a Naval Aviator on February 2, 1943. He reported for further training at N.A.S. Melbourne, and then on April 20, 1943, to the Carrier Qualification Training Unit, Norfolk, Virginia. On completion of this training he reported to Fighting 17 on May 12, 1943.

His nickname in the squadron was "Fatso," and that was how he signed his name on squadron photos. While with Fighting 17, Lt. (jg) Ellsworth took part in seventy-one combat missions over Japanese territory and was awarded the Distinguished Flying Cross. He was credited with two confirmed Japanese aircraft destroyed and one probable. He was also credited with destroying a Japanese bomber during a strafing attack on Ballale airfield on October 30, 1943.

He was promoted to Lt. (jg) on March 1, 1944, and upon his return home from combat he was detached from Fighting 17 on April 2, 1944.

L – R: Uncle Bill Padgett and John Kleinman after a turkey hunt. The other two people are unknown. *Courtesy Dale P. Logsdon and Frances Kleinman Rowland.*

John Kleinman, wife Frances, and turkeys. *Courtesy Dale P. Logsdon and Frances Kleinman Rowland.*

Ens. John Orrin Ellsworth at Bougainville in 1944. *Courtesy National Archives.*

John Ellsworth with his aircraft #18 on the second tour at Bougainville in 1944. *Courtesy U.S. Naval Historical Centre / M. W. "Butch" Davenport Collection.*

While he was on shore leave he married Dolores Marie Vollmer on April 24, 1944, and on May 9, 1944, he reported to Headquarters Squadron, Fleet Air Wing, stationed at N.A.A.S. Elizabeth City, NC. Whilst flying an FM-2 Wildcat at 13:15, on June 3, 1944, he crashed ten miles south of the base. According to the report:

"The Pilot opened the hood and removed his helmet in order to overcome some abnormal physical disability, but this action did not restore him to normal state. The Pilot was unable to pull out of the dive and not able to extricate himself from the falling plane and unable to bail out."

Lt. (jg) Ellsworth had only been married just over a month when he died.

In addition to the Distinguished Flying Cross he was awarded the Navy Unit Commendation, Asiatic - Pacific Campaign Medal, American Campaign Medal, and WWII Victory Medal.

Lt. Donald Allan "Stinky" Innis
Plane Crash June 20, 1944

Don Innis was born on November 14, 1915, in Nevada, Missouri. He was known as "Stinky" in the Navy, which is believed to have come from his days serving at Guadalcanal.

He entered Nevada High School in September 1929 and graduated from there on May 17, 1933. He was then educated at the University of Missouri, starting there in September 1934.

He worked his way through the University of Missouri as a waiter at the Daniel Boone Tavern, Columbia, and during the summer months worked for three summers for the Radio Springs Park, Nevada, Missouri, as a life guard. He also worked two summers on construction jobs; one for the Pan Handle Eastern Pipeline Co. of Kansas City, Missouri, and the other for a company in North Carolina.

Donald Allan Innis joined Fighting 17 in October 1943. He served at Guadalcanal in 1942. *Courtesy U.S. Navy.*

Don Innis beside sign on Bougainville in 1944. *Courtesy Vought / U.S. Naval Historical Center / M.W. "Butch" Davenport Collection.*

Upon leaving the University of Missouri he was employed for two and a half years as a Credit Correspondent by the Liquid Carbonic Corporation of Chicago, IL. Other than the basic R.O.T.C. training that he received at the University of Missouri he had no previous military or Navy training. Innis joined the Naval Reserve, enlisting on October 29, 1940, and on February 1, 1941, his enlisted service was terminated to accept his appointment as an Aviation Cadet. He reported to N.A.S. Pensacola and then N.A.S. Miami for training and was commissioned as an Ensign on July 16, 1941. He was designated a Naval Aviator on September 8, 1941, and reported to Advanced Carrier Training Group, N.A.S. Norfolk, Virginia, on October 24, 1941.

He reported on January 3, 1942, to Fighting Squadron Five, and on May 20, 1942, along with VF-5, was ordered to Commander Aircraft South Pacific and reported on September 2, 1942. He was wounded in action on September 13, 1942, following air combat against Japanese aircraft at Guadalcanal. He was hit by gunfire and his aircraft burst into flames, resulting in burns of the face, neck, arms, and legs. The medical report stated:

Lt. Don Innis died on June 20, 1944, in the Salton Sea, California, on a routine flight in an F6F Hellcat. *Courtesy U.S. Navy*

"He had first and second degree burns of the face, neck, right ear, right arm and forearm, left wrist and both legs, and a laceration of the skin of the dorsum of the left hand overlying the distal halves of the second and third metacarpal bones. The right conjunctiva was inflamed."

Lt. (jg) Innis was admitted to U.S. Naval Base Hospital, Number Two, Base Roses on September 14, 1942. On September 29, 1942, he was admitted to hospital from the U.S.S. *Solace* with an indefinite duration of stay in hospital. He was promoted to Lt. (jg) on October 1, 1942, and was detached from VF-5 on December 24, 1942.

He reported to U.S. Navy Camden, New Jersey, for duty in connection of fitting out a vessel on January 1, 1943, and then reported to VF-24 on March 31, 1943. He was promoted to Lt. on October 1, 1943, and detached from VF-24 and assigned to Fighting 17 on October 13, 1943. He served two tours with Fighting 17 and after an accident was given the role as Squadron Duty Officer.

He was detached from Fighting 17 on April 3, 1944, and reported to N.A.S. San Diego for duty involving flying in the Aircraft Ordnance Development Unit at Inyokern, California.

He was killed in a crash in an F6F Hellcat on June 20, 1944, in the Salton Sea, California, whilst on routine operations.

The Commander of the U.S. Naval Ordnance Test Station, Inyokern, California, wrote to his mother with the sad news on June 21, 1944.

"Dear Mrs Innis,

It is with the deepest sympathy that I write you regarding your son, Donald, who was instantly killed in an airplane crash yesterday.

Donald was assigned to duty with the Aviation Ordnance Development Unit attached to this station. His time has been devoted to test flights in connection with the development of a new weapon for aircraft. He has been of material assistance to this most important work.

I feel a deep personal loss in the death of this fine young man. I found Donald to be at all times extremely capable, intelligent, and most thorough in the performance of his duties. His behaviour was always above reproach, indicating that his home surroundings and general upbringing were of the very best. He was well liked and respected by officers and men alike. All hands on this station join me in expressing our sympathy for you in this great sorrow.

These are sad days for a great many Americans who have lost their loved ones in the service of our country. We must all remember that these costly sacrifices are the price of freedom, and continue to bend our every effort to shortening this war.

Sincerely yours

S E Burroughs, Jr.
Captain U.S. Navy."

Lt. Innis was awarded the American Defense Service Medal, Asiatic - Pacific Campaign Medal, Purple Heart for wounds received on September 13, 1942, Presidential Unit Citation (U.S.S. *Belleau Wood*) and Bronze Star (First Marine Division), and World War II Victory Medal.

Lt. (jg) William Preston Meek
Plane Crash July 23, 1944

William Preston Meek was born on June 9, 1921, in Long Beach, California. He attended Covina Union High School from 1936 to 1940 and then studied at Chaffey Junior College, Ontario, California, where he entered on September 16, 1940, and graduated on June 12, 1942. While there he majored in aeronautics.

During the summer, from June 19, 1941, to September 19, 1941, he was an employee of the Douglas Aircraft Company of Santa Monica, California, although he resigned his position to continue his aeronautical course at Chaffey Junior College.

Bill took and completed the Primary Course of the Civilian Pilot Training which was given in the Fall Session of 1941 to 1942, where Arthur C. Nelson of Nelson Flying Service, Ontario, California, had this to say on February 13, 1942.

Bill Meek at High School. *Courtesy the Meek Family Collection.*

Bill Meek as a young boy in his Navy suit. *Courtesy the Meek Family Collection.*

Bill Meek after graduation from Covina Union High School in 1940. *Courtesy the Meek Family Collection.*

"We have found him to be friendly, honest, capable and conscientious in all of his flying activities. He has a pleasing personality plus the ability to get along with men of his own age and interests."

Bill Meek applied to the Navy in March 1942, and on August 10, 1942, became an Aviation Cadet. He was commissioned as an Ensign on April 16, 1943, and became a Naval Aviator on April 28, 1943. He trained at N.A.S. Corpus Christi and then went to N.A.S. Jacksonville for further training. He reported to the Atlantic Fleet and then C.A.S.U. Twenty One on June 17, 1943, and then VF-52 on August 15, 1943. He reported to Fighting 17 on August 29, 1943.

While in the Solomon Islands serving with Fighting 17, Meek received news that his father George Preston Meek had died on November 7, 1943. As the sole surviving son Bill could have come home, but he wrote a couple of letters home in December 1943 after his leave in Australia expressing how he felt.

Bil Meek in the summer of 1943, just prior to joining Fighting 17. *Courtesy the Meek Family Collection.*

Bill Meek graduated as an Ensign at N.A.S. Corpus Christi, Texas, in April 1943. *Courtesy the Meek Family Collection.*

"Dear Jonesy,

I sure do appreciate you taking care of my mother. I would like to come home, but I am out here so I had better stay and do my part.

My mother said something about writing Jerry to see if I could get some leave. That would be foolish. I have my part out here to do and I am going to stay and do it."

This gives an indication of the sort of man Bill was and his commitment to the service of his country.

Bill Meek served two tours with Fighting 17 in the Solomon Islands, flying 112.3 combat hours in his first tour. On his second tour up to February 21, 1944, he completed 22 combat sorties flying 13 missions to Rabaul and 64.7 combat hours. He was credited with one Japanese Zeke destroyed.

He returned home and was detached from Fighting 17 on April 2, 1944, and after a short leave reported to VF-84 on May 4, 1944.

While on leave he married "*Almost the girl next door*," Delpha Levon Meek, his childhood sweetheart.

Ensign Bill Meek in the summer of 1943 at N.A.S. Corpus Christi. *Courtesy the Meek Family Collection.*

Bill Meek married his childhood sweetheart Delpha, "*who was almost the girl next door,*" when he returned from combat with Fighting 17 in April 1944. *Courtesy the Meek Family Collection.*

On July 1, 1944, he was promoted to Lt. (jg).

Lt. (jg) Meek died at sea ¼ mile south of Los Coronados Islands on July 23, 1944, at 13:45 after a mid - air collision with another FG-1 Corsair piloted by Ensign Archie Beene whilst they were engaged in combat offensive - defensive division tactics. At about 8000 feet over the local sea operating area the aircraft were seen to crash in mid - air. One wing was torn off of each aircraft by the collision and both spun violently into the sea. No attempt to jump was observed in the case of either pilot. Neither pilot's body could be recovered. Lt. (jg) Meek was given a posthumous award of the Air Medal in November 1944 for his actions with Fighting 17. The citation quotes:

"As pilot, attached to a fighter squadron during action against enemy Japanese forces in the Solomon Islands and Bismarck Archipelago areas from October 27, 1943 to March 8, 1944, Lieutenant Meek is cited for meritorious achievement.

Intercepted by an overwhelming force of hostile fighters while acting as escort for a bombing strike against Tobera, January 28, he fought gallantly despite great odds, pressing home his attack vigorously and shooting down one Japanese Zero.

Ensign Bill Meek at Bougainville in early 1944. *Courtesy National Archives.*

His splendid airmanship and outstanding devotion to duty throughout this engagement and during numerous other combat missions in this vitally strategic area were in keeping with the highest traditions of the United States Naval Service."

In addition to the Air Medal, Lt. (jg) Meek was awarded the Navy Unit Commendation, Asiatic - Pacific Area Campaign Medal with two Bronze Stars, American Campaign Medal and World War II Victory Medal.

Lt. (jg) Doris Clyde "Chico" Freeman
Kamikaze Attack May 11, 1945

Doris Clyde "Chico" Freeman was born in Los Angeles, California, on April 18, 1920. The name Doris was his father and grandfather's name.

"Chico's" father was known as Clyde Freeman and served in the U.S. Marine Corps in WWII as a 1st Sergeant. He was a broker with A.W. Coote at time of his son's birth. His mother was Mary Jane (Berkman) Freeman.

"Chico" was called "Jack" by a nurse who took care of him during an illness when he was a baby, and since that time he was called Jack by all the family until such time as he started school, where he was known as Clyde Freeman, and later on he adopted the name Clyde Jack Freeman.

During his high school days he was an active member of the football team for three years. Swimming was also a favourite sport of his, and although he was a very capable swimmer he was never fast enough to compete on the swimming team.

Lt. (jg) D. C. "Chico" Freeman who later made ace with VF-84, at Bougainville in 1944. *Courtesy National Archives.*

At Oceanside Junior College he participated in spring football and track. His summer jobs consisted of washing cars, digging ditches, selling articles and mining.

"Chico" was educated at University High Los Angeles and studied there from 1935 to 1938. He then entered Manual Arts High School in Los Angeles in February 1938 and graduated on February 3, 1939. He attended Los Angeles City College in 1939 and Carlsbad Junior College, and also attended Los Angeles City College and Ventura Junior College. He had studied briefly at Santa Barbara State College in March 1941 but withdrew with an honourable dismissal.

On February 25, 1942, he enlisted in the U.S. Naval Reserve and then had his enlistment terminated on May 27, 1942, to accept appointment as an Aviation Cadet from May 15, 1942. He reported to N.A.S. Corpus Christi, Texas, for training and was designated a Naval Aviator on October 8, 1942. On October 30, 1942, he was commissioned as an Ensign to rank from October 1, 1942, and reported to N.A.S. Miami for pre-operational training, and on December 11, 1942, reported to N.A.S. Jacksonville for further training.

On March 11, 1943, he reported to the Carrier Qualification Training Unit, Norfolk, Virginia, and then to Fighting 17. On October 1, 1943, he was promoted to Lt. (jg).

During his first tour he flew 132 combat flying hours, and when he resumed combat on his second tour he flew 68.8 combat hours up to February 21, 1944, with 21 combat sorties completed. He flew 14 missions to Rabaul and scored two confirmed and two probable victories with Fighting 17.

He was recommended for the Distinguished Flying Cross and the citation in part states:

"In action over Empress Augusta Bay, Bougainville, on November 21, 1943, he flew one of four Corsairs which attacked six Zekes, of which he shot down two. On 18 November he took part in the remarkable flight lasting six hours and forty five minutes which resulted in the recovery of Lt. (jg) R. S. Anderson. In 36 days he flew 39 sorties, a total of 132 hours of combat flying. His devotion to duty, his great courage in the face of superior enemy forces, and his skilful airmanship were in keeping with the highest traditions of the U. S. Naval Service."

On April 3, 1944, he reported to Fleet Air West Coast, N.A.S. San Diego, and was then assigned to VF-84. He saw service against the Japanese home islands, and on February 17, 1945, destroyed a Tony in the Tokyo Area. On April 13, 1945, Freeman shot down a Sonia over Okinawa, and on April 17, 1945, shot down a George aircraft over Okinawa. He scored two Nates on April 28, 1945, and his final victories were two Nates on May 11, 1945.

His final total was nine confirmed Japanese planes destroyed, and with John M. Smith was the joint leading ace of VF-84.

After returning from his successful mission "Chico" Freeman died at about 10:45 on May 11, 1945, after a Kamikaze attack on the U.S.S. *Bunker Hill*, and was buried at sea on April 12,

1945. Captain G.A. Seitz wrote this about Lt. Freeman on May 25, 1945:

"Lt. Freeman was one of our ablest fighter pilots, aggressive and determined in all his attacks against the enemy. His endless flow of wit and his abundant store of good humor always served to give his squadron a lift when it was most needed. We shall miss him greatly aboard this ship."

In addition to the Distinguished Flying Cross he was awarded with Fighting 17 he was awarded three further DFCs, the Purple Heart, seven Air Medals, the Asiatic - Pacific Area Campaign Medal, Navy Unit Commendation, Presidential Unit Citation and World War II Victory Medal.

Lt. Cdr. Harry Andrew "Dirty Eddie" March, Jr.
Pneumonia March 2, 1946

Harry Andrew March, Jr, was born in East Liverpool, Ohio, on February 2, 1919. He was ranked number one in junior tennis in Washington, D.C., when aged fifteen and had a National ranking as a junior. He even played the famous Bill Tilden in an exhibition match.

He was educated at the University of North Carolina and attended from September 1936 to June 1940. He graduated with a B.A. Degree in Physical Education in the class of 1940. He qualified for the Olympic team of 1940 in the 400 hurdles and was named on the All American Track Team, and was the National Pentathlon Champion of 1940. Harry would have gone to the 1940 Olympics, which were cancelled as a consequence of the war. He won the National A.A.U. Pentathlon Championship in Philadelphia during his senior year at the University of North Carolina and held a number of records in track events.

On December 16, 1940, he enlisted in the U.S. Naval Reserve as a Seaman Second Class.

He began his elimination flight training on March 6, 1941, as an Aviation Cadet and reported to N.A.S. Jacksonville for training. He was ordered to N.A.S. Miami for further training and reported on August 21, 1941. On September 23, 1941, he was designated a Naval Aviator, and on November 6, 1941, was commissioned as an Ensign.

Harry was then ordered to the Advanced Carrier Training Group, Pacific Fleet at N.A.S. San Diego for temporary duty, reporting there on November 29, 1941. He was further ordered to Fighting Squadron Six, and reported on June 15, 1942. According to his family the nickname "Dirty Eddie" was something to do with his black beard he grew while based at Guadalcanal. It may have also had something to do with the conditions there, which were primitive due to the intense fighting involved with this island.

He was promoted to Lt. (jg) on October 1, 1942, and on December 19, 1942, he was detached from Fleet Air Command, West Coast and ordered to Fleet Air Detachment, N.A.S. New York, and then on December 31, 1942, to Fighting Squadron Twenty Four based on the U.S.S. *Belleau Wood*.

On September 24, 1943, he was ordered to Air Force Pacific Fleet and reported on September 28, 1943, to the Fourteenth Naval District, Pearl Harbor, and further ordered to N.A.S. Barber's Point, Oahu.

He had married Elsa Smedes March as soon as Ensigns were allowed to do so, and their daughter Mary Elizabeth March was born on September 29, 1943.

He was appointed Lt. for temporary service from October 1, 1943, and then when he completed his temporary duty in Carrier Aircraft Service Unit One he was ordered to Fighting 17.

During his service with Fighting 17 Lt. March was recommended by Tom Blackburn for the Navy Cross on March 14, 1944, with the following report:

"For extraordinary heroism while participating in aerial combat. Lt. March as a member of four squadrons which have operated in the South Pacific under frequently difficult and occasionally hazardous conditions, has seen action intermittently since June 10, 1942, in a series of campaigns ranging from Guadalcanal to New Britain, from aircraft carriers until bases were established and then from the bases themselves. In the early stages of the severe Guadalcanal campaign his flight of six F4F's attacked a force of enemy bombers which attacked our transports. During this action he shot down one of the six Vals destroyed. Again, on August 24, 1942, he was one of the five fighters who repulsed a determined

Harry Andrew "Dirty Eddie" March, Jr., was appointed an Ensign in August 1941. *Courtesy the March Family.*

enemy attack on the U.S.S. Enterprise and in this action he shot down one Jap torpedo plane. Following this, he operated from the U.S.S. Saratoga and Guadalcanal, where his squadron was in almost daily contact with the enemy. Then, after participating in 3 more actions while in VF-24, Lt. March began his second tour of combat as a member of VF-17. As a flight leader, during the squadron's second tour of combat, Lt. March flew 24 combat sorties, of which 18 were escort missions or fighter sweeps over the Rabaul Area, and on 8 of which he encountered enemy aircraft. On 28 January, the bombers he was escorting in a Rabaul strike were intercepted by a swarm of enemy fighters which Lt. March attacked without regard for the odds against him. The attack was so well timed and executed that the enemy attack was repulsed. During the melee Lt. March shot down 2 Zekes. His untiring devotion to duty, his heroic conduct in a long series of action which mark the progress of the whole Solomons Campaign, his steady and experienced leadership, and his intelligent airmanship were in keeping with the highest traditions of the U.S. Naval Service."

On April 3, 1944, he was detached from the Pacific Fleet and ordered to N.A.S. Jacksonville. On May 6, 1944, he reported to N.A.A.S. Green Cove Springs, and then on May 16, 1945, he reported to Air Force Atlantic Fleet, N.A.S. Norfolk, and on May 21, 1945, to Bombing Fighting Squadron 74 at Camp Edwards, Massachusetts. On October 3, 1945, he was appointed Lt Cdr., and on December 14, 1945, served on the U.S.S. *Midway*.

Lt. Cdr. March applied to join the regular Navy, and according to a report dated November 12, 1945, was highly recommended. After the war in February 1946 Harry went to Chapel Hill, N.C., to participate in the University of North Carolina indoor track meet as part of his training for the 1948 Olympics. Suddenly he became acutely ill with chills and a very high fever on February 23, 1946. He was admitted to the University of North Carolina Infirmary, Chapel Hill, N.C., where a diagnosis of Pneumonia was given. Despite large doses of Penicillin being administered Harry's illness grew rapidly worse and he was in need of specialist care; however, the nearest Naval hospital was the U.S. Naval Hospital, Portsmouth, VA, which was over 200 miles away. Harry was far too ill to transfer to the Naval hospital, so he was therefore sent by private ambulance from the University of North Carolina Infirmary to Watts Hospital, Durham, N.C., a civilian hospital about 12 miles away. Despite intensive care Lt. Cdr. Harry March died at 04 00 on March 2, 1946. He was just 27 years old.

Harry Andrew "Dirty Eddie" March, Jr., at Bougainville in 1944. *Courtesy National Archives.*

Lt. Cdr. March was awarded the Distinguished Flying Cross, Air Medal with one Gold Star, Navy Unit Commendation, Presidential Unit Citation (U.S.S. *Enterprise*), Presidential Unit Citation (First Marine Division), Asiatic - Pacific Area Campaign Medal with one Bronze Star, American Defense Service Medal and World War II Victory Medal. He was also an ace with five confirmed victories. He left a devoted wife Elsa and their young daughter Mary.

Cdr. Lemuel Doty Cooke
Plane Crash May 17, 1950

Lemuel Doty Cooke was born on October 7, 1916, in Hernando, Mississippi; his middle name of Doty was a family name descending from England, as the Doty's came over on the Mayflower to America.

Lem Cooke went to school in Hernando, Mississippi, and left to attend the Marion Military Institute in Marion, Alabama. On July 9, 1935, Lem Cooke was appointed a Midshipman at the U.S. Naval Academy, Annapolis, Maryland, and was commissioned as an Ensign on June 1, 1939. He followed his older brother Eb Smith Cooke to Annapolis.

Lem was a very good football player, but had to have his teeth fixed to pass the medical, which they arranged for him as he was so good at football. He won the Thompson Trophy Cup at the Naval Academy in his senior year in 1939 for football and baseball. According to the Naval Academy, the Thompson Trophy is presented to:

"The midshipman, declared by the Association's Athletic Committee to have done the most during the year for the promotion of athletics at the Naval Academy. The award was the highest form of recognition the Naval Academy Athletic Association can bestow upon a student-athlete."

He reported to the U.S.S. *Ranger* on June 24, 1939, and then to N.A.S. Pensacola, Florida, on October 2, 1941. He was promoted to Lt. (jg) on November 1, 1941, and designated a Naval Aviator on February 22, 1942. On April 21, 1942 he reported to the aviation unit of U.S.S. *South Dakota* and was promoted as temporary Lt. on June 15, 1942. He was then assigned to Patrol Squadron 211 on February 28, 1943, and to Fighting 17 on March 5, 1943.

Lem Cooke as a young boy with his family. Lem is on the end right in the back row. *Courtesy Robert P. Cooke III.*

He was awarded the Distinguished Flying Cross for his service with Fighting 17; the Citation read as follows:

"For heroism and extraordinary achievement in aerial flight as Pilot of a Fighter Plane in Fighting Squadron Seventeen during operations against enemy Japanese forces in the vicinity of Bougainville, Solomon Islands, from November 18 to 22, 1943. Completing his twentieth mission during this period, Lt. Cdr. (then Lt.) Cooke participated in attacks against enemy troop concentrations, airfields and gun positions. On one occasion, he destroyed a Japanese plane on the ground. By his skill and courage in the face of hostile anti-aircraft fire, he contributed materially to the infliction of damage on the enemy. His airmanship throughout was in keeping with the highest traditions of the U.S. Naval Service."

After his combat tour with Fighting 17 he reported to Fighting Squadron 38 as Commanding Officer on January 28, 1944. While with VF-38 he received a Gold Star in lieu of his second DFC. The citation in part read:

"For heroism and extraordinary achievement in aerial flight during operations against enemy Japanese forces in the Solomon Islands and Bismarck Archipelago Areas, from February 12 to 18, 1944. Completing his fortieth mission during this period, Lt. Cdr. (then Lt.) Cooke participated in attacks against enemy airfields and shipping near Rabaul and in patrol flights during the invasion of Green Island. On one occasion, he strafed and set afire a radar station on Rabaul. By his skilled airmanship in the face of hostile anti-aircraft fire and aerial opposition, he aided materially in inflicting damage on the enemy."

He returned home after his tour with VF-38 and reported to Naval Operational Training, N.A.S. Jacksonville on April 15, 1944, and was then assigned permanent duty on June 23, 1944, at Naval Auxiliary Air Station, Green Cove Springs, Florida.

On January 6, 1945, he reported to N.A.S. Miami, Florida, and to Bombing Fighting Squadron 74 on May 22, 1945. He assumed command of Bombing Fighting Squadron 74 on May 24, 1945, but saw no further action due to the cessation of hostilities.

On September 23, 1946, he reported to the Staff of Commander Air Atlantic and was promoted to Lt. Cdr. on October 1, 1947, to rank from March 15, 1944. On April 27, 1949, he reported to Aircraft Development Squadron Three at N.A.S. Atlantic City, New Jersey, and on August 31, 1949, accepted his appointment as temporary Commander.

Cdr. Cooke had passed his physical in April 1950, as he was going to be a test pilot. While waiting to report as a test pilot, he was practicing for the armed forces parade when his jet aircraft

Lemuel Doty Cooke as a midshipman in 1935. Doty was a family name. *Courtesy Robert P. Cooke III.*

lost power and he crashed on May 17, 1950, in Atlantic City, New Jersey. He is buried at Arlington National Cemetery. Cdr. Cooke's first wife Barbara died in childbirth and had a son, Lem Cooke, Jr. He later remarried and had two further children.

In addition to two DFCs Cdr. Cooke was awarded eight Air Medals, a Letter of Commendation with Ribbon (CINPAC), the Navy Unit Commendation (U.S.S. *South Dakota*), the Navy Unit Commendation (VF-17), American Defense Service Medal with "Fleet" clasp, American Campaign Medal, Asiatic - Pacific Campaign Medal and World War II Victory Medal.

Lt. Cdr. Earl May, Jr.
Plane Crash October 22, 1951

Earl May, Jr. was born in Milwaukee, Wisconsin, on June 1, 1920. He attended Thomas Jefferson Grammar School in West Allis, Wisconsin, from 1926 to 1934, and then went to Nathan Hale Junior High School from 1934 to 1936 and West Allis High School from 1936 to 1937. He then studied at William Horlick High School from 1937 to 1938 in Racine, Wisconsin, and Bay View High School from 1938 to 1939 in Milwaukee, Wisconsin.

On September 7, 1938, Earl enlisted in the Wisconsin National Guard and served as a Private in the 121st Field Artillery. He was honourably discharged until September 7, 1939.

Lem Cooke studied at the U.S. Naval Academy, Annapolis, Maryland, and graduated in 1939. *Courtesy Robert P. Cooke III.*

Lt. Lem Cooke at Espiritu Santo in October 1943. *Courtesy Vought / Lennard Edmisten.*

Earl May, Jr., and his brother Del in 1936. *Courtesy Del and Pat May Collection.*

Earl May, Jr., and the "Flying Badgers" during primary training in 1942 at N.A.S. Glenview, Illinois. Earl back row 7th from left, "Hap" Bowers front row 6th from left. *Courtesy Del and Pat May Collection.*

L – R: "Ginger" and Bill Landreth and Thelma and Earl May taken in late 1944 just before Bill and Earl left for the Pacific with VBF-10 aboard the carrier *Intrepid*. Bill and Earl were good friends, and were each other's Best Man at their weddings. A few months later Bill was forced down over Honshu, Japan, and was a prisoner of war for the duration. *Courtesy Del and Pat May Collection.*

Earl and Thelma May in late 1944. *Courtesy Del and Pat May Collection.*

He attended Marquette University from 1939 to 1941 in Milwaukee, Wisconsin, and then Milwaukee Extension Division in 1941 to 1942. His Major was Pre Dental and his Minor English. He was employed by the Railway Express Agency as a clerk from 1940 to 1941, and on February 9, 1942, he enlisted in the U.S. Naval Reserve in Chicago, IL. On May 28, 1942, his enlistment was terminated to accept his appointment as an Aviation Cadet and he reported to N.A.S. Corpus Christi. On October 8, 1942, he was designated a Naval Aviator, and the next day was commissioned as an Ensign.

On October 16, 1942, he reported to N.A.S. Miami for pre-operational training and was then ordered to the Carrier Qualification Training Unit, Norfolk, Virginia, on November 26, 1942.

He was further ordered for duty with Fighting Squadron 17 and was a founder member or "Plank Owner" when it was commissioned on January 1, 1943. On October 13, 1943, he was promoted to Lt. (jg).

On his first tour with Fighting 17 Earl flew 143.9 combat hours, and on his second tour he flew 75.4 combat hours up to February 21, 1944, with twenty-one combat sorties completed. He flew sixteen missions to Rabaul and shot down Zekes on January 27 and 29, 1944. He scored again with a Zeke on February 9, 1944, and on February 18, 1944, scored a further two Zekes. He concluded his scoring on February 19, 1944, with three Zekes on one mission to take his final score to eight confirmed victories. In his two tours with Fighting 17 Earl was awarded the Silver Star and Distinguished Flying Cross.

After returning to the States and a well earned leave he reported to N.A.A.S. Green Cove Springs on May 6, 1944, for duty as an instructor. On August 28, 1944, he reported to Fighting Squadron Ten in N.A.S. Atlantic City, and on November 20, 1944, was appointed to the regular Navy.

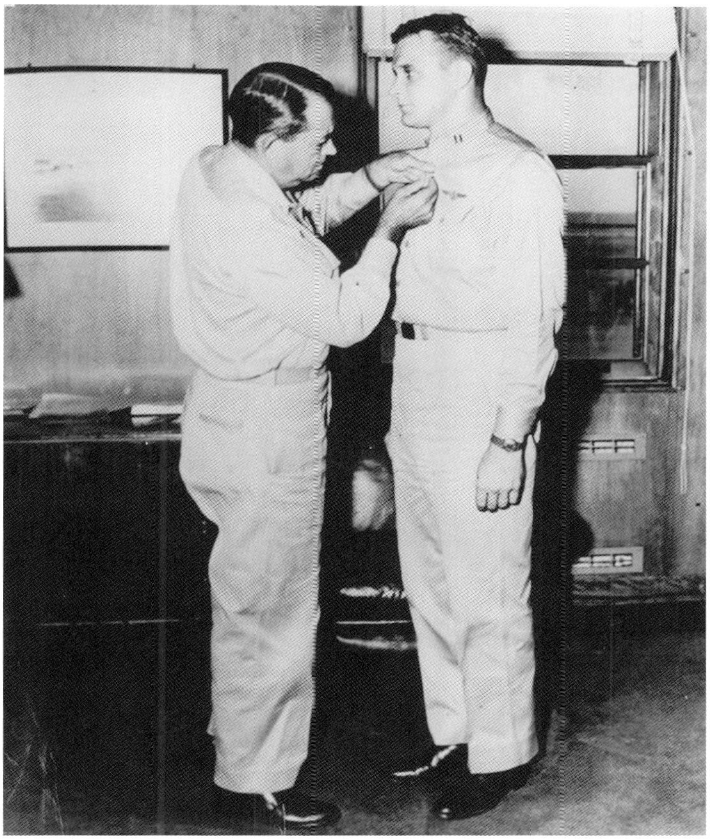

Lt. Earl May, Jr., receiving the Air Medal and Gold Star in lieu of a second Distinguished Flying Cross while serving with VBF-10. *Courtesy Del and Pat May Collection.*

Lt. Cdr. Earl May, Jr. A memorial portrait commissioned by his father and painted by Charles W. Thwaites, a Milwaukee artist. *Courtesy Del and Pat May Collection.*

Earl married Thelma Wright May on September 11, 1944, prior to going into combat again with VBF-10.

On January 2, 1945, he reported to Bomber Fighter Squadron Ten, based on the U.S.S. *Intrepid*, where he served in combat against the Japanese home islands and Okinawa campaign, being awarded a second DFC to add to the one he was awarded with Fighting 17. He was also awarded two Air Medals covering the period March 18, 1945, to April 17, 1945.

On November 20, 1945, he was ordered to N.A.S. Glenview and then to N.A.S. Corpus Christi for temporary duty on February 26, 1946. He then reported to N.A.A.S. Rodd Field, Corpus Christi, on June 5, 1946, and was ordered on December 3, 1947, to N.A.S. Jacksonville for transportation to N.A.S. Roosevelt Roads, Puerto Rico. On January 18, 1948, he was ordered to Aircraft Development Squadron Three (VX-3). Whilst attached to ADS Three, May reported to the Naval School All Weather Flight, N.A.S. Corpus Christi, from September 21, 1950, to November 15, 1950. On June 21, 1951, May was detached from VX-3 and ordered to N.A.S. Patuxent River, Maryland. Amongst those serving at "Pax River" at the time was the future astronaut Alan B. Shepard.

On August 29, 1951, May was promoted as Lt. Cdr. U.S. Navy.

Lt. Cdr. May died on October 10, 1951, when he crashed in an F8F-1 Bearcat at high speed from high altitude. He was believed to be unconscious due to loss of oxygen or carbon monoxide poisoning. The aircraft crashed at Saw Mill Road, Cedarville, New Jersey. Local residents have been caring for Earl May's crash site to this day.

Lt. Cdr. May's remains were transported to Milwaukee and buried at Wanderer's Rest Cemetery, now called Lincoln Memorial Cemetery. His parents, Earl Sr. and Norma, who died just a few weeks apart in 1965, now lie beside him. He left a widow Thelma, a son Richard E. May, a daughter Carol Ann May, and a brother Del. Millville Army Airfield Museum has a display in May's memory and Lawrence Township Historical Society has dedicated a road sign to mark the crash site.

Lt. Cdr. May, in addition to the Silver Star and Distinguished Flying Cross, was awarded a Gold Star in lieu of a second Distinguished Flying Cross, two Air Medals, Navy Unit Commendation, Asiatic - Pacific Campaign Medal with three stars, American Campaign Medal, Navy Occupation Service Medal "Asia" clasp, Philippine Liberation Ribbon with two Bronze Stars and the World War II Victory Medal.

Note: Ensigns Bill Burnham and Sam Carlton died during Fighting 17's training, but no records appear to exist to clarify just what happened.

2

Corpus Christi

Nearly 75% of the pilots who served with Fighting 17 were stationed at Corpus Christi. The base was given the nickname "*Corpus Crapsi*."

Naval aviation had rapidly developed in the 1930s, and facilities to support this expansion were needed. Amongst the sites developed was an area near Corpus Christi, Texas. From the outset the base was planned as an air station for the training of naval aviators. The local weather conditions were deemed very favorable, in that flying time could be maximised for training purposes.

Naval Air Station (N.A.S.) Corpus Christi was commissioned on March 12, 1941. Amongst those present at the ceremony was Congressman (and future President of the United States) Lyndon Johnson.

Training commenced at N.A.S. Corpus Christi in April 1941, with the first class of Aviation Cadets graduating on November 1, 1941. During the war years Corpus Christi produced thousands of naval aviators, amongst them future astronaut John Glenn and future President of the United States George Bush (Sr.), who was the youngest cadet ever to graduate. More than 35,000 aviators earned their wings at N.A.S. Corpus Christi by the end of WWII. Corpus Christi was the only base that provided training right through from primary, into intermediate, and on to advanced training all on one site. At one time it was the largest pilot training facility in the world. In 1972, Naval Air Training Command Headquarters moved from Pensacola to Corpus Christi and Training Air Wing Four was formed. The station's airfield was named Truax Field on August 6, 1986. This was in honor of Lt. Myron Milton Truax, United States Navy, although it is not the only airfield known as Truax Field. The training program is currently 18 months long due to the advances in technology in modern warfare. This compares to four months in WWII. Around 400 new aviators qualify every year. N.A.S. Corpus Christi is also home to the Helicopter Mine Countermeasures Squadron Fifteen. In addition, enlisted and civilian personnel serving the Navy, Marine Corps, Air Force, Coast Guard, Army, and Customs Service are based there.

For Navy Aviation Cadets in World War II, Primary flight training consisted of six stages: A to F. After each stage you had a flight check. If you failed you would have to re-check. If you failed the re-check you were dropped from the program and would be "washed out."

The following photographs contain images of activities at Naval Air Station (N.A.S.) Corpus Christi, Texas, during the early 1940s. *Courtesy National Naval Aviation Museum.*

A Stage consisted of approximately 10-14 hours dual time, after which you would be expected to go solo in a PT-17 Stearman.

B Stage was composed of basic upper air work and general handling, short field landings and side-slips to landing, altitude maintenance and holding compass headings.

C Stage taught the fundamentals of aerobatics. The SNV-1 Vultee "Vibrator" was one of the aircraft used.

D Stage was the final check before advanced training.

E Stage moved on to basic formation flying.

F Stage was night flying.

For Advanced Flight Training aircraft such as the SNV were used primarily for instrument flight training and navigation. North American SNJs were used for formation flying and fighter tactics with mock dog fights. If they passed this stage the pilots were then sent to operational training in fighters, usually in F4F Wildcats or F6F Hellcats.

3

Chance Vought

Designed in response to the U.S. Navy's competition for a high performance fighter, the Chance Vought F4U Corsair was unusual, in that it went against the then in-line engine precedent for fighters that was demonstrated by the Messerschmitt 109, Spitfire, North American P-51, and the Curtiss P-40 Warhawk. The Corsair was designed around the new Pratt & Whitney R2800, which with its 2,000 horsepower was at the time the most powerful engine put in a fighter. The huge 13ft propeller needed for the R2800, and the need to avoid long and potentially bouncy and fragile undercarriage legs led to the unique W-shaped wing and the nickname that followed it – "the bent wing bird." First flown in 1940, the Corsair was not an immediate success due to the long "hose nose" and rear-set cockpit and the resulting effect on visibility for the pilot, coupled with problematic low speed handling qualities. The Corsair was the first American fighter to exceed 400 miles per hour. However, there were many landing accidents, and although the aircraft was put into production, the U.S. Navy would not approve it for use on carriers.

The first Corsairs to see combat were land based Marine Corps units at Guadalcanal. It was at Guadalcanal that Corsairs first demonstrated their aerial superiority over the vaunted Japanese Zero that had outperformed all U.S. fighters before the Corsair.

Chance Vought Chief Experimental Test Pilot Boone Guyton in 1943. *Courtesy Peter S. Guyton.*

This is a photograph of the Chance Vought Factory in Stratford, Connecticut, which was the birthplace of the Corsairs. Vought employment stood at 4,450 in 1940, and by 1943 had increased to 13,447. *Courtesy National Naval Aviation Museum.*

Vought's production began slowly, partially due to the number of changes implemented before the program began: the cockpit was moved three feet aft to accommodate more fuel and the engine bay was redesigned to accommodate the updated R-2800-8 engine, providing 2,000 horsepower on take-off. *Courtesy National Naval Aviation Museum.*

In 1944 alone more than 5,000 Corsairs were produced. This was more than three times the whole production of Vought aircraft before the war years. *Courtesy National Naval Aviation Museum.*

After Guadalcanal Corsairs took part in almost every major campaign in the Pacific. Corsairs also flew with the Royal Navy in the Atlantic, Pacific and Indian Oceans and also with the Royal New Zealand Air Force in the Pacific. Fighting 17 provided proof, under battle conditions, of the suitability of the F4U for carrier operations when they were first into combat flying off a carrier with the Corsair in the Battle of the Solomon Sea in November 1943.

Continually developed, and with problems gradually ironed out, the Corsair became a formidable fighting machine and a mainstay for the U.S. Navy on carriers in the war against the Japanese home islands. It was called "Whistling Death" by the Japanese. In the course of shooting down 2,140 enemy aircraft, only 189 Corsairs were lost in aerial combat – a ratio of better than 11:1.

The conclusion of WWII and the introduction of jet fighters did not spell the end of the Corsair's combat career. Between 1946 and 1950 Corsairs still served with the U.S. 6th and 7th Fleet. During the Korean War Corsairs flew low-altitude fighter-bomber close air support missions. The last of the F4U Corsair line was supplied to the *Aeronavale*, the French Navy, where it saw combat in Indo-China, Suez and Algeria. The Corsair served with the *Aeronavale* until 1964, twenty-six years after it was designed. A long and distinguished career for any fighter.

Opposite: F4U-1 final assembly. 11,798 Corsairs were produced during WWII. *Courtesy National Naval Aviation Museum.*

By the end of 1944 Chance Vought was turning out 300 Corsairs a month, or one complete airplane every 82 minutes. Vought built 2,814 of the F4U-1s. *Courtesy National Naval Aviation Museum.*

Final assembly of an F4U Corsair. *Courtesy Vought.*

When Fighting 17 went into combat in October 1943 they flew the F4U-1A fifth production aircraft, which included a number of modifications. Each change necessitated considerable research, engineering and testing at Vought. *Courtesy National Naval Aviation Museum.*

Corsairs on line awaiting delivery. *Courtesy National Naval Aviation Museum.*

Ten F4U-1 Corsairs having been accepted by the Navy waiting to be delivered. *Courtesy National Naval Aviation Museum.*

Chance Vought test pilots in 1942. *Courtesy Peter S. Guyton.*

Powered by a 2,000 horsepower Pratt and Whitney R2800 engine, this streamlined fighting ship of the skies, the FG-1 Corsair, stands poised on the apron of the Goodyear Aircraft Corporation at Akron. *Courtesy Goodyear Aircraft Corporation / the Burriss Family.*

F4U- A, 3/4 front right side view. *Courtesy Vought.*

F4U-1A, right side view. *Courtesy Vought.*

F4U-1A, front view. *Courtesy Vought.*

F4U-1, 3/4 front left side view. Dive test aircraft. *Courtesy Vought.*

F4U-1, 3/4 rear right side view. Dive test aircraft. *Courtesy Vought.*

Ray DeLeva (Left) and "Butch" Davenport in front of "Big Hog." Ray DeLeva was a Field Service Technician for Chance Vought for 40 years and retired in 1973. *Courtesy Vought.*

A Vought Service Representative with Fighting 17 Engineering Officer "Butch" Davenport (Right). *Courtesy Vought.*

Ray DeLeva (Left) with another Vought Representative in front of "Big Hog," Tom Blackburn's aircraft. *Courtesy Vought.*

Ray DeLeva pointing to the squadron scoreboard with another Vought Service Representative on Bougainville in 1944. *Courtesy Vought.*

F4U, Killer of the Sky. This lone sinister looking Vought Corsair of the U.S. Navy is heightened by the somber background and leaden sea as it is banking before diving down toward a target somewhere in the South Pacific. *Courtesy U.S. Navy photo / Vought.*

F4U, Killers in the Sky. These U.S. Navy Chance Vought Corsairs (F4Us) wheel about before attacking a target somewhere in the South Pacific. Corsairs, flown by Navy and Marine Corps pilots, played a significant role in smashing Japanese air power in the Pacific theater. *Courtesy U.S. Navy photo / Vought*

4

Fighting 17 in Training

After Fighting 17 was commissioned on January 1, 1943, Tom Blackburn had nine months to get the squadron ready for combat in the then brand new Chance Vought Corsair. When the squadron was first commissioned they only had about ten SNJ advanced trainers and eight F4Fs. The F4Fs were used to give the new pilots fighter hours before moving up to the F4U.

Corsairs arrived in mid-February 1943 with many trips to the factory to pick up the new F4U-1s, and the squadron had a full complement by mid March.

Once they had become familiar with this powerful new fighter they then had to qualify for carrier landings. This was made all the more difficult due to the long "hose nose" and pronounced bounce on landing. To become carrier qualified the pilot had to fly five touchdowns and arrests; not an easy task whilst still getting to grips with such a new and formidable aeroplane as the Corsair was. Lt. Cdr. Tom Blackburn worked and trained the men hard and instilled a team ethic. He also stressed the importance of gunnery as, after all, the aim of air combat is to shoot down the enemy. Blackburn "*Worked their tails off*" to be proficient in all these areas. From Blackburn's experience fuel saving techniques and instrument training to prevent losses from disorientation were given a priority along with night flying, low level work on the water, and target acquisition techniques.

Nothing was missed to help hone the skills of Fighting 17 pilots that were going to be tested when facing the Japanese. It was a tall order, and there was the loss of a number of pilots in training, as is often the case as combat units prepare themselves for war. This is reflected in the In Memoriam chapter of this book.

"Hap" Bowers in flight gear. He entered N.A.S. Glenview, Illinois, as a Cadet in February 1942. *Courtesy Alexandra Bowers.*

"Hap" Bowers on May 25, 1942, after he had transferred to N.A.S. Corpus Christi. *Courtesy Alexandra Bowers.*

"Hap" Bowers on July 1, 1942, at N.A.S. Corpus Christi. *Courtesy Alexandra Bowers.*

"Hap" Bowers received his wings on October 16, 1942, at N.A.S. Corpus Christi. *Courtesy Alexandra Bowers.*

"Hap" Bowers celebrating becoming an Ensign in October 1942. *Courtesy Alexandra Bowers.*

"Hap" Bowers in October 1942 as a young Ensign. *Courtesy Alexandra Bowers.*

Fighting 17 pilots Jack Chasnoff, "Andy" Anderson and Mills Schanuel during training. Chasnoff middle row 5th from left. Anderson front row 2nd from left. Schanuel front row 5th from left. *Courtesy the Chasnoff Family.*

Bob Kieffer in 1942 as an Aviation Cadet at N.A.S. Corpus Christi, Texas. *Courtesy the Kieffer Family.*

Bob Kieffer in 1942 as an Aviation Cadet. *Courtesy the Kieffer Family.*

Aerial photograph showing part of Naval Operating Base, Norfolk, VA, including the Naval Training Center in the foreground and seaplane hangars at the top of the photograph. The wooden training ship *Electric* is visible at the bottom of the photograph. *Courtesy National Museum of Naval Aviation.*

Jim Halford in cold weather suit in early 1943. *Courtesy the James A. Halford Collection.*

A formation of SB2C-1s of Bombing Squadron Seventeen (VB-17) pictured in flight, probably in the vicinity of Norfolk, Virginia. The first squadron to receive the Helldiver, VB-17 experienced some growing pains with the type, losing numerous aircraft while operating from shore and aboard the U.S.S. *Bunker Hill* (CV-17) during the carrier's shakedown cruise. While flying from *Bunker Hill* on November 11, 1943, the squadron introduced the aircraft to combat during a raid on Rabaul. *Courtesy National Museum of Naval Aviation.*

A formation of SB2C-1s of Bombing Squadron Seventeen (VB-17) pictured in flight, probably in the vicinity of Norfolk, Virginia. *Courtesy National Museum of Naval Aviation.*

Low level flying by one of Fighting 17's Corsairs, probably at Norfolk in the spring of 1943. *Courtesy Tom Blackburn Collection.*

N.A.S. Floyd Bennett Field, where Fighting 17 collected F4Us and ferried them back to N.A.S. Norfolk. *Courtesy National Museum of Naval Aviation*

Another view of N.A.S. Floyd Bennett Field, where Fighting 17 collected their F4Us and ferried them back to N.A.S. Norfolk. *Courtesy National Museum of Naval Aviation.*

An F4U-1 of Fighting 17 on the U.S.S. *Charger* during carrier suitability tests in March 1943. *Courtesy Robert Lawson Photograph Collection, National Museum of Naval Aviation / U.S. Navy photo.*

One of Fighting 17's F4U-1s on the U.S.S. *Charger* during carrier landing qualifications in Chesapeake Bay in March 1943. *Courtesy Robert Lawson Photograph Collection, National Museum of Naval Aviation / U.S. Navy photo*

One of Fighting 17's F4U-1s about to touch down on the deck of the U.S.S. *Charger* in Chesapeake Bay during the squadron's initial carrier landing qualifications in March 1943. *Courtesy Robert Lawson Photograph Collection, National Museum of Naval Aviation / U.S. Navy photo.*

Another view of one of Fighting 17's F4U-1s on the U.S.S. *Charger* during carrier landing qualifications in Chesapeake Bay in March 1943. *Courtesy Robert Lawson Photograph Collection, National Museum of Naval Aviation / U.S. Navy photo.*

SB2C-3 of Bombing Squadron 82 (VB-82) pictured after going over the side of the U.S.S. *Charger* (CVE-30) during training operations off the East Coast. The pilot, Lt. O. R. Brown, received minor head injuries. Note that there was no gunner on the flight, standard practice during carrier qualification flights. *Courtesy National Museum of Naval Aviation.*

An F6F-3 Hellcat after going over the side during carrier qualifications on board U.S.S. *Charger* (CVE-30) operating in Chesapeake Bay. *Courtesy National Museum of Naval Aviation.*

Another view of an F6F-3 Hellcat after going over the side during carrier qualifications on board U.S.S. *Charger* (CVE-30) operating in Chesapeake Bay. *Courtesy National Museum of Naval Aviation.*

A TBF/TBM Avenger after crashing during carrier qualifications on board U.S.S. *Charger* (CVE-30) operating in Chesapeake Bay. *Courtesy National Museum of Naval Aviation.*

SB2U-2 with Scouting Squadron Forty Two (VS-42) pictured on the deck of U.S.S. *Charger* (CVE-30) after a crash landing. The pilot was Ens. C. N. Rohmann. *Courtesy Robert Lawson Photograph Collection, National Museum of Naval Aviation.*

An F6F-3 Hellcat aircraft of VF-2 is on the very edge of the flight deck of U.S.S. *Charger* (CVE-30). The aircraft is tilted, resting on the port wing. Twelve crewmen are on the port wing in what appears to be an attempt to stop the aircraft going over the side. *Courtesy Robert Lawson Photograph Collection, National Museum of Naval Aviation.*

An OS2U Kingfisher seaplane is craned aboard the auxiliary carrier U.S.S. *Charger* (CVE-30), a former merchantman converted to an aircraft carrier. *Courtesy National Museum of Naval Aviation.*

Hal Jackson in 1943. *Courtesy Hal and Barbara Jackson.*

A division of Fighting 17's F4U-1s early in 1943. *Courtesy Vought.*

"Timmy" Gile leading a flight of F4U-1s off Manteo, NC, in the spring of 1943. *Courtesy Robert Lawson Photograph Collection, National Museum of Naval Aviation / U.S. Navy photo.*

Naval Auxiliary Air Station, Manteo, NC. Notice the water coming in on Runway Four. *Courtesy Harry Bridges, Dare County Regional Airport Museum.*

Another view of Naval Auxiliary Air Station, Manteo, NC. *Courtesy Harry Bridges, Dare County Regional Airport Museum.*

James Alex Halford, Jr., was one of a few combat veterans that Fighting 17 relied on when going into combat for the first time. *Courtesy the James A. Halford Collection.*

Lt. (jg) James A. Halford, Jr., receiving a Gold Star to his Distinguished Flying Cross in April 1943. *Courtesy the James A. Halford Collection.*

Lt. (jg) James A. Halford, Jr., was awarded a Distinguished Flying Cross for his actions at the Battle of Midway and a Gold Star to his D.F.C. for his service at Guadalcanal. This was presented in April 1943. *Courtesy the James A. Halford Collection.*

James A. Halford, Jr., fought with Fighting Five in the intense combat at Guadalcanal in September 1942. Halford is in the front row 5th from left, with his helmet in front of him. *Courtesy the James A. Halford Collection.*

Bob Kieffer in April 1943. *Courtesy the Kieffer Family.*

Two future aces, "Big Jim" Streig and "Chico" Freeman, in June 1943. *Courtesy the Kieffer Family.*

Ray and Dolly Ferguson and Pat and Bob Kieffer in June 1943 at the Monticello Hotel. *Courtesy the Kieffer Family.*

The Beach Club, Nags Head, North Carolina, May 1943. *Courtesy the Kieffer Family.*

Bob Kieffer in June 1943. *Courtesy the Kieffer Family.*

Bob Kieffer and his dog "Nasty" in June 1943. *Courtesy the Kieffer Family.*

Fighting 17 dinner party at Nags Head Beach in June 1943. *Courtesy the Kieffer Family.*

Dinner party at the Gilbert's at Nags Head in June 1943. *Courtesy the Kieffer Family.*

Another view of a Fighting 17 dinner party at Nags Head Beach in June 1943. *Courtesy the Keffer Family.*

"Tuffy" Henderson, "Big Jim" Streig, Doug Gutenkunst, Lou Kelley, "Andy" Anderson and Jack Chasnoff at the beach in spring 1943. *Courtesy the Chasnoff Family.*

Joy and "Andy" Anderson at the beach in spring 1943. *Courtesy the Anderson Family.*

Doug Gutenkunst at the beach in spring 1943. *Courtesy the Chasnoff Family.*

Jack and Alice Chasnoff in the spring of 1943. *Courtesy the Chasnoff Family.*

"Tuffy" Henderson, "Big Jim" Streig, Doug Gutenkunst, Lou Kelley, "Andy" Anderson and Jack Chasnoff at the beach in spring 1943. *Courtesy the Chasnoff Family.*

Far left: "Teeth" Burriss relaxing on the beach in the spring of 1943. *Courtesy Vought.*

Left: James A. Halford Jr., and his aircraft, probably at Norfolk in the spring of 1943. Note number 13 under engine cowling. *Courtesy the James A. Halford Collection.*

Another view of James A. Halford, Jr., and his aircraft, probably at Norfolk in the spring of 1943. Note number 13 under engine cowling. *Courtesy the James A. Halford Collection.*

James A. Halford, Jr., in his Corsair in the spring of 1943. *Courtesy the James A. Halford Collection.*

Two views of Ensign "Tim" Gile in front of his parent's house in Jaffrey, NH, in 1941. He was based at N.A.S. Miami at the time. *Courtesy the Gile Family.*

Robert "Andy" Anderson received his wings at N.A.S. Corpus Christi, Texas, then reported to Miami, Florida, to train as a fighter pilot. *Courtesy the Anderson Family.*

September 29, 1943, N.A.S. Jacksonville. Training Flight. Rear Row L – R: Lt. Cdr. J. C. Kelly, Ens. G. M. Keller, Jr., Ens. E. E. Beeler, and Ens. J. B. Black. Front row L – R: Ens. R. M. Lang, Ens. J. C. Dixon, Ens. D. R. McQueen and Ens. N. G. Baumgarden. Dixon, McQueen, Keller and Beeler all reported to Fighting 17 in January 1944 as replacement pilots. *Courtesy U.S. Navy photo.*

Lou Fitzgerald 3rd from left back row. In training at N.A.S. Melbourne on September 1, 1943, prior to reporting to Fighting 17. *Courtesy the Fitzgerald Family.*

John M. Smith as a young Ensign in the summer of 1943. *Courtesy John M. Smith Collection.*

Mervin Ward "Ace" Cole in the summer of 1942. *Courtesy the Cole Family.*

Harvey "Matty" Matthews as a young Ensign at Pensacola in the summer of 1943. *Courtesy the Matthews Family.*

Ward Cole with his mother in 1943. *Courtesy the Cole Family.*

Future Fighting 17 pilots and Pensacola graduates Harvey Matthews and Ward Cole at a friend's wedding in the summer of 1943. Back Row L – R: Matthews 2nd from left, Cole 3rd from left. *Courtesy the Matthews Family.*

Don McQueen in February 1942. *Courtesy the McQueen Family.*

Don McQueen on October 30, 1943, shortly before he reported to Fighting 17. *Courtesy the McQueen Family.*

Don McQueen, second from left, with parents and family on October 30, 1943. *Courtesy the McQueen Family.*

Don McQueen with his father Robert McQueen. *Courtesy the McQueen Family.*

Ensign Don McQueen with neighborhood military friends. McQueen 5th from left. *Courtesy the McQueen Family.*

Ensign Don McQueen with a girlfriend. *Courtesy the McQueen Family.*

Howard McClain Burriss in flight gear probably in the summer of 1942. *Courtesy the Burriss Family.*

L – R: Two young Ensigns. Harvey Matthews and a buddy in 1943. *Courtesy the Matthews Family.*

Ensign Louis Marsden Kelley in 1942. He was one of many Fighting 17 pilots who trained at N.A.S. Corpus Christi. *Courtesy Sarah Bradshaw Lewis.*

Louis Marsden Kelley in 1942. He graduated from Junior College and then applied to the Navy for flight training. *Courtesy Sarah Bradshaw Lewis.*

Edward Bennett Turner as a Young Ensign in 1941. *Courtesy U.S. Navy photo via the Edward Bennett Turner Family.*

Ensign John H. Cantrell in 1942. *Courtesy U.S. Navy photo via the Cantrell Family.*

5

Shakedown Cruise

With the introduction of the new Essex class carriers and their air groups equipped with new combat aircraft the writing was on the wall for the Japanese.

The U.S.S. *Bunker Hill* was built in Quincy, Massachusetts, and it was commissioned on May 24, 1943. Her air group, Carrier Air Group Seventeen, had been commissioned on the first of January 1943 at N.A.S. Norfolk with Commander M. P. "Bags" Bagdanovich as Air Group Commander. Its four squadrons (VB-17, VF-17, VS-17 and VT-17) worked hard in the spring to prepare when the ship was ready. VT-17 operated the Grumman TBF Avenger, however, the new Curtiss SB2C-1 Helldivers of VB-17 were far from ready. One VB-17 pilot said that the aircraft had "*more bugs than an oriental flophouse*." The Vought F4U-1 Corsairs of VF-17 were also new to the fleet and had many problems to be ironed out.

On June 28, 1943, flight operations commenced in Chesapeake Bay, and Air Group 17 prepared for combat operations in the Pacific. On July 13, 1943, the *Bunker Hill* sailed for the shakedown cruise to Trinidad, in the Gulf of Paria. This was designed to mesh the air group as a team and run the bugs out of the ship. This was also the last chance for Blackburn to decide on the team he would take into combat, and a number of changes were made prior to leaving for Pearl Harbor. This also included delivery of new F4U-1A Corsairs.

The *Bunker Hill* returned to Norfolk on August 10, 1943, and Air Group 17 and the ship made their final preparations to go to war. In September the *Bunker Hill* left for the Pacific and the war. At Pearl Harbor, Fighting 17 was replaced by F6Fs and became a land - based squadron in the Solomon Islands. This was due to logistics, as the Marines had parts for the Corsairs in the islands, whereas the Navy could not support the only carrier based Corsair squadron at that time.

One of Fighting 17's F4U-1s on the U.S.S. *Bunker Hill* during her shakedown cruise in July 1943. *Courtesy Robert Lawson Photograph Collection, National Museum of Naval Aviation / U.S. Navy photo.*

This Fighting 17 F4U-1 was piloted by Ensign Ray Ferguson who had just made the 1000th landing aboard the U.S.S. *Bunker Hill* (CV-17), July 28, 1943. *Courtesy Tailhook Collection / National Archives.*

Ensign Ray Ferguson, who had just made the 1000th landing aboard the U.S.S. *Bunker Hill* (CV-17), July 28, 1943. *Courtesy U.S. Navy photo via the Ferguson Family.*

Ens. F.A. "Andy" Jagger. Hook point failure. July 26, 1943. Due to a design fault the tailhooks snapped when they came into contact with the steel drain channels upon landing. If the hook caught an arresting wire they were lifted clear of the deck. If they missed a wire they caught the drain channel and snapped. A new hook was designed and the problem was resolved. *Courtesy Robert Lawson Photograph Collection, National Museum of Naval Aviation / U.S. Navy photo.*

A barrier crash (#10) on the U.S.S. *Bunker Hill* in July 1943. *Courtesy Robert Lawson Photograph Collection, National Museum of Naval Aviation / U.S. Navy photo.*

One of Fighting 17's F4U-1s (#24) flipping over on its back on the U.S.S. *Bunker Hill* in July 1943. *Courtesy Robert Lawson Photograph Collection, National Museum of Naval Aviation / U.S. Navy photo.*

One of Fighting 17's birdcage canopy F4U-1s on the U.S.S. *Bunker Hill* during her shakedown cruise in July 1943. *Courtesy Robert Lawson Photograph Collection, National Museum of Naval Aviation / U.S. Navy photo.*

Another view of one of Fighting 17's birdcage canopy F4U-1s on the U.S.S. *Bunker Hill* during her shakedown cruise in July 1943. *Courtesy Tailhook Collection.*

SB2C-1 of Bombing Squadron Seventeen (VB-17) pictured during approach for recovery aboard U.S.S. *Bunker Hill* (CV-17) during operations in the Caribbean. *Courtesy Robert Lawson Photograph Collection, National Museum of Naval Aviation.*

SB2C-1 Helldiver of Bombing Squadron Seventeen (VB-17) takes a wave-off during flight operations aboard U.S.S. *Bunker Hill* (CV-17) in the Caribbean. The first squadron to receive the Helldiver, VB-17 experienced some growing pains with the type, losing numerous aircraft while operating from shore and aboard U.S.S. *Bunker Hill* (CV-17) during the carrier's shakedown cruise. *Courtesy Robert Lawson Photograph Collection, National Museum of Naval Aviation.*

SB2C-1 of Bombing Squadron Seventeen (VB-17) pictured after losing its tail during recovery aboard U.S.S. *Bunker Hill* (CV-17) during operations in the Caribbean. *Courtesy Robert Lawson Photograph Collection, National Museum of Naval Aviation.*

Lt. (jg) James A. Halford's (3½ kills in VF-5 & 6 in 1942) aircraft on the U.S.S. *Bunker Hill* July 9, 1943. *Courtesy Robert Lawson Photograph Collection, National Museum of Naval Aviation / U.S. Navy photo.*

F4U-1 Corsair "17-F-24" of Fighting 17 on its back following a carrier landing mishap aboard U.S.S. *Bunker Hill* in August 1943. *Courtesy Tailhook Collection.*

Tom Blackburn flying in Lem Cooke's F4U-1A. The #29 aircraft later became famous as "Ike" Kepford's aircraft, but when the first tactical organisation was introduced in the spring of 1943, Lem Cooke was allocated this aircraft. *Courtesy the Tom Blackburn Collection.*

F4U-1A of Fighting 17 landing on the deck of the U.S.S. *Bunker Hill* on September 14, 1943. *Courtesy Robert Lawson Photograph Collection, National Museum of Naval Aviation / U.S. Navy photo.*

F4U-1As of Fighting 17 on the U.S.S. *Bunker Hill*'s fl ght deck going through the Panama Canal on September 17, 1943. *Courtesy Robert Lawson Photograph Collection, National Museum of Naval Aviation / U.S. Navy photo.*

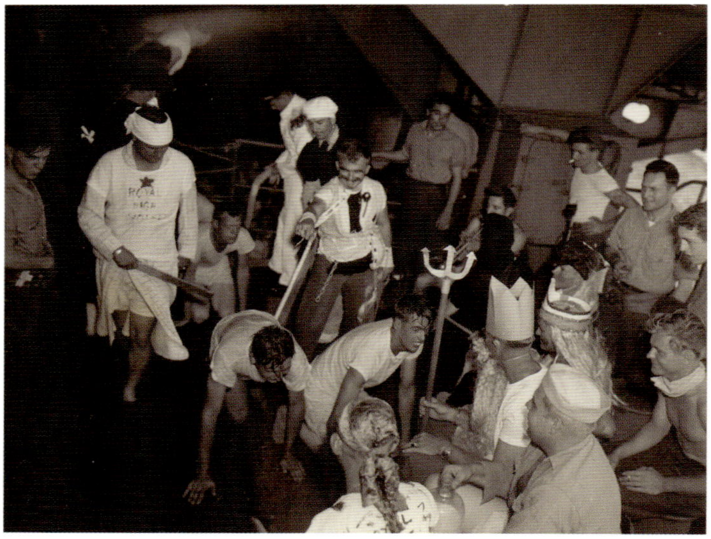

The traditional "Crossing the Line" (Equator) ceremony, where "Pollywogs" (seamen who have not crossed the equator) are initiated by "Shellbacks" (seamen who have crossed the equator). *Courtesy the Anderson Family.*

Another photo of the "Crossing the Line" ceremony. It has been a long naval tradition to initiate "Pollywogs" upon their first crossing of the Equator. *Courtesy Alexandra Bowers.*

Another photo of the "Crossing the Line" ceremony, where there is no escape from the initiation. *Courtesy the Anderson Family.*

Another photo of the "Crossing the Line" ceremony. Not sure whether this "Pollywog" is enjoying the procedure. *Courtesy the Anderson Family.*

Another photo of the "Crossing the Line" ceremony. "Dirty Eddie" March was the Royal Barber and cut about 300 heads of hair. Messing everyone's hair up in general. *Courtesy the Burriss Family.*

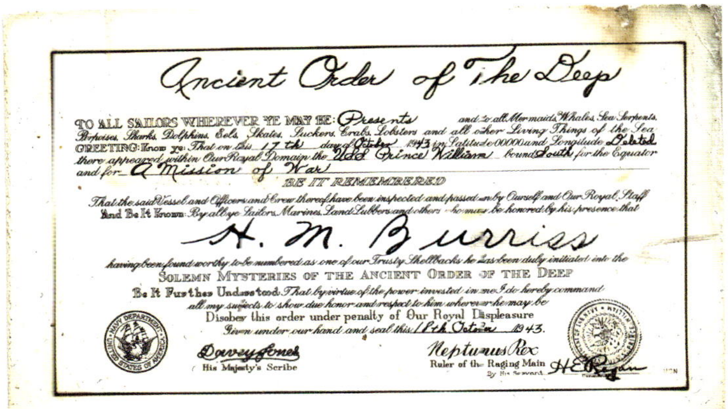

Ancient Order of The Deep

TO ALL SAILORS WHEREVER YE MAY BE: Presents and to all Mermaids, Whales, Sea Serpents, Porpoises, Sharks, Dolphins, Eels, Skates, Suckers, Crabs, Lobsters and all other Living Things of the Sea GREETING: Know ye: That on this 17th day of October 1943 in Latitude 00000 and Longitude Deleted there appeared within Our Royal Domain the USS Prince William bound South for the Equator and for A Mission of War

BE IT REMEMBERED

That the said Vessel and Officers and Crew thereof have been inspected and passed on by Ourself and Our Royal Staff And Be It Known: By all ye Sailors, Marines, Land Lubbers and others who may be honored by his presence that

H. M. Burriss

having been found worthy to be numbered as one of our Trusty Shellbacks he has been duly initiated into the SOLEMN MYSTERIES OF THE ANCIENT ORDER OF THE DEEP

Be It Furthes Undsestood: That by virtue of the power invested in me I do hereby command all my subjects to show due honor and respect to him wherever he may be

Disobey this order under penalty of Our Royal Displeasure

Given under our hand and seal this 18th October 1943.

Davey Jones — His Majesty's Scribe

Neptunus Rex — Ruler of the Raging Main — By His Servant H E Regan

Ancient order of the deep for "Teeth" Burriss on the U.S.S. *Prince William*, October 17, 1943. *Courtesy the Burriss Family.*

6

Ondongo - Place of Death

After being detached from the U.S.S. *Bunker Hill* Fighting 17 was ordered to Ondongo, New Georgia, which to the locals meant Place of Death, and arrived on October 27, 1943.

Rabaul was the main Japanese outpost in the Southwest Pacific and had a perfect anchorage and natural base for shipping in Simpson Harbor.

In order to bring Rabaul into range of U.S. Forces they landed at Bougainville, and Fighting 17's first combat was to support the landings on Empress Augusta Bay, Bougainville, on November 1, 1943. The aim being to establish a beachhead and build airstrips which could be used to launch attacks against Rabaul.

Fighting 17's task was not only to support the landings at Bougainville, but also to protect the American forces, thereby neutralizing the Japanese Air Force in the Bougainville area.

They supported a carrier strike on Rabaul on November 5, 1943, and another major carrier task force was launched on November 11, 1943, which was one of the significant missions for Fighting 17. They flew from land bases to cover the carriers while a strike went into Rabaul. They landed and refuelled on the carriers and were over the carriers to protect them when the Japanese launched their strike. This was done with great success, and Fighting 17 scored 18.5 victories and ensured the carriers were not damaged.

This was the first time Corsairs had been operated off a carrier in combat in WWII despite being unproven for carrier operations at this time.

Most Fighting 17 pilots averaged over 100 hours of combat flying on the first tour. They were relieved on December 2, 1943, and headed to Australia for a much needed rest.

Fighting 17 at Ford Island, Pearl Harbor, prior to being deployed into action. Photo taken on October 12, 1943. Don Innis is missing from the group, as he reported to Fighting 17 the next day. Front Row: Schub, Wharton, Gile, Killefer, Kropf, Jagger, Cordray, Davenport. 2nd Row: Burriss, Baker, Jackson, Kleinman, Hedrick, Blackburn, Hogan, Bowers. 3rd Row: Cooke, Anderson, Meek, Malone, Chasnoff, Schanuel, Ellsworth, Beacham, Freeman, Cunningham, Kurlander, Hill, Keith, Landreth, Bell. Top Row: Dunn, Gutenkunst, March, Halford, Gilbert, Henning, Kelley, Kepford, Streig, Pillsbury, May, Hall, Popp. Of the forty-three pilots manning the squadron prior to first combat, ten were killed while serving with Fighting 17. *Courtesy the Tom Blackburn Collection.*

William "Country" Landreth at Pearl Harbor in October 1943. Fighting 17 outward bound at Ford Island. *Courtesy the Landreth Family Collection.*

Mel "Kurly" Kurlander, who served with Fighting 17 on both tours of combat. *Courtesy Mel Kurlander.*

Hotel Mud Plaza, Ondonga, November 1943. NB. In the Fighting 17 combat reports and war diary it is referred to as Ondongo, not Ondonga. *Courtesy Vought.*

Harry Andrew "Dirty Eddie" March, Jr. Fighting 17 ace with five victories. March reported to Fighting 17 on October 5, 1943. *Courtesy the March Family.*

F4Us of Fighting 17 at Munda, New Georgia, at the start of the first combat tour in November 1943. *Courtesy Vought.*

Jack Chasnoff sitting on his Corsair at Ondongo late in 1943. *Courtesy the Chasnoff Family.*

Ready Hut, Ondongo in November 1943. Back row L – R: Schub, Schanuel, Hedrick, Ellsworth, Landreth, Anderson Hill and Herrmann. Front Row L – R: Cunningham, Baker (in front of Cunningham), Jackson, Cordray, Kelley, Hogan, Chasnoff, and Jagger. Jagger had just returned from a mission. *Courtesy Vought / the Anderson Family.*

Tom Blackburn in Corsair "Big Hog" running up on line. *Courtesy U.S. Naval Historical Center / M. W. "Butch" Davenport Collection.*

Doug Gutenkunst (Left) and Bob Hogan (Right) at Ondongo in November 1943. The man in the center is unknown. *Courtesy Vought.*

Doug Gutenkunst (Left) and Bob Hogan (Right) outside Hog Hollow, Ondongo, in November 1943. *Courtesy Vought.*

Lem Cooke, Bob Hogan, Mel Kurlander, and Doug Gutenkunst (behind Kurlander) at Hog Hollow, Ondongo, November 1943. *Courtesy Vought.*

L – R: Davenport, Cooke, Hogan, and Gutenkunst in front of Hog Hollow, Ondongo, November 1943. *Courtesy Vought.*

#33 - Lonesome Polecat. As aircraft were lost or damaged, Butch Davenport's aircraft #33, was wrecked and was replaced new with #9 his final aircraft. *Courtesy U.S. Naval Historical Center / M. W. "Butch" Davenport Collection.*

Paul Cordray Fighting 17 ace with six victories at Ondongo in November 1943. *Courtesy Vought.*

Above: Roger Hedrick and his aircraft. An exceptional fighter pilot and Naval Officer. *Courtesy U.S. Naval Historical Center / M. W. "Butch" Davenport Collection.* Bottom left: Tom Blackburn taxiing out in "Big Hog" at Munda in November 1943. *Courtesy U.S. Naval Historical Center / M. W. "Butch" Davenport Collection.* Bottom right: Fighting 17 ace "Timmy" Gile at Ondongo in November 1943. *Courtesy U.S. Naval Historical Center / M. W. "Butch" Davenport Collection.*

Tom Blackburn in Japanese officer's hat on November 15, 1943. *Courtesy U.S. Naval Historical Center / M. W. "Butch" Davenport Collection.*

A division of Corsairs with #34 "L.A. City Limits" flown by "Chico" Freeman in the foreground. *Courtesy U.S. Naval Historical Center / M. W. "Butch" Davenport Collection.*

Hal Jackson at Ondongo, in November 1943. *Courtesy Vought.*

Jack Chasnoff beside his aircraft in November 1943 at Ondongo. *Courtesy the Chasnoff Family.*

Fighting 17 F4U Corsairs. *Courtesy Vought.*

Ray Beacham walking away from his Corsair. *Courtesy Harry Bridges, Dare County Regional Airport Museum.*

Lt. (jg) Robert "Andy" Anderson in flight gear. *Courtesy the Anderson Family.*

Jack Chasnoff in his aircraft showing two Japanese victory flags. *Courtesy the Chasnoff Family.*

"Hap" Bowers and Dan Cunningham in "Command Car," New Georgia in 1943. *Courtesy U.S. Naval Historical Center / M. W. "Butch" Davenport Collection.*

L – R: "Dirty Eddie" March, Tom Killefer, and "Big Jim" Streig at Ondongo in November 1943. *Courtesy Vought / Lennard Edmisten.*

Tom Blackburn at Ondongo, New Georgia, in November 1943. The bullet holes that resulted from Roger Hedrick's accidental shooting at Blackburn on 11 November have just been recently patched. *Courtesy Vought / Lennard Edmisten / the Tom Blackburn Collection / U.S. Naval Historical Center / M. W. "Butch" Davenport Collection.*

L – R: Hal Jackson, "Ike" Kepford and Paul Cordray at Ondongo in November 1943. *Courtesy Robert Lawson Photograph Collection, National Museum of Naval Aviation / U.S. Navy photo.*

Two aces, "Big Jim" Streig behind "Ike" Kepford. *Courtesy Robert Lawson Photograph Collection, National Museum of Naval Aviation / U.S. Navy photo.*

Second division of "Butch" Davenport's flight en route to Bougainville. *Courtesy U.S. Naval Historical Center / M. W. "Butch" Davenport Collection.*

Whit Wharton standing next to his Corsair. *Courtesy U.S. Naval Historical Center / M. W. "Butch" Davenport Collection.*

L – R: "Andy" Anderson and "Timmy" Gile at Ondongo in November 1943. *Courtesy U.S. Naval Historical Center / M. W. "Butch" Davenport Collection.*

"Butch" Davenport in the cockpit of his Corsair with one of his ground crew. *Courtesy U.S. Naval Historical Center / M. W. "Butch" Davenport Collection.*

Jack Chasnoff at Ondongo in November 1943. *Courtesy the Chasnoff Family.*

A rare photo of "Ike" Kepford in plane #7 early in the first tour. Most of the photos of Kepford were with his famous #29. *Courtesy U.S. Naval Historical Center / M. W. "Butch" Davenport Collection.*

"Chico" Freeman with his F4U-1A "L.A. City Limits," his favorite picture. *Courtesy Robert Lawson Photograph Collection, National Museum of Naval Aviation / U.S. Navy photo.*

"Andy" Jagger, Duke Henning, and Bill Popp at New Georgia in 1943. *Courtesy U.S. Naval Historical Center / M. W. "Butch" Davenport Collection.*

"Butch" Davenport on right with one of his ground crew. *Courtesy Vought / Lennard Edmisten.*

Jack Chasnoff in the cockpit of his Corsair. *Courtesy the Anderson Family.*

Admiral William F. "Bull" Halsey pictured with Senator David I. Walsh, D-Mass, Chairman of the Senate Committee on Naval Affairs, on board U.S.S. *Missouri* (BB-63). Fighting 17 flew cover on Admiral Halsey on October 28, 1943, and November 12, 1943, whilst he was flying to the Russell Islands and Bougainville. *Courtesy National Museum of Naval Aviation.*

A group of Fighting 17 pilots. *Courtesy Alexandra Bowers.*

Tom Killefer in battle dress at Ondongo in November 1943. *Courtesy Vought / Lennard Edmisten.*

Fighting 17 Ready Room. L – R: "Big Jim" Streig (leaning), "Hap" Bowers, Tom Blackburn, Dan Cunningham (head in hands), Tom Killefer and "Ike" Kepford, New Georgia in 1943. *Courtesy U.S. Naval Historical Center / M.W. "Butch" Davenport Collection.*

Above: Basil Duke Henning, Air Combat Information Officer. *Courtesy the Henning Family.* Above right: L – R: "Timmy" Gile, "Big Jim" Streig, Tom Killefer, Doug Gutenkunst and Tom Blackburn, at Ondongo in November 1943. *Courtesy U.S. Naval Historical Center / W. W. "Butch" Davenport Collection.* Right: Dan Cunningham in #22, his aircraft for the first tour at Ondongo. *Courtesy Robert Lawson Photograph Collection, National Museum of Naval Aviation / U.S. Navy photo.*

Fighting 17 officers in front of Ready Quonset, New Georgia. Back Row L - R: Jack Chasnoff, "Hap" Bowers, Duke Henning, Hal Jackson, "Chico" Freeman and "Windy" Hill. Front Row L - R: "Andy" Anderson, Bob Hogan, Johnny Kleinman and Lou Kelley. *Courtesy Vought / the Anderson Family.*

A group of Fighting 17 officers at the ready hut in Ondongo, November 1943. "Chuck" Pillsbury is looking around the door. *Courtesy Vought.*

Corsair "Big Hog" running up on line. *Courtesy U.S. Naval Historical Center / M. W. "Butch" Davenport Collection.*

Tom Blackburn with Jack Hospers, Chance Vought Service Representative at Ondongo in November 1943. *Courtesy Robert Lawson Photograph Collection, National Museum of Naval Aviation / U.S. Navy photo.*

Ready Room. Group of ten officers in front of Ready Quonset, New Georgia. Back Row L - R: Jack Chasnoff, "Hap" Bowers, Duke Henning, Hal Jackson, "Chico" Freeman and "Windy" Hill. Front Row L - R: "Andy" Anderson, Bob Hogan, Johnny Kleinman and Lou Kelley. *Courtesy U.S. Naval Historical Center / M. W. "Butch" Davenport Collection.*

Fighting 17 Ready Room. L – R: "Big Jim" Streig, "Hap" Bowers, Tom Killefer, Tom Blackburn, "Ike" Kepford and Dan Cunningham, New Georgia in 1943. *Courtesy U.S. Naval Historical Center / M. W. "Butch" Davenport Collection.*

Tom Blackburn sitting in "Big Hog." *Courtesy U.S. Naval Historical Center / M. W. "Butch" Davenport Collection.*

Tom Blackburn standing beside "Big Hog." *Courtesy U.S. Naval Historical Center / M. W. "Butch" Davenport Collection.*

Jim Halford in "Command Car." *Courtesy U.S. Naval Historical Center / M. W. "Butch" Davenport Collection.*

Jack Chasnoff with his Plane Captain. *Courtesy U.S. Naval Historical Center / M. W. "Butch" Davenport Collection.*

Fighting 17 personnel at Ondongo in November 1943. *Courtesy Vought.*

Jack Chasnoff in the cockpit of his aircraft. *Courtesy Vought.*

Fighting 17, Ready Room. L – R: Schub, Davenport, Chasnoff, March, Kepford, Blackburn, Wharton (kneeling), Kurlander (kneeling), Streig and Hogan. Ondongo, November 15, 1943. *Courtesy Robert Lawson Photograph Collection, National Museum of Naval Aviation / U.S. Navy photo / Joyce Wharton.*

L – R: Don Malone, a Marine General, Mills Schanuel, Tom Blackburn and Mel Kurlander at Ondongo in November 1943. *Courtesy Alexandra Bowers.*

Corsair #30 was originally assigned to "Teeth" Burriss, who named all of his aircraft "Barb" after his girlfriend. It is unclear in this photo whether it is Burriss or his aircraft. *Courtesy Vought.*

Bill Meek and "Chico" Freeman inspecting a wrecked Japanese aircraft on Kolumbangaru. *Courtesy Vought.*

A wrecked Japanese Zero on Kolumbangaru. *Courtesy Vought.*

Another wrecked Japanese aircraft. *Courtesy Vought.*

"Timmy" Gile at Ondongo in November 1943. *Courtesy Vought.*

A group of Fighting 17 personnel. *Courtesy Vought.*

"Ike" Kepford and Duke Henning at New Georgia in 1943. *Courtesy U.S. Naval Historical Center / M.W. "Butch" Davenport Collection.*

Dan Cunningham in flight gear, ready to go, at Ondongo in November 1943. He flew #22 on the first tour. *Courtesy Vought.*

An early photo of "Chico" Freeman with aircraft #7. He later went on to fly #34. *Courtesy U.S. Naval Historical Center / M. W. "Butch" Davenport Collection.*

Paul Cordray on the wing of #19. He took this number after "Andy" Anderson was shot down in November 1943. *Courtesy Robert Lawson Photograph Collection, National Museum of Naval Aviation / U.S. Navy photo.*

Two Fighting 17 aces, "Ike" Kepford and "Big Jim' Streig. *Courtesy Vought.*

"Dirty Eddie" March in front of #29 early in the first tour of Fighting 17 at Ondongo in November 1943. *Courtesy Vought.*

"Big Jim" Streig and Tom Killefer at Ondongo in November 1943. *Courtesy Robert Lawson Photograph Collection, National Museum of Naval Aviation / U.S. Navy photo.*

7

Carriers and Ships

Fighting 17 originally served on the U.S.S. *Bunker Hill* as part of Air Group 17. They were detached to support the landings on Empress Augusta Bay as a land based squadron. This was not due to the unsuitability of the Corsair on the carrier but due to logistics. With only one squadron of Corsairs serving on a carrier in the Pacific they could not be supported with the spare parts they needed. Therefore they were assigned to the Solomon Islands, where the Marines were operating Corsairs and parts were available. It was some time before carriers were able to support Corsair squadrons.

Fighting 17 flew combat air patrol to support carrier operations over the U.S.S. *Saratoga* on 5 November and the U.S.S. *Independence*, U.S.S. *Essex* and U.S.S. *Bunker Hill* in the Battle of the Solomon Sea on November 11, 1943.

View of the strike on Rabaul taken by Commander Joseph C. Clifton from the cockpit of his F6F-3 Hellcat, November 5, 1943. *Courtesy Commander Joseph C. Clifton Photograph Album, National Museum of Naval Aviation.*

Another view of the strike on Rabaul taken by Commander Joseph C. Clifton from the cockpit of his F6F-3 Hellcat, November 5, 1943. *Courtesy Commander Joseph C. Clifton Photograph Album, National Museum of Naval Aviation.*

Another view of the strike on Rabaul taken by Commander Joseph C. Clifton from the cockpit of his F6F-3 Hellcat, November 5, 1943. *Courtesy Commander Joseph C. Clifton Photograph Album, National Museum of Naval Aviation.*

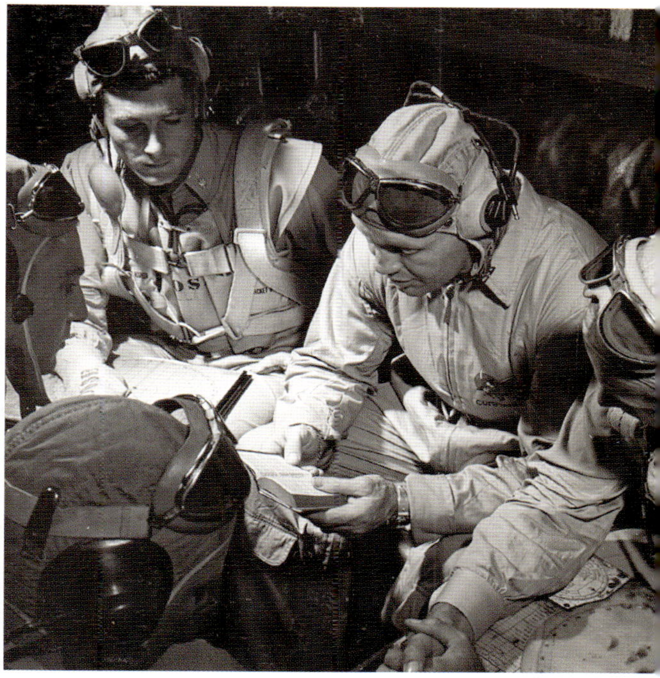

Commander Joseph C. Clifton reads from the bible while surrounded by pilots of Fighting Squadron 12 in a ready room on board the carrier U.S.S. *Saratoga* (CV-3). This was taken prior to the launch of a strike against Rabaul on November 5, 1943. *Courtesy Commander Joseph C. Clifton Photograph Album, National Museum of Naval Aviation.*

Scene on the flight deck of the carrier U.S.S. *Saratoga* (CV-3) after the return of Air Group 12 pilots from a strike against Rabaul, November 5, 1943. *Courtesy Commander Joseph C. Clifton Photograph Album, National Museum of Naval Aviation.*

Rear Admiral Ted Sherman talks with Commander Joseph C. Clifton on board U.S.S. *Saratoga* (CV-3) after the latter's return from a strike against Rabaul, November 5, 1943. *Courtesy Commander Joseph C. Clifton Photograph Album, National Museum of Naval Aviation.*

The aircraft carrier U.S.S. *Saratoga* (CV-3) pictured at sea. *Courtesy Commander Joseph C. Clifton Photograph Album, National Museum of Naval Aviation.*

Another view of the aircraft carrier U.S.S. *Saratoga* (CV-3) pictured at sea in 1944. *Courtesy Commander Joseph C. Clifton Photograph Album, National Museum of Naval Aviation.*

The veteran U.S.S. *Saratoga* (CV-3) underway with aircraft on her deck. *Courtesy National Museum of Naval Aviation.*

A view from the starboard side of the U.S.S. *Saratoga* (CV-3). *Courtesy National Museum of Naval Aviation.*

The veteran U.S.S. *Saratoga* (CV-3) presents this view to one of her planes at the conclusion of a mission in the Pacific. At the time of the photo this hardy carrier was fighting the Japanese in the Pacific. *Courtesy National Museum of Naval Aviation.*

A near miss on the carrier U.S.S. *Bunker Hill* (CV-17) during an attack by Japanese aircraft off the Mariana Islands on June 19, 1944. *Courtesy Cdr. Francis Gilreath Scrapbook, National Museum of Naval Aviation.*

Another view of the near miss on the carrier U.S.S. *Bunker Hill* (CV-17) during an attack by Japanese aircraft off the Mariana Islands on June 19, 1944. *Courtesy Cdr. Francis Gilreath Scrapbook, National Museum of Naval Aviation.*

Off Okinawa May 11, 1945. The U.S.S. *Bunker Hill* is under attack at 14:09 by a Japanese aircraft believed to be a Judy. It was set on fire by anti-aircraft fire and exploded upon crashing into the sea astern. *Courtesy Captain Carlos W. Wieber Photograph Album, National Museum of Naval Aviation.*

Off Okinawa May 11, 1945. U.S.S. *Bunker Hill* already burning badly from the first Kamikaze hit is attacked by a second. *Courtesy Captain Carlos W. Wieber Photograph Album, National Museum of Naval Aviation.*

Another view of the Kamikaze attack on May 11, 1945. U.S.S. *Bunker Hill* (CV-17) already burning from one kamikaze plane was hit by another. *Courtesy Captain Carlos W. Wieber Photograph Album, National Museum of Naval Aviation.*

U.S.S. *Wilkes Barre* (left) flames a third attacker over U.S.S. *Bunker Hill*. Carrier at right is U.S.S. *Randolph*. *Courtesy National Museum of Naval Aviation.*

U.S.S. *Charles S. Sperry* and U.S.S. *Wilkes Barre* assist in bringing the U.S.S. *Bunker Hill* fires under control. *Courtesy National Museum of Naval Aviation.*

Broadside view of U.S.S. *Essex* (CV-9). *Courtesy Captain Carlos W. Wieber Photograph Album, National Museum of Naval Aviation.*

San Francisco Bay, April 15, 1945. U.S.S. *Essex* (CV-9) in her new war paint departs Hunter Point Navy Yard bound for the Pacific. *Courtesy Captain Carlos W. Wieber Photograph Album, National Museum of Naval Aviation.*

Photograph of the Kamikaze attack against the U.S.S. *Essex* off the Philippines. *Courtesy Captain Carlos W. Wieber Photograph Album, National Museum of Naval Aviation.*

U.S.S. *Independence* (CVL-22) pictured in port at an unidentified location. *Courtesy U.S.S. Independence Photo Album, National Museum of Naval Aviation.*

U.S.S. *Independence* (CVL-22) underway. *Courtesy Al Hiegel, Historian, U.S.S. Independence (CVL 22) Reunion Group.*

U.S.S. *Independence* (CVL-22) aerial view in 1943. *Courtesy Al Hiegel, Historian, U.S.S. Independence (CVL 22) Reunion Group.*

U.S.S. *Independence* (CVL-22) in rough seas in 1944. *Courtesy Al Hiegel, Historian, U.S.S. Independence (CVL 22) Reunion Group.*

U.S.S. *Independence* (CVL-22) stern view in 1943. *Courtesy Al Hiegel, Historian, U.S.S. Independence (CVL 22) Reunion Group.*

Battle of Solomon Sea, November 11, 1943. *Courtesy Al Hiegel, Historian, U.S.S. Independence (CVL 22) Reunion Group.*

Another view of the Battle of Solomon Sea, November 11, 1943. *Courtesy Al Hiegel, Historian, U.S.S. Independence (CVL 22) Reunion Group.*

An F6F Hellcat pictured in the catwalk after an errant landing on board the light carrier U.S.S. *Independence* (CVL-22). *Courtesy U.S.S. Independence Photo Album, National Museum of Naval Aviation.*

Flight deck crewman swarm around an F6F Hellcat after an errant landing on board the light carrier U.S.S. *Independence* (CVL-22), 1944-1945. *Courtesy U.S.S. Independence Photo Album, National Museum of Naval Aviation.*

An F6F Hellcat approaches the crash barrier that will stop the aircraft in the event it misses the arresting wires on the flight deck of the light carrier U.S.S. *Independence* (CVL-22), 1944-1945. *Courtesy U.S.S. Independence Photo Album, National Museum of Naval Aviation.*

An F6F-5N Hellcat pictured in the catwalk on board the light carrier U.S.S. *Independence* (CVL-22) after an errant landing, 1944-1945. *Courtesy U.S.S. Independence Photo Album, National Museum of Naval Aviation.*

View of a TBF/TBM Avenger making a high approach for recovery on board the light carrier U.S.S. *Independence* (CVL-22), 1944-1945. *Courtesy U.S.S. Independence Photo Album, National Museum of Naval Aviation.*

View of a TBF/TBM Avenger nosing over after making an errant recovery on board the light carrier U.S.S. *Independence* (CVL-22), 1944-1945. *Courtesy U.S.S. Independence Photo Album, National Museum of Naval Aviation.*

8

Life in the Islands

Lennard "Red" Edmisten, part of Fighting 17's ground crew, describes the living conditions:

"Our camp ground was in a coconut grove and we were told they belonged to Palmolive. We weren't supposed to cut any trees down as the military would have to pay for them. I thought that was rather funny! Our tents were in a soggy hole that water ran through every time it rained. The Marines had pitched our tents and I am ***quite sure*** *they knew how wet it could be. We finally got ditches dug to run the water outside the tents. We had six men to a tent and they were supposed to hold eight. It was so hot and muggy that we stretched the side out to let more air in. This also gave us more area to move around in.*

The floors were dirt and mud depending on the weather. We were always on the lookout for boards to make a little platform to get in and out of our bunks. We also got some old packing crates to make crude lockers for our gear. We found a piece of plywood for a table and some ammo cans for stools. We had cots to sleep on with mosquito netting over them, and could you believe we were issued double down arctic sleeping bags? Anyway they served as a mattress. The showers were about a block away and consisted of a wooden platform with a dozen or so shower heads. No walls, no roof, no hot water and setting in a lake to run off soapy water. Lucky they also issued us rubber boots that came about knee high. Most of us used them for shower shoes to get on and off the shower platform. Couldn't find any other use for the boots.

We were issued green pants and shirts - I think they were for the Seabees. Most of us cut the legs from the pants making shorts and sleeves and long tail from the shirts. Sun helmets were mostly used to shed rain and sun. When you met a stranger - first thing you ask was what branch of the service he was in. Couldn't tell Navy personnel from Marines, Army or Seabees. Most of us grew beards - pilots and enlisted personnel. There was little saluting and everyone used first name or nicknames.

We ate in the Marine chow hall and their food wasn't all that good. Most servicemen complain about the spam they ate overseas. I don't remember ever eating it - our island got all the Vienna sausages. We had them boiled, fried, stewed in tomatoes and even served to us in the can. We gave them the nickname 'Ondongo Round Steak.' I don't know what the batter was made out of but it wouldn't even melt when we washed our mess kits in barrels of boiling hot water.

We usually went into large bunkers and had our night meal, usually K Rations. One night a driver on a Seabee truck joined us in our bunker. When he saw our chow - he offered us some coffee and sandwiches that were left over from his delivery to some guys working on the flight strip. When he found out we could get him Plexiglass and aluminium from our crashed planes - he started making a regular food delivery. The material we gave him was highly prized by the troops to make jewellery and knife handles."

George Mauhar remembers the food well:

"A lot of dehydrated food - butter you had to roll bread around it so it didn't stick to your mouth. Dehydrated eggs and potatoes. Potatoes were okay if you fried them. A lot of Spam, sausages - small canned sausages. Once in a while fresh meat from Australia, Goat meat or Mutton.

I admired the Seabees, they knew how to live and work. I got acquainted with one of their Chiefs and they had an ice making machine. I ate with the Seabees. We had what you call a listrus bag. A big canvas bag that you put water into and then something like Iodine. You were thirsty all the time and your stomach distended due to this. Once in a while we'd get beer. Pilots would fly and get some occasionally. The beer was put where the gun heaters had been taken out. Then the pilots would fly and cool the beer!"

Roger Hedrick outside Bougainville tents. *Courtesy U.S. Naval Historical Center / M. W. "Butch" Davenport Collection.*

Living conditions at Bougainville. *Courtesy Lennard Edmisten.*

Left: Bougainville tents. "*We city Navy types were really roughing it at this point,*" recalled "Butch" Davenport. *Courtesy U.S. Naval Historical Center / M. W. "Butch" Davenport Collection.* Right: These shacks serve as quarters for Fighting 17 pilots at Bougainville. Four men to each shack. Three weeks after this picture was taken the Japanese shelled the base heavily. The "Fearsome Foursomes Inn," Ondongo, Duke Henning Prop. Inhabitants Duke Henning, Chief bar tender, Lyle Herrmann, Officer in charge of social distress, "Stinky" Innis Officer in charge of snatch and other incidentals, "Dirty Eddie" March Officer in charge of theft and assistant bar tender. *Courtesy the Tom Blackburn Collection / National Archives.*

Hog Hollow No. 3. Living conditions at Bougainville. *Courtesy the Tom Blackburn Collection.*

These shacks serve as quarters for Fighting 17 pilots at Bougainville. *Courtesy the Tom Blackburn Collection / National Archives.*

Amateur barbers prevented Fighting 17 pilots from becoming long haired whilst stationed on Bougainville. The client apparently about to lose an ear is Lt. B. D. Henning, a Yale professor before he became an intelligence officer. Lt. D. A. "Stinky" Innis of Nevada, MO, clips while Lt. (jg) Earle C. Peterson of Coronado, California, cocks a critical eye over his can of fruit juice. Lt. H. A. "Dirty Eddie" March, Jr., of Washington, D.C. definitely is not interested in the performance. *Courtesy the Tom Blackburn Collection / National Archives.*

Despite the primitive conditions Fighting 17 officers had to keep up appearances. "Stinky" Innis trimming Duke Henning's beard. *Courtesy the Tom Blackburn Collection*

"Stinky" Innis finishing off trimming Duke Henning's beard. *Courtesy the Henning Family.*

Ward "Ace" Cole keeping an eye on the laundry in February 1944 on Bougainville. *Courtesy Vought.*

Tom Blackburn and the weekly laundry. *Courtesy U.S. Naval Historical Center / M.W. "Butch" Davenport Collection.*

Living conditions for Fighting 17 pilots at Bougainville. *Courtesy the Tom Blackburn Collection.*

Despite flying combat missions, Lt. Walter Schub still has to make sure he does his laundry. *Courtesy the Tom Blackburn Collection.*

A Fighting 17 pilot uses homemade shower set up at quarters on Bougainville. *Courtesy U.S. Naval Historical Center / M. W. "Butch" Davenport Collection.*

The non-stop poker game with $3.00 limit per game on "Scramble Alert." *Courtesy Vought.*

Fighting 17 and VF (N) pilots in ready room at Bougainville. *Courtesy the Tom Blackburn Collection.*

Fighting 17 pilots celebrate the day's achievements at their mess hut on Bougainville. Earlier in the day of February 19, 1944, Fighting 17 pilots shot down sixteen Japanese aircraft. *Courtesy National Archives.*

A group of Fighting 17 pilots relaxing on Bougainville in 1944. *Courtesy Alexandra Bowers.*

"Dirty Eddie" March, Wally Schub, "Country" Landreth, "Ike" Kepford, Don McQueen and Dan Cunningham relaxing with a beer between missions. *Courtesy Alexandra Bowers.*

"Dirty Eddie" March with camera, Wally Schub, "Country" Landreth, Don McQueen and Dan Cunningham. *Courtesy Alexandra Bowers.*

Dan Cunningham, "Dirty Eddie" March, "Stinky" Innis and Hal Jackson. *Courtesy Alexandra Bowers.*

Wally Schub, Dan Cunningham, Don McQueen and Mills Schanuel enjoying a beer on Bougainville. *Courtesy Alexandra Bowers.*

Wally Schub, Dan Cunningham and Don McQueen making the most of a beer at Bougainville. *Courtesy Alexandra Bowers.*

Mills Schanuel and Wally Schub with beer at Bougainville. *Courtesy Alexandra Bowers.*

"Hap" Bowers, George Keller, "Big Jim" Streig, and Whit Wharton at Bougainville. *Courtesy Alexandra Bowers.*

Bill Meek, Bobby Mims and "Ike" Kepford at Bougainville in 1944. *Courtesy Vought.*

Standing: "Beads" Popp, "Big Jim" Streig and Whit Wharton. Crouching: "Hap" Bowers and George Keller at Bougainville. *Courtesy Alexandra Bowers.*

Harold Bitzegaio in a foxhole at Bougainville. *Courtesy Vought.*

A Fighting 17 pilot catches up on his sleep in his quarters on Bougainville in February 1944. Note the flight gear hanging by cots. *Courtesy National Archives.*

Two Fighting 17 pilots catch up on their mail in their quarters tent on Bougainville, February 1944. They are (L - R) Lt. Merl W. Davenport, and Ens. Don McQueen. *Courtesy National Archives.*

"Hap" Bowers with one of the Seabees on Bougainville. *Courtesy Alexandra Bowers.*

Signpost on Bougainville to thoughts of home. *Courtesy Vought.*

Fighting 17 aces Tom Blackburn and "Dirty Eddie" March at Bougainville in January 1944. *Courtesy the Tom Blackburn Collection.*

9

Ground Crew

When Fighting 17 arrived in the Solomon Islands it was generally thought that the Marines looked after their aircraft. George Mauhar, Leading Crew Chief, explains:

"*When we first got there we relieved a Marine squadron. Their aircraft were gone, but the ground crew were still there, and they helped us get indoctrinated, not on the airplanes, we had our own mechanics who were superior to what the Marines had as far as I'm concerned. The Marines and Fighting 17 Plane Captains worked together but they were only there for about a week. Then they went. From then on we were on our own.*

We had a group called A.C.O.R.N. that were a kind of support. They weren't aircraft mechanics, but welders, craftsmen, etc. We did all our own maintenance. The Marines helped us for a week or so. They were just awaiting orders to leave."

Fighting 17 took along with them 67 ground crew when they were detached from the U.S.S. *Bunker Hill*; the rest stayed aboard. C.A.S.U. personnel were added to the numbers and contributed to the maintenance of the aircraft, as Fighting 17 did not have the full complement of ground crew required to service a squadron.

The following is an example of the checks performed by the ground crew on the F4Us. This was issued in December 1943.

Work to be done on Fighting 17 Aircraft type F4U-1

Engines:
1. Check harness for weak or burned out leads.
2. Check entire ignition system mags, etc.
3. Check push rod housings for oil leaks.
4. Check all quick disconnects. oil return lines, diverter valves and oil coolers for oil leaks.
5. Inspect all drains for metal filings.
6. Check super chargers (visual) for wearing away of blower vanes.
7. Check and clean out entire duct system; blow out sand etc, check for duct leaks.
8. Check emergency fuel pumps – grease or replace as necessary (those that have seen considerable use).
9. Check engine instruments replacing bad ones; fuel gauges, cylinder head, temperature gauges.

Structural:
1. Check all planes throughout for structural failures or near failures.
2. Raise wings and check hinge pins, locking pins and linkages for fractures, operation and greasing.
3. Check control cables for fraying, binding, stretching, etc.
4. Check tab control cables and tab gears for slipping and wear and loose cables.
5. Smooth out any skin fractures and replace puffy filling around blast tube openings where necessary.
6. Touch up all paint work where necessary.

The following memo was issued in January 1944:

Operations Memorandum

1. All aircraft assigned to air activities on Bougainville will be given standard periodic checks. These checks will be commenced upon return of the first major mission each day and every effort will be made for completion prior to daylight the following day.

Not more than ten percent of the planes assigned a unit will be out of commission for this purpose at any one time during daylight hours. During the hours of darkness, up to fifty percent may be out for check, depending on the tactical situation.

2. Newly assigned planes will be combat checked immediately upon delivery by the ferry pilot and prior to their first combat mission.

3. Field Commanders and Squadron Commanders are responsible that this procedure is carried out. **These checks are absolutely essential for successful combat operations.**

Lennard "Red" Edmisten AMMH1c. in October 1944 at hydraulic school, Chicago, Illinois. "Red" served with Fighting 17 as part of their ground crew in the Solomon Islands. *Courtesy Lennard Edmisten.*

Ground crew at Ondongo, November 15, 1943. Front Row L – R: J. A. "Johnny" Craig S2c, Lennard R. "Red" Edmisten AMM2c, T. B. Fisher AMM3c, E. W. Gober AMM1c, E. W. Flynn AMM3c. Back Row L – R: E. R. McLean S1c, D. D. McLaughlin AMM3c, T. S. "Tommy" Pitts AMM2c, G. C. Duke S1c. *Courtesy Lennard Edmisten / U.S. Naval Historical Center / M. W. "Butch" Davenport Collection.*

Ground crew at Ondongo, November 1943. Front row 3rd from left B. Murray ACMM. *Courtesy Lennard Edmisten / U.S. Naval Historical Center / M. W. "Butch" Davenport Collection.*

Ground crew at Ondongo, November 1943. L – R: Second from left L. W. Jordan AMM3c, fourth from left B. Murray ACMM. *Courtesy Lennard Edmisten.*

Ground crew at Ondongo, New Georgia, November 1943. Front row 3rd from left J. H. Gafford AMM3c. *Courtesy Lennard Edmisten.*

Ground crew at Ondongo, November 1943. Front row 3rd from left H. M. Gill AMM3c. Back row 4th from left T. S. Pitts AMM2c. *Courtesy Lennard Edmisten / U.S. Naval Historical Center / M. W. "Butch" Davenport Collection.*

"Hap" Bowers and ground crew at Bougainville with his plane #23. *Courtesy Alexandra Bowers.*

Ground crew at Ondongo, November 1943. Maintenance crews of Fighting 17. These very few, dedicated young men, literally made Fighting 17's accomplishments possible. *Courtesy Lennard Edmisten / U.S. Naval Historical Center / M. W. "Butch" Davenport Collection.*

Ground crew with "Butch" Davenport on an F4U-1A of Fighting 17. *Courtesy Vought.*

Another view of ground crew on "Butch" Davenport's F4U-1A. *Courtesy Vought.*

Mel Kurlander (center) and ground crew. *Courtesy Mel Kurlander.*

"Butch" Davenport and Crew Chief George Mauhar in front of a Corsair. *Courtesy Robert Lawson Photograph Collection, National Museum of Naval Aviation / U.S. Navy photo.*

Battle damage to an F4U-1A of Fighting 17. *Courtesy Robert Lawson Photograph Collection, National Museum of Naval Aviation / U.S. Navy photo.*

"Butch" Davenport's aircraft after "Windy" Hill's crash landing. *Courtesy Robert Lawson Photograph Collection, National Museum of Naval Aviation / U.S. Navy photo.*

Another view of "Butch" Davenport's aircraft #9 after "Windy" Hill's crash landing. *Courtesy Vought.*

Another view of "Butch" Davenport's aircraft after "Windy" Hill's crash landing. *Courtesy Vought.*

In this photo you can clearly see the extent of the damage to Kepford's F4U. *Courtesy Robert Lawson Photograph Collection, National Museum of Naval Aviation / U.S. Navy photo.*

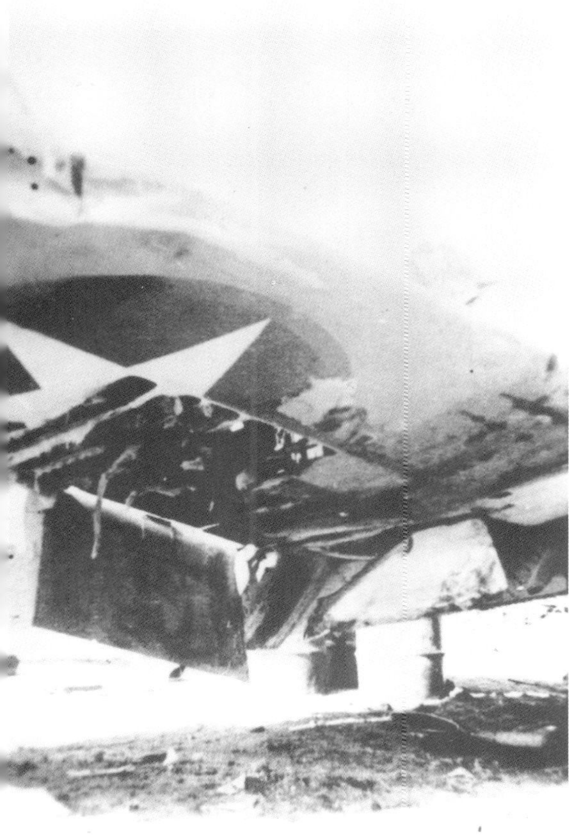

Left: Damage to one of "Ike" Kepford's aircraft. *Courtesy Robert Lawson Photograph Collection, National Museum of Naval Aviation / U.S. Navy photo.*

Right: "Ike" Kepford's aircraft after crash landing. *Courtesy Robert Lawson Photograph Collection, National Museum of Naval Aviation / U.S. Navy photo.*

Another view of "Ike" Kepford's crashed aircraft. *Courtesy Robert Lawson Photograph Collection, National Museum of Naval Aviation / U.S. Navy photo.*

"Ike" Kepford's wrecked aircraft at Bougainville in 1944. *Courtesy Robert Lawson Photograph Collection, National Museum of Naval Aviation / U.S. Navy photo.*

"Big Jim" Streig and his ground crew. *Courtesy Lennard Edmisten.*

"Hap" Bowers and ground crew beside his aircraft at Bougainville. *Courtesy Alexandra Bowers.*

Ground crew at Bougainville. *Courtesy Vought.*

Ground crew at Bougainville, February 1944. George Mauhar first left. *Courtesy Robert Lawson Photograph Collection, National Museum of Naval Aviation / U.S. Navy photo.*

Ground crew at Bougainville. *Courtesy Vought.*

L. W. Jordan AMM3c adds "Kill" flags to the squadron's scoreboard, bringing the total to 154 Japanese planes destroyed. Photo taken at Bougainville. Note censored squadron number above its Skull and Crossbones emblem. *Courtesy Robert Lawson Photograph Collection, National Museum of Naval Aviation / U.S. Navy photo.*

Ordnancemen service .50 cal. machine guns in the wing of one of Fighting 17's F4U-1A Corsair fighters at Bougainville in February 1944. Note cut-off toes in one man's boots. *Courtesy National Archives.*

Squadron ground crew await the return of their planes from an attack on Rabaul, February 1944. Fighting 17 was then based on Bougainville. Note the tape over muzzles of F4U-1A's .50 cal. machine guns. *Courtesy National Archives.*

Once the Corsairs had left on a mission it was left to the ground crew to wait for their safe return. Bougainville 1944. *Courtesy the Tom Blackburn Collection.*

Two Fighting 17 personnel relax prior to take off from Piva airstrip, Bougainville, for a raid on Rabaul, February 1944. Aircraft is an F4U-1A Corsair. Note smoking volcano in the distance and pierced steel mat on the airfield's runway. *Courtesy National Archives.*

Ground crewmen ride the wings of Fighting 17 F4U-1A Corsair fighters as they taxi into take off position for a raid on Rabaul, February 1944. Fighting 17 was then operating out of Bougainville. *Courtesy National Archives.*

Yeoman Harry U. Meeteer updates the squadron's flight logs at its Bougainville base, February 1944. *Courtesy National Archives.*

Harry Meeteer (second from left) and squadron flight logs. *Courtesy the Tom Blackburn Collection.*

Air Combat Information Officer Basil Duke Henning. *Courtesy the Henning Family.*

Air Combat Information Officer Basil Duke Henning had to ensure all combat reports were recorded and compiled. *Courtesy the Tom Blackburn Collection.*

Operations Room on Bougainville, February 16, 1944. *Courtesy the Tom Blackburn Collection.*

Squadron briefing at Bougainville in 1944. *Courtesy the Tom Blackburn Collection.*

Mechanics swarm over Lt. (jg) Tom Killefer's aircraft, which made an emergency landing on the strip at Nissan Island, Green Islands group. It had not been officially opened and he landed before all machinery was off the strip. March 6, 1944. *Courtesy Robert Lawson Photograph Collection, National Museum of Naval Aviation / U.S. Navy photo.*

Another view of Tom Killefer's aircraft at Nissan Island on March 6, 1944. *Courtesy Robert Lawson Photograph Collection, National Museum of Naval Aviation / U.S. Navy photo.*

10

Carrier Air Service Unit (C.A.S.U.) 12

Carrier Air Service Units were set up by the Navy to service combat aircraft for the U.S. carriers and island bases. The C.A.S.U. personnel maintained the aircraft and A.C.O.R.N. (Aircraft Overhaul Repair Navy) furnished the materials and equipment and looked after the housekeeping and conveniences for squadrons. A.C.O.R.N. is an airfield assembly designed for rapid repair, installation and operation of a landplane and seaplane air base, or in conjunction with amphibious operations, for repair and operation of a captured enemy airfield. In such island set-ups, C.A.S.U.s usually confined themselves to servicing, re-arming and minor repairing of squadron aircraft based on that island. When the squadrons left the C.A.S.U. remained, awaiting the next visiting squadron.

Overhauls and major repairs were made by aircraft repair and overhaul units in rear areas.

C.A.S.U.s were trained to work on carrier type aircraft, and the mission of C.A.S.U. 12 was to prepare and flight test new aircraft prior to sending to Navy squadrons in the Pacific. They were also responsible for repairing aircraft after battle damage and had specialists in props, instruments, plane captains, metalsmiths, hydraulics and ordnance.

One of these specialists was Thomas Junior Carpenter, AMM, who trained as an electrician and worked on Lt. (jg) Earl May's aircraft at Bougainville. May became an ace with Fighting 17, scoring eight victories.

It was C.A.S.U. 12s job to support the Navy and Marine fighters and bombers at three airstrips on Bougainville. Plane Captain Charlie Dixon had this to say:

"I was in C.A.S.U. 12 when we went to Bougainville after the Marines took over. We put up tents like the Marines and lived there. The Seabees built two strips in about three weeks and then Fighting 17 and a Marine squadron was across the strip. Fighting 17 needed some Plane Captains and I don't know how I did it, but I bluffed it. I knew a little from gunnery school in Norman, Oklahoma and I had a Marine ordnance man who took care of the guns for three planes. Most of the mechanics had left when I met 'Butch' Davenport, they got the rest from C.A.S.U. 12 out of Guadalcanal. When we got to Bougainville I was picked by 'Butch.' You are a pilot's belt boy and I took care of #9, #33 and new #9. I fuelled up the plane, checked the oil and kept the cockpit clean with no cigarette butts anywhere ('Butch' did not like that). Every morning before a strike I turned the plane up and checked it out, supercharger, prop pitch of 2700 RPM's. I had a Marine ordnance man to handle the guns and my job was to tape the six gun holes up with masking tape to keep the coral dust out.

They usually escorted B-24s from Guadalcanal to Rabaul. In the morning 'Butch' arrived (and rest of the pilots), I put his chute in the plane and strapped him in (I had a hard time lifting it) as I just weighed 116lbs and was barely sixteen years old."

C.A.S.U. 12 served with Fighting 17 until the squadron was relieved in March 1944.

Earl May and ground crew in front of his assigned aircraft #27. Middle man in the photo is Earl May's Plane Captain Thomas Carpenter AMM2c. On the left is Norm Growchowski. *Courtesy Del and Pat May Collection.*

Climbing into Higgins boats. *Courtesy CASU 12 Association via Greg Pruis.*

Unloading supplies and gear on to the beach. *Courtesy CASU 12 Association via Greg Pruis.*

Another view of unloading supplies and gear on to the beach. *Courtesy CASU 12 Association via Greg Pruis.*

A wrecked aircraft on the beach. *Courtesy CASU 12 Association via Greg Pruis.*

A group of CASU 12 personnel. *Courtesy CASU 12 Association via Greg Pruis.*

A line of F4U Corsairs. *Courtesy CASU 12 Association via Greg Pruis.*

A line of F6F Hellcats. *Courtesy CASU 12 Association via Greg Pruis.*

A couple of CASU 12 personnel. *Courtesy CASU 12 Association via Greg Pruis.*

CASU 12 mechanics maintaining and repairing an aircraft. *Courtesy CASU 12 Association via Greg Pruis.*

Hitching a lift on the bomb truck. *Courtesy CASU 12 Association via Greg Pruis.*

Four of CASU 12's men doing their weekly laundry. *Courtesy CASU 12 Association via Greg Pruis.*

Four CASU 12 personnel. It was the job of these men to make sure everything went smoothly with the ground operations. *Courtesy CASU 12 Association via Greg Pruis.*

A foxhole in case of bomb attack. *Courtesy CASU 12 Association via Greg Pruis.*

Weekly laundry and living conditions. *Courtesy CASU 12 Association via Greg Pruis.*

CASU 12 personnel. These men were vital to the success of ground operations. *Courtesy CASU 12 Association via Greg Pruis.*

The resourceful men of CASU 12 with a homemade motorcycle. *Courtesy CASU 12 Association via Greg Pruis.*

A sailor of CASU 12 with a homemade motorcycle. *Courtesy CASU 12 Association via Greg Pruis.*

CASU 12 Hydraulics shop. *Courtesy CASU 12 Association via Greg Pruis.*

A group of CASU 12 personnel. The men on the ground played an important part in keeping the aircraft in combat condition. *Courtesy CASU 12 Association via Greg Pruis.*

The chapel on either Guadalcanal or Bougainville. *Courtesy CASU 12 Association via Greg Pruis.*

Movie screen and a time to relax. *Courtesy CASU 12 Association via Greg Pruis.*

The parachute loft *Courtesy CASU 12 Association via Greg Pruis.*

Island living conditions. *Courtesy CASU 12 Association via Greg Pruis.*

One of CASU 12's tents. *Courtesy CASU 12 Association via Greg Pruis.*

Shower time for CASU 12. *Courtesy CASU 12 Association via Greg Pruis.*

Into the water hole for a swim. *Courtesy CASU 12 Association via Greg Pruis.*

A couple of CASU 12 personnel relax. *Courtesy CASU 12 Association via Greg Pruis.*

A group of CASU 12 personnel on Bougainville. *Courtesy CASU 12 Association via Greg Pruis.*

A group of CASU 12 personnel. The men on the ground kept the aircraft maintained and repaired, and were vital to combat operations. *Courtesy CASU 12 Association via Greg Pruis.*

Another group of CASU 12 personnel. *Courtesy CASU 12 Association via Greg Pruis.*

"Butch" Davenport's ground crew in front of #9, their responsibility. Two fine young men, but "Butch" Davenport always suspected that the one on the left was only 15 years old. "Butch" was close, as the one on the left is Charlie Dixon, aged 16! *Courtesy U.S. Naval Historical Center / M. W. "Butch" Davenport Collection.*

Charlie Dixon, AMM3c, CASU 12, wearing "Butch" Davenport's flight suit at Bougainville in 1944. *Courtesy Charles E. Dixon.*

"Butch" Davenport and Plane Captain Charlie Dixon (aged 16) with #9 at Bougainville, 1944. Dixon was given this responsibility by Davenport despite his young age. *Courtesy U.S. Naval Historical Center / M. W. "Butch" Davenport Collection.*

11

New Zealand Fighter Wing

The role of the New Zealand Fighter Wing was to support U.S. forces against the Japanese in the Solomon Islands. It was agreed that the U.S. Navy would provide new combat aircraft to the R.N.Z.A.F., and the squadrons were eventually supplied with Corsairs, Avengers, Venturas, Dauntless Dive Bombers and Catalinas.

In October 1943 the New Zealand Fighter Wing was established at Ondongo, New Georgia, with Wing Commander Freeman as Commanding Officer. The R.N.Z.A.F. were now within range of the Japanese bases in southern Bougainville and less than 400 miles from Rabaul.

Fighter operations from Ondongo were directed by Colonel Bryce, U.S.M.C., for the first three weeks, and he was responsible for the RNZAF Wing, the 70th Fighter Squadron U.S.A.A.F. and U.S. Navy Fighter Squadron 17.

The priority for the R.N.Z.A.F.'s operations in 1944 on Bougainville was the Japanese stronghold of Rabaul. The main focus of operations was to cover Allied bombers and conduct fighter sweeps of the area. When the Japanese withdrew their forces from Rabaul in early 1944, their role changed to fighter bomber operations.

As the U.S. forces moved on through the islands toward Japan the R.N.Z.A.F. harassed Japanese ground forces left behind on the islands. Agreement was reached at the start of 1945 for the R.N.Z.A.F. to support operations with the Australians and Americans.

At the end of the war twenty-four R.N.Z.A.F. squadrons had served in the Pacific Theater.

ComAirSoPac Conference, Espiritu Santo, in July 1943. L - R: Air Commodore S. Wallingford, Rear-Admiral O. B. Hardison, Vice-Admiral W. L. Ainsworth, Vice-Admiral A. W. Fitch, Major General R. J. Mitchell, Major General N. F. Twining and Brigadier General B. C. Lockwood. *Courtesy RNZAF Official, Air Force Museum of New Zealand.*

A group of officers beside the New Zealand Fighter Wing scoreboard. Ondongo, New Georgia, November 1943. L - R: Air Commodore M. W. Buckley CBE, Air Commodore S. Wallingford, Wing Commander T. O. Freeman DSO, DFC, unknown airman, Sir Cyril Newall GCB, OM, GCMG, CBE, AM and Major General H. E. Barrowclough, New Zealand Army. *Courtesy RNZAF Official, Air Force Museum of New Zealand.*

An airman paints the 57th victory flag onto the New Zealand Fighter Wing scoreboard. Ondongo, New Georgia, November 1943. *Courtesy RNZAF Official, Air Force Museum of New Zealand.*

Servicing Unit maintenance area during inspection by the New Zealand Governor General, Sir Cyril Newall. Ondongo, New Georgia, November 1943. *Courtesy RNZAF Official, Air Force Museum of New Zealand.*

Group of 17 Squadron Pilots involved in the first bomber assault on Rabaul. Ondongo, New Georgia. L - R: Pat Bradley, Ian Speedy, Doug Jones, Don Williams, Peter Worsp, Johnny Mills, Guy Newton, Alex George (partly obscured), Bruce Thomson, R.H. Covic, Jack Edwards, B.A. McHardie. December 19, 1943. *Courtesy RNZAF Official, Air Force Museum of New Zealand.*

Aerial oblique of the Ondongo airstrip, New Georgia, 1944. *Courtesy RNZAF Official, Air Force Museum of New Zealand.*

Pilot Officer McBride (Intelligence Officer) interrogates a group of 18 Squadron pilots after their return from an operation. Torokina, Bougainville, in February 1944. L - R: Pilot Officer J. A. McBride, unknown, Flying Officer A. R. Walker, Pilot Officer R. A. MacKinder, Flying Officer B. L. Hoskin, Sergeant D. W. Kidd and Squadron Leader J. A. Oldfield. Names supplied by Keith Gibson - 18 Squadron. *Courtesy RNZAF Official, Air Force Museum of New Zealand.*

Ground Staff Camp on Bougainville, January 1944. The airmen's mess is in the background. *Courtesy RNZAF Official, Air Force Museum of New Zealand.*

Grumman TBF Avenger takes-off from Bougainville with Mt. Bagana in the distance, 1944. *Courtesy RNZAF Official, Air Force Museum of New Zealand.*

Armorers loading ammunition into the magazines of a New Zealand Fighter Wing Curtiss P-40 Kittyhawk. Presumed to be Torokina, Bougainville, 1944. *Courtesy RNZAF Official, Air Force Museum of New Zealand.*

New Zealand Fighter Wing Curtiss P-40 Kittyhawk taxiing out at Bougainville in 1944. *Courtesy Vought.*

Number Ten Servicing Unit personnel maneuver a Pratt and Whitney (Ventura) engine on a gantry. Piva, Bougainville, in 1944. *Courtesy RNZAF Official, Air Force Museum of New Zealand.*

Number Two Servicing Unit Curtiss P-40 Kittyhawk taking off. Torokina, Bougainville, in 1944. *Courtesy RNZAF Official, Air Force Museum of New Zealand.*

Royal New Zealand Air Force Lockheed PV-1 Ventura squadron dispersal area on Bougainville. Presumed to be Number Ten Servicing Unit aircraft. NZ4515, NZ4518 and NZ4503 amongst aircraft in view in 1944. *Courtesy RNZAF Official, Air Force Museum of New Zealand.*

Lockheed PV-1 Venturas on Piva, Bougainville. Aircraft on charge to Number Ten Servicing Unit, NZ4518 and NZ4503, visible in 1944. *Courtesy RNZAF Official, Air Force Museum of New Zealand.*

Ground crew attach a 1,000 pound bomb onto a Two Squadron Lockheed PV-1 Ventura before a raid on Rabaul, Green Island. *Courtesy RNZAF Official, Air Force Museum of New Zealand.*

Air to air view of a Royal New Zealand Air Force Lockheed PV-1 Ventura strike on Rabaul. *Courtesy RNZAF Official, Air Force Museum of New Zealand.*

Air to air view of Lockheed PV-1 Ventura NZ4608, of 1 Squadron, over Rabaul. *Courtesy RNZAF Official, Air Force Museum of New Zealand.*

Aerial view of a bombing raid over Rabaul. *Courtesy RNZAF Official, Air Force Museum of New Zealand.*

12

Bougainville and Rabaul

After rest and recreation in Australia, Lt. Cdr. Blackburn had to train and absorb replacement pilots into the squadron. When they were first commissioned in January 1943 they had nine months to train prior to first combat. Before their second tour flying missions into Rabaul they only had a few weeks to get the new pilots ready. Some were experienced but some were not, and therefore it was a difficult time for all. When Fighting 17 returned to combat on January 26, 1944, they faced an entirely different challenge. The Americans had taken only a small part of the island of Bougainville, the rest being held by the Japanese. This meant when American aircraft took off the Japanese would radio their base at Rabaul and tell them how many aircraft were coming and when. The enemy would then be waiting for them to arrive, and instead of being hunters they were the hunted. The enemy opposition was fierce, and although Fighting 17's primary mission was to protect the bombers they scored many aerial victories. After losses in the first few missions it was clear something had to be done about the Japanese getting through, so Blackburn devised a new tactic called "Roving High Cover." This was designed to attack and break up the Japanese fighters before they could get to the bombers. This was highly successful and a significant factor in Fighting 17's success in the air.

From January 26, 1944, to January 30, 1944, Fighting 17 shot down 60.5 Japanese aircraft and 19 probables. This gives an indication of how important Rabaul was to the Japanese and the lengths they went to in defending it.

The intense combat continued until February 19, 1944, when enemy air opposition ceased over the skies of Rabaul. Fighting 17 continued flying missions until they were relieved on March 7, 1944.

Lt. (jg) Robert "Bobby" Mims at Bougainville in 1944. Mims returned to Fighting 17 on December 5, 1943, after recovering from illness. *Courtesy National Archives.*

Ens. John M. Smith at Bougainville in 1944. Smith reported to Fighting 17 on December 8, 1943. *Courtesy National Archives.*

Lt. (jg) Harold James "Bitz" Bitzegaio at Bougainville in 1944. Bitzegaio reported to Fighting 17 on December 10, 1943. *Courtesy National Archives.*

Ens. Louis Allen Fitzgerald reported to Fighting 17 on December 22, 1943. *Courtesy the Fitzgerald Family.*

Ens. Harmond Becker Richardson, Jr., at Bougainville in 1944. Richardson reported to Fighting 17 on January 3, 1944. *Courtesy National Archives.*

Lt. (jg) R. L. Mills at Bougainville in 1944. Mills reported to Fighting 17 as Squadron Duty Officer on January 3, 1944. *Courtesy National Archives.*

Oscar Ivan Chenoweth, Jr., at Bougainville in February 1944. He shot down a Zeke with VF-38, then added another 7.5 victories with Fighting 17. *Courtesy National Archives.*

Ens. James Cass Dixon at Bougainville in 1944. Dixon reported to Fighting 17 on January 10, 1944. *Courtesy National Archives.*

Edward Ellsworth Beeler in the cockpit of his Corsair in 1944. Beeler reported to Fighting 17 on January 11, 1944. *Courtesy Edward E. Beeler Collection.*

Ens. Donald Roy McQueen reported to Fighting 17 on January 10, 1944. *Courtesy the McQueen Family.*

Ens. Mervin Ward "Ace" Cole reported to Fighting 17 on January 11, 1944. *Courtesy National Archives.*

Lt. Cdr. Lionel Thiel "Mac" McQuiston. McQuiston reported to Fighting 17 as a Lt. on January 18, 1944. *Courtesy Della McQuiston.*

Lt. (jg) Earle Carpenter "Pete" Peterson, Jr., at Bougainville in February 1944. Peterson reported to Fighting 17 on January 22, 1944. *Courtesy National Archives.*

SBD-5s assigned to an unidentified Marine Corps Squadron taxi on a runway on Bougainville just prior to launching on a combat mission. Note the bombs visible beneath the wings of some of the aircraft. *Courtesy Robert Lawson Photograph Collection, National Museum of Naval Aviation.*

"Big Jim" Streig at Bougainville in 1944. *Courtesy National Archives.*

Robert "Windy" Hill at Bougainville in 1944. *Courtesy National Archives.*

SBDs from an unidentified squadron pictured en route to their home base after an attack against the Japanese naval base at Rabaul. *Courtesy Robert Lawson Photograph Collection, Nationcl Museum of Naval Aviation.*

SBD-5s assigned to Composite Squadron 40 (VC-40) pictured at Piva Uncle Airstrip, Torokina, prior to taking off on a strike against Talili Bay, Rabaul. The strike group that day consisted of 54 SBDs and 36 TBF Avengers, with launch beginning at 10:00 and the attack commencing at 12:00. *Courtesy Robert Lawson Photograph Collection, National Museum of Naval Aviation.*

A formation of SBD-5s assigned to Composite Squadron 40 (VC-40) pictured in flight near the squadron's home base at Torokina. VC-40 was one of a handful of Navy Dauntless squadrons that supported the bombing campaign against Rabaul. *Courtesy Robert Lawson Photograph Collection, National Museum of Naval Aviation.*

SBD-5 assigned to unidentified squadron pictured in flight over Munda. *Courtesy Robert Lawson Photograph Collection, National Museum of Naval Aviation.*

"Hap" Bowers with his assigned Corsair #23 for the second tour on Bougainville. *Courtesy Alexandra Bowers.*

SBD-5s assigned to Composite Squadron 40 (VC-40) based at Torokina, pictured en route to bomb a Japanese target, probably at Rabaul. Note the weathered paint scheme on the aircraft is the result of the hot and humid conditions in the Solomon Islands. *Courtesy Robert Lawson Photograph Collection, National Museum of Naval Aviation.*

A Marine Corps SBD en route to a bombing mission against Vunakanau Airfield on Rabaul. *Courtesy Robert Lawson Photograph Collection, National Museum of Naval Aviation.*

Illustrating just how the dive bomber got its name, this Douglas Dauntless plummets downward, releases its bomb, then begins to pull out of its near vertical descent. The camera catches the aircraft immediately after the ordnance was released. *Courtesy Robert Lawson Photograph Collection, National Museum of Naval Aviation.*

Group at Bougainville. L – R: Bill Popp, Hal Jackson, John M. Smith, "Tim" Gile, Mills Schanuel, Don Innis, "Ike" Kepford and Roger Hedrick. Hedrick was 6' 2" and 140lbs when this photo was taken. *Courtesy U.S. Naval Historical Center / M. W. "Butch" Davenport Collection / the Hedrick Family.*

"Hap" Bowers at Bougainville in 1944. *Courtesy Alexandra Bowers.*

Tom Killefer in Bobby Mims' aircraft early in the second tour at Bougainville. NB. In my previous book *The Skull and Crossbones Squadron* the aircraft was stated as Burriss' aircraft, which is incorrect. *Courtesy U.S. Naval Historical Center / M. W. "Butch" Davenport Collection.*

Donald Allan "Stinky" Innis at Bougainville. His nickname was believed to have come from Guadalcanal, where he served in 1942. *Courtesy Alexandra Bowers.*

"Hap" Bowers, "Fatso" Ellsworth and "Big Jim" Streig on Bougainville, where they were living in the same tent. *Courtesy Alexandra Bowers*

"Country" Landreth with his assigned Corsair #39, which he flew on the second tour at Bougainville. *Courtesy Vought.*

Hal Jackson and Duke Henning in front of the squadron scoreboard. *Courtesy Vought.*

Lt. Walter John "Wally" Schub at Bougainville 1944. Schub had the reputation of not losing a man who flew in his division throughout the war. *Courtesy National Archives.*

"Big Jim" Streig, Fighting 17 ace with 5.5 victories. *Courtesy Jim Streig.*

Lt. Basil Duke Henning at Bougainville in 1944. *Courtesy National Archives.*

Back Row L – R: Chenoweth, Kurlander, Killefer and Cunningham. Front Row L – R: Unknown and Bitzegaio with camera. *Courtesy Vought.*

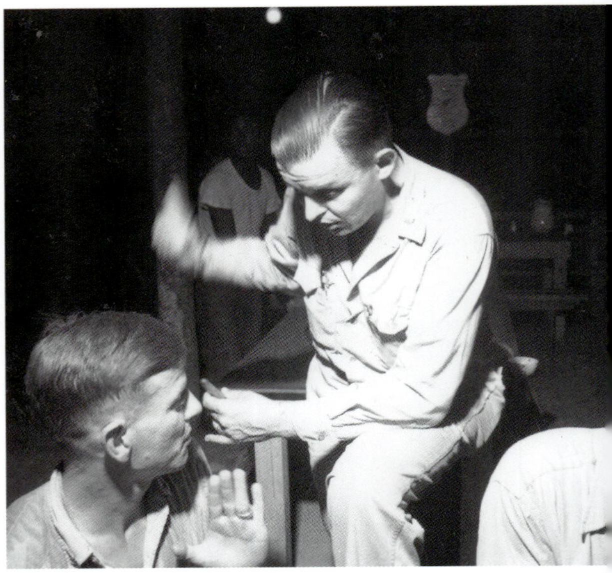

Squadron Commanding Officer Lt. Cdr. Tom Blackburn (Left) discusses a raid on Rabaul with another officer after returning to his unit's base on Bougainville, February 1944. *Courtesy National Archives.*

Ens. Don McQueen at Bougainville in 1944. *Courtesy National Archives.*

PBY Catalina pictured on patrol. Fighting 17 escorted PBY "Dumbos" on many missions to rescue survivors on their first tour in October and November 1943. *Courtesy National Museum of Naval Aviation.*

Lt. (jg) Robert Hal Jackson. *Courtesy National Archives.*

A group of Fighting 17 pilots in a photo which was taken between December 22, 1943, and January 5, 1944. Back Row L – R: Ellsworth, Cordray, Freeman, Gile, Dunn, Hedrick, Kepford, Landreth, Jagger, and Hill. Front Row. L – R: Cooke, J. M. Smith, Cunningham, Fitzgerald, Wharton and Schanuel. *Courtesy U.S. Naval Historical Center / M. W. "Butch" Davenport Collection.*

Wilbert Peter "Beads" Popp in the "Command Car." *Courtesy Alexandra Bowers.*

Basil Duke Henning, Air Combat Information Officer, relaxing at the beach. *Courtesy U.S. Naval Historical Center / M. W. "Butch" Davenport Collection.*

Harold J. Bitzegaio and Plane Captain at Bougainville. *Courtesy Vought / Harold J. Bitzegaio.*

Roger Hedrick sitting on the wing of his Corsair. *Courtesy Lennard Edmisten / Vought / U.S. Naval Historical Center / M. W. "Butch" Davenport Collection.*

Whit Wharton sitting on Corsair #26. *Courtesy Alexandra Bowers.*

Robert "Windy" Hill in a Corsair. *Courtesy Alexandra Bowers.*

Robert "Windy" Hill and "Hap" Bowers by Corsair #34. *Courtesy Alexandra Bowers.*

Earl May and his wingman "Beads" Popp. *Courtesy Alexandra Bowers.*

Whit Wharton in front of Corsair #34. *Courtesy Alexandra Bowers.*

Ear May and "Hap" Bowers at Bougainville. May and Bowers were both from Wisconsin. *Courtesy Alexandra Bowers.*

A group of Fighting 17 pilots in front of an F4U-1A. *Courtesy U.S. Naval Historical Center / M. W. "Butch" Davenport Collection.*

"Hap" Bowers in aircraft #23, which he flew for the second tour from Bougainville. *Courtesy Alexandra Bowers.*

Robert "Windy" Hill at Bougainville taxiing his F4U-1A. *Courtesy Robert Lawson Photograph Collection, National Museum of Naval Aviation / U.S. Navy photo.*

"Hap" Bowers and Earl May by Earl's plane, #27. *Courtesy Alexandra Bowers.*

"Hap" Bowers in the cockpit of his aircraft, which was part of Roger Hedrick's flight. *Courtesy Alexandra Bowers.*

Robert "Windy" Hill and "Hap" Bowers by the squadron scoreboard. *Courtesy Alexandra Bowers.*

Ready to go! Back row L – R: March, Gilbert, and Schub. Front row L – R: Wharton, Jagger, and Bitzegaio. January 1944. *Courtesy Robert Lawson Photograph Collection, National Museum of Naval Aviation / U.S. Navy photo.*

Harold Bitzegaio at Bougainville in January 1944. *Courtesy Harold J Bitzegaio / Robert Lawson Photograph Collection, National Museum of Naval Aviation / U.S. Navy photo.*

A group of Fighting 17 pilots in Command Car. *Courtesy Lennard Edmisten / Vought / U.S. Naval Historical Center / M. W. "Butch" Davenport Collection.*

Hal Jackson at Bougainville in 1944. *Courtesy Hal and Barbara Jackson.*

Fighting 17 pilots back from the February 19, 1944, raid on Rabaul congregate at headquarters at Bougainville. The squadron shot down 16 aircraft without the loss of a man, although one pilot was given up for lost until he returned three quarters of an hour late. *Courtesy U.S. Naval Historical Center / M. W. "Butch" Davenport Collection.*

"Hap" Bowers with gun drawn. *Courtesy U.S. Naval Historical Center / M.W. "Butch" Davenport Collection.*

"Butch" Davenport, Skull and Crossbones ace with 6.25 victories, stands in front of his aircraft, #9 "Lonesome Polecat." *Courtesy U.S. Naval Historical Center / M. W. "Butch" Davenport Collection.*

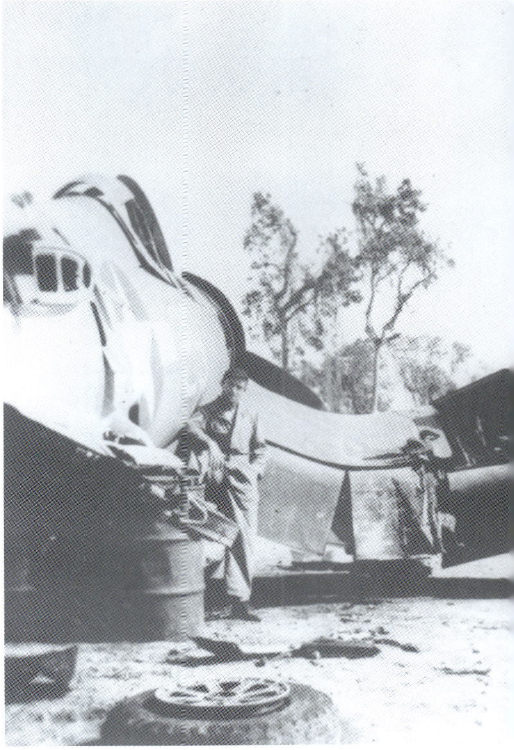

"Ike" Kepford and his F4U-1A. Note the flaps burned by exploding ammunition cans. Piva Yoke, January 31, 1944. *Courtesy Robert Lawson Photograph Collection, National Museum of Naval Aviation / U.S Navy photo.*

Ray Beacham, "the Kitty Hawk Kid," sitting in his Corsair. *Courtesy Harry Bridges, Dare County Regional Airport Museum.*

Tom Blackburn in front of the squadron scoreboard at Bougainville early in 1944. *Courtesy Robert Lawson Photograph Collection, National Museum of Naval Aviation / U.S. Navy photo.*

Ray Beacham on left in front of the squadron scoreboard at Bougainville in February 1944. The other pilot is believed to be Don "Stinky" Innis. *Courtesy Robert Lawson Photograph Collection, National Museum of Naval Aviation / U.S. Navy photo.*

Earle C. "Pete" Peterson in his Corsair. *Courtesy Earle C. Peterson, Jr. Collection.*

Popp, Smith, Jackson and Kurlander on Bougainville in 1944. *Courtesy Lennard Edmisten.*

Group of Fighting 17 pilots in front of scoreboard. Back Row L – R: Bill Meek, "Windy" Hill, "Butch" Davenport, Mel Kurlander and "Fatso" Ellsworth. Middle Row L – R: "Hap" Bowers, Ray Beacham and Harmond Richardson, Jr. Front Row L – R: "Chico" Freeman and Don Innis. *Courtesy the Anderson Family / Vought / U.S. Naval Historical Center / M. W. "Butch" Davenport Collection.*

"Hap" Bowers outside squadron office in flight gear. *Courtesy Alexandra Bowers.*

Fighting 17 personnel are briefed in the ready tent by Intelligence Officer Lt. B. D. Henning (at right) before a raid on Rabaul in February 1944. In center, seated is Fighting 17 Commanding Officer Lt. Cdr. Tom Blackburn. The squadron was then based on Bougainville. *Courtesy National Archives.*

Earl May, Unknown and Paul Cordray at Bougainville in 1944. *Courtesy Del and Pat May Collection.*

"Butch" Davenport's aircraft "Lonesome Polecat." *Courtesy the Deveney family.*

A group of Fighting 17 pilots by the squadron scoreboard at Bougainville. *Courtesy the Anderson Family / Vought.*

Lt. (jg) Earl May, Fighting 17 ace with eight victories to his credit. *Courtesy National Archives.*

Three Fighting 17 officers chatting in front of the unit's scoreboard at Piva airstrip, Bougainville, February 1944. They are (L - R) Lt. Basil Duke Henning, Lt. Merl W. Davenport, and Lt. (jg) R. L. Mills. *Courtesy National Archives.*

Lt. Cdr. Tom Blackburn, Commanding Officer of Fighting Squadron 17, receives the Distinguished Flying Cross from Major General Ralph J. Mitchell, U.S.M.C., in a ceremony on Bougainville, in February 1944. Behind them is the Fighting 17 scoreboard showing 130 Japanese planes claimed shot down by the squadron at that time. *Courtesy National Archives.*

From above left (clockwise): Another view of Lt. Cdr. Tom Blackburn, Commanding Officer of Fighting Squadron 17, receiving the Distinguished Flying Cross from Major General Ralph J. Mitchell, U.S.M.C., in a ceremony on Bougainville in February 1944. *Courtesy National Archives.*

"Country" Landreth, "Fatso" Ellsworth, "Butch" Davenport and "Windy" Hill at Bougainville in 1944. *Courtesy U.S. Naval Historical Center / M. W. "Butch" Davenport Collection.*

Whit Wharton and Wally Schub at Bougainville in 1944. *Courtesy Robert Lawson Photograph Collection, National Museum of Naval Aviation / U.S. Navy photo.*

Below: "Chico" Freeman leading a section of F4U-1As. *Courtesy Robert Lawson Photograph Collection, National Museum of Naval Aviation / U.S. Navy photo.*

Officers pose with the unit's scoreboard on Bougainville in February 1944. The Commanding Officer, Lt. Cdr. Tom Blackburn, is in the front row, center. At the time Fighting 17 was credited with 130 Japanese planes shot down. Courtesy National Archives.

"Chico" Freeman sitting on the wing of #34. *Courtesy U.S. Naval Historical Center / M. W. "Butch" Davenport Collection.*

Squadron Commanding Officer Lt. Cdr. Tom Blackburn after his return from a successful raid on Rabaul in mid-February 1944. The squadron was then based on Bougainville. *Courtesy National Archives*

"Country" Landreth and Carl Gilbert in front of the squadron scoreboard on Bougainville in 1944. *Courtesy Robert Lawson Photograph Collection, National Museum of Naval Aviation / U.S. Navy photo.*

"Beads" Popp with his #28 at Bougainville in 1944. *Courtesy the Popp Family.*

"Andy" Jagger in his Corsair #36 at Bougainville in 1944. *Courtesy Robert Lawson Photograph Collection, National Museum of Naval Aviation / U.S. Navy photo.*

An F4U-1A of Fighting 17 taxiing out for a raid on Rabaul in February 1944. #35 was normally flown by Harold Bitzegaio. *Courtesy Robert Lawson Photograph Collection, National Museum of Naval Aviation / U.S. Navy photo.*

Tom Blackburn, Commanding Officer of Fighter Squadron 17 and one of its leading "aces." He is credited with shooting down eleven Japanese aircraft, plus five "probables," whilst flying F4U-1A "Corsair" fighters with Fighting 17 in the Solomons, November 1943 and January-February 1944. *Courtesy National Archives.*

Back row. L – R: May, Jackson, Einar, Smith, Meek, Mills, Kincaid and Henning. Front row. L – R: Schub, Cordray, Kepford, Kurlander, Hedrick, Killefer and Hill. Bougainville in February 1944. *Courtesy Hal and Barbara Jackson / Vought.*

Lt. (jg) Carl Gilbert at Bougainville in 1944. *Courtesy National Archives.*

John M. Smith, "Beads" Popp, Duke Henning, and Mel Kurlander at Bougainville. *Courtesy Robert Lawson Photograph Collection, National Museum of Naval Aviation / U.S. Navy photo.*

Tom Killefer in front of Corsair #5 on March 6, 1944. *Courtesy Robert Lawson Photograph Collection, National Museum of Naval Aviation / U.S. Navy photo.*

Squadron Commanding Officer Lt. Cdr. Tom Blackburn stands before the unit's scoreboard at Piva airstrip, Bougainville, in February 1944. Note Skull and Crossbones emblem with F4U Corsair silhouettes flanking. *Courtesy National Archives.*

L – R: Les Kincaid, Mel Kurlander, Jim Dixon, John M. Smith, "Beads" Popp, Roger Hedrick, Earl May, "Oc" Chenoweth and Harmond Richardson at Bougainville in 1944. *Courtesy Robert Lawson Photograph Collection, National Museum of Naval Aviation / U.S. Navy photo.*

Roger Hedrick's aircraft running up on line. It was thought Tom Blackburn's aircraft was the only one with the number under the cowl, but this photo shows Hedrick's with the # 17 clearly marked under the cowl also. *Courtesy Lennard Edmisten / Vought / U.S. Naval Historical Center / M. W. "Butch" Davenport Collection.*

Ens. F. A. "Andy" Jagger on Bougainville in 1944. *Courtesy National Archives.*

Pilot Lt. (jg) Dan Cunningham (Left) explains details of Fighting 17's successful raid on Rabaul to Lt. Duke Henning, Air Intelligence Officer. In the center are Lt. (jg) E. Peterson and Ens. M. W. Cole. *Courtesy National Archives.*

Pilot Lt. Oscar Chenoweth describes his activities to Air Intelligence Officer Lt. Duke Henning after returning from a raid on Rabaul. *Courtesy National Archives.*

Lt. "Oc" Chenoweth (Left) and Lt. (jg) Earle Peterson (Center) with Lt. Basil Duke Henning after a Rabaul strike in February 1944. *Courtesy Robert Lawson Photograph Collection, National Museum of Naval Aviation / U.S. Navy photo.*

"Hap" Bowers on Bougainville in 1944. *Courtesy National Archives.*

Hedrick, Smith, Matthews, Bowers, Herrmann, Gile and Ellsworth at Bougainville in February 1944. *Courtesy Lennard Edmisten / U.S. Naval Historical Center / M.W. "Butch" Davenport Collection.*

Chicago's Pride - Dan Cunningham, winner of the Navy Cross for shooting down four Japanese planes in one day on February 19, 1944. *Courtesy National Archives.*

Lt. (jg) R. L. Mills, Squadron Duty Officer at Bougainville in 1944. *Courtesy National Archives.*

Lt. (jg) Mills Schanuel at Bougainville in 1944. *Courtesy National Archives.*

Ens. Louis Fitzgerald at Bougainville in 1944. *Courtesy National Archives.*

Don Innis and "Butch" Davenport beside #9 "Lonesome Polecat" at Bougainville in 1944. *Courtesy Robert Lawson Photograph Collection, National Museum of Naval Aviation / U.S. Navy photo.*

Ensign "Andy" Jagger of Southampton, NY, describes an aerial victory made over Rabaul to Lt. H. A. March of Washington, D.C., in February 1944. This famous photo by Navy estimate has been reprinted more often than any image of any other Naval aviator. *Courtesy National Archives.*

Lt. (jg) Ira C. "Ike" Kepford stands beside his F4U-1A Corsair shortly after being rotated from combat duty in the Central Solomons. He became the U.S. Navy's then-leading "ace," credited with sixteen kills plus one probable. Note his .45 automatic pistol and sixteen Japanese flags painted on his aircraft. *Courtesy National Archives.*

Medal presentations to Fighting 17 pilots in February 1944 at Bougainville. *Courtesy Vought.*

Lt. (jg) Earle C. "Pete" Peterson next to Corsair #31. *Courtesy Earle C. Peterson, Jr. Collection.*

Ensign Jack Evans Diteman reported to Fighting 17 on February 13, 1944. *Courtesy the Diteman Family.*

Ensign Richard Martin "Dick" Einar, Jr., reported to Fighting 17 on February 13, 1944. *Courtesy Rick and Cathy Einar.*

L – R: Robert Einar, mother Mildred Einar and "Dick" Einar. "Dick" Einar's brother Robert was killed in action in 1945. *Courtesy Rick and Cathy Einar.*

Ensign Harvey "Matty" Matthews, Class 3B at N.A.S Pensacola in the summer of 1943. Matthews reported to Fighting 17 on February 13, 1944. *Courtesy the Matthews Family.*

Ensign Harvey "Matty" Matthews' Naval Aviator Certificate. *Courtesy the Matthews Family.*

DEPARTMENT OF THE NAVY

Date 2 July 1943

NAVAL AVIATOR NO. P-406

This Certifies that

Harvey MATTHEWS

Ensign A-V(N) USNR

born 22 *day of* August 192

having fulfilled the conditions prescribed by the United States Navy Department, was appointed a

NAVAL AVIATOR

on 2 July 1943

G. D. MURRAY

COMMANDANT N.A.T.C. PENSACOLA, FLA

(Seal)

Received

(Rank and Service)

Lt. (jg) William "Country" Landreth at Bougainville in 1944. *Courtesy National Archives.*

Roger Hedrick at Bougainville in February 1944. *Courtesy Robert Lawson Photograph Collection, National Museum of Naval Aviation / U.S. Navy photo.*

Mervin Ward "Ace" Cole at Bougainville in 1944. *Courtesy National Archives.*

Robert "Windy" Hill receives a medal from a Marine General in February 1944 at Bougainville. Twelve other personal awards would follow. *Courtesy Vought.*

Lt. (jg) Tom Killefer at Bougainville in 1944. *Courtesy National Archives.*

"Ike" Kepford, Mills Schanuel and Hal Jackson. *Courtesy U.S. Naval Historical Center / M. W. "Butch" Davenport Collection.*

Lt. Cdr. Roger Hedrick, Fighting 17 Executive Officer and ace with nine Japanese aircraft shot down. He later went on to score another three victories as Commanding Officer of VF-84. *Courtesy National Archives.*

Lt. Cdr. Tom Blackburn stands in front of Fighting 17 as General Ralph Mitchell (left foreground) reads the citation. F4U aircraft in background on Bougainville. *Courtesy National Archives.*

Ens. Whitfield Carlisle Wharton, Jr., at Bougainville in 1944. *Courtesy National Archives.*

"Ike" Kepford's Corsair #29 parked on Bougainville in 1944. *Courtesy Vought.*

"Ike" Kepford hamming it up. *Courtesy U.S. Naval Historical Center / M. W. "Butch" Davenport Collection.*

Ens. M. M. "Kurly" Kurlander at Bougainville in 1944. *Courtesy National Archives.*

Ensign Whit Wharton next to his Corsair. *Courtesy Vought.*

Fighting 17's "Skipper," Lt. Cdr. Tom Blackburn, walks toward his Corsair before taking off to attack Rabaul in February 1944. Fighting 17 was then operating out of Bougainville. Note #1 marking on Blackburn's plane. *Courtesy Robert Lawson Photograph Collection, National Museum of Naval Aviation / U.S. Navy photo.*

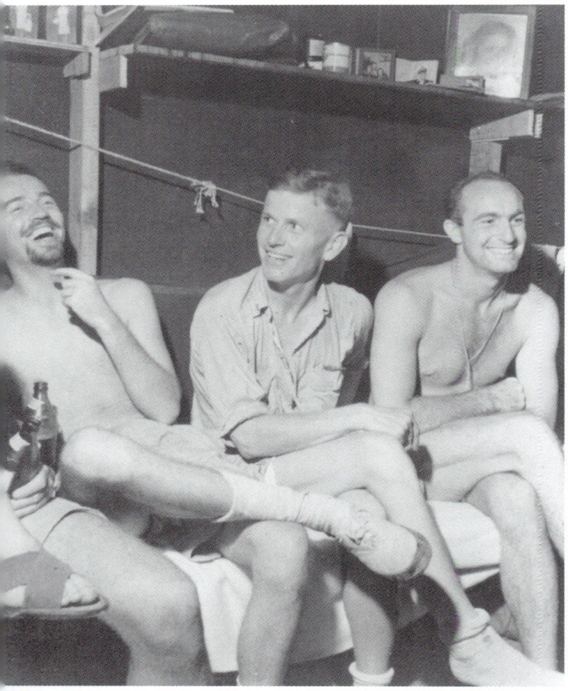

Duke Henning, Tom Blackburn and "Ike" Kepford relaxing after a mission. Photo dated February 19, 1944. *Courtesy U.S. Naval Historical Center / M. W. "Butch" Davenport Collection.*

Ensign Don McQueen next to the squadron scoreboard in February 1944. *Courtesy the McQueen Family.*

"Country" Landreth on Bougainville in 1944. *Courtesy Robert Lawson Photograph Collection, National Museum of Naval Aviation / U.S. Navy photo.*

Ensign Jack Diteman on Bougainville in 1944. *Courtesy National Archives.*

Lou Fitzgerald standing next to his Corsair on Bougainville in 1944. *Courtesy Vought.*

"Dick" Einar on Bougainville in 1944. *Courtesy National Archives.*

Don McQueen relaxing with a beer on Bougainville in 1944. *Courtesy Alexandra Bowers.*

"Ike" Kepford taxies out of its revetment for a strike on Rabaul. Delayed in getting away, he was unable to overtake Fighting 17 and when near Rabaul turned back. He had his own little Jap party instead. *Courtesy Robert Lawson Photograph Collection, National Museum of Naval Aviation / U.S. Navy photo.*

"Bitz" Bitzegaio and Whit Wharton standing beside a sign on Bougainville in 1944. *Courtesy Vought / the Anderson Family / Harold J. Bitzegaio.*

Cemetery on Bougainville. *Courtesy Vought / the Anderson Family.*

Ray Beacham sitting in his Corsair. *Courtesy Harry Bridges, Dare County Regional Airport Museum.*

"Big Jim" Streig with his #3 Corsair. *Courtesy U.S. Naval Historical Center / M. W. "Butch" Davenport Collection.*

Ensign Lou Fitzgerald on Bougainville in 1944. *Courtesy National Archives.*

Wilbert Peter "Beads" Popp on Bougainville in 1944. *Courtesy National Archives.*

"Ike" Kepford returns to Piva Yoke, 45 minutes late from his eventful mission of February 19, 1944. *Courtesy Robert Lawson Photograph Collection, National Museum of Naval Aviation / U.S. Navy photo.*

The leading ace of Fighting 17 was Lt. (jg) Ira. C. "Ike" Kepford with sixteen victories. He is shown here flying his raised canopy F4U-1A near Bougainville in the Solomon Islands in March 1944. *Courtesy Robert Lawson Photograph Collection, National Museum of Naval Aviation / U.S. Navy photo.*

"Bitz" Bitzegaio and "Country" Landreth at the Bougainville beachhead perimeter. The area beyond the sign was held by the Japanese. *Courtesy Vought / the Anderson Family / Harold J. Bitzegaio.*

Lt. (jg) I. C. "Ike" Kepford's F4U-1A parked on Bougainville, February 19, 1944. *Courtesy Robert Lawson Photograph Collection, National Museum of Naval Aviation / U.S. Navy photo.*

Roger Hedrick sitting in his aircraft #17 shown with nine victories. *Courtesy Robert Lawson Photograph Collection, National Museum of Naval Aviation / U.S. Navy photo.*

"Ike" Kepford leading a division of Fighting 17 Corsairs near Bougainville in March 1944. #29 "Ike" Kepford. #8 Hal Jackson. #3 "Big Jim" Streig has an old Star & Bar insignia, perhaps with the red outline that was replaced with blue the previous summer. #28 Wilbert Peter "Beads" Popp. This is one of the best known photos from World War II. *Courtesy Robert Lawson Photograph Collection, National Museum of Naval Aviation / U.S. Navy photo.*

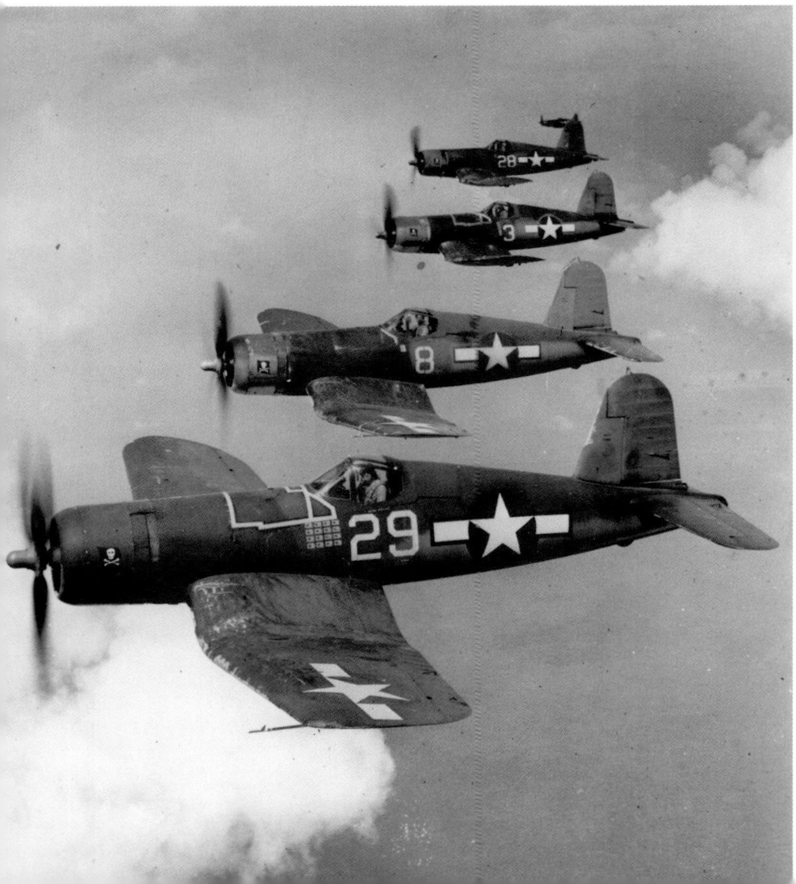

Espiritu Santo, March 1944. Full squadron of Fighting 17 - the last time they will see these fine aircraft together. Fighting 17 are headed home after flying in from Bougainville. *Courtesy U.S. Naval Historical Center / M. W. "Butch" Davenport Collection.*

Another view of the squadron flying in from Bougainville, Espiritu Santo, March 1944. Full squadron of Fighting 17 - the last time they will see these fine aircraft together. *Courtesy U.S. Naval Historical Center / M. W. "Butch" Davenport Collection.*

"Chico" Freeman leading a section of F4U-1As. *Courtesy Robert Lawson Photograph Collection, National Museum of Naval Aviation / U.S. Navy photo.*

Lt. (jg) Ira C. Kepford in the cockpit of his F4U-1A Corsair on the day Fighting 17 raided Rabaul on February 19, 1944. *Courtesy National Archives.*

Lt. (jg) Ira C. "Ike" Kepford poses by the cockpit of his Vought F4U Corsair in March 1944. From November 1943 to February 1944 he shot down sixteen Japanese aircraft to become the Navy's then leading ace. *Courtesy National Archives.*

Tom Blackburn and Gus Wildhelm, skipper of VF (N) 75, at Bougainville early in 1944. *Courtesy Robert Lawson Photograph Collection, National Museum of Naval Aviation / U.S Navy photo.*

J. C. Duke, plane captain AMM 3c, and Lt. Cdr. Roger Hedrick in March 1944, Piva Yoke Fighter Strip, Bougainville. *Courtesy the Hedrick Family.*

L – R: Jimmy Dixon (sitting on jeep), Dan Cunningham, and "Oc" Chenoweth at Bougainville, 1944. *Courtesy Vought.*

Lt. C. D. "Timmy" Gile, Fighting 17 ace with eight Japanese aircraft shot down. *Courtesy National Archives.*

Earl May in #8 after a February 26, 1944, mission. *Courtesy Del and Pat May Collection.*

Dan Cunningham with his aircraft #15 showing seven Japanese flags, on Bougainville in 1944. He flew #15 on the second tour. *Courtesy Robert Lawson Photograph Collection, National Museum of Naval Aviation / U.S. Navy photo.*

"Butch" Davenport, Fighting 17 Engineering Officer and ace with 6.25 Japanese aircraft to his credit. *Courtesy National Archives.*

Paul Cordray from Texas shot down six Japanese aircraft while serving with Fighting 17. He scored another with VBF-10 when he destroyed a Zeke on April 16, 1945, near Kikai Airfield, Japan. *Courtesy National Archives.*

Bobby Mims, Fighting 17 ace with six victories. *Courtesy Vought.*

Harry "Dirty Eddie" March and "Country" Landreth. *Courtesy U.S. Naval Historical Center / M. W. "Butch" Davenport Collection.*

"Big Jim" Streig, Fighting 17 ace with 5.5 victories. *Courtesy U.S. Naval Historical Center / M. W. "Butch" Davenport Collection.*

John M. Smith, who later made ace with VF-34. *Courtesy John M. Smith Collection.*

"Chico" Freeman at Bougainville early in 1944. *Courtesy Robert Lawson Photograph Collection, National Museum of Naval Aviation / U.S. Navy photo.*

13

On with the War

After Fighting 17 returned home at the end of March 1944 the squadron was de-commissioned and the pilots had a welcome spot of leave. Many of the pilots formed the nucleus of two squadrons: VF-84 and VF/VBF-10.

VF-84 served with distinction on the U.S.S. *Bunker Hill* until the carrier was put out of action by a Kamikaze attack on May 11, 1945. VF/VBF-10 also served with honor on the U.S.S. *Intrepid*, which suffered a similar fate. Other pilots continued to serve overseas until the end of the war. Those who did not see action again served as combat instructors and other assignments at various bases in the U.S.

VF-17 was officially reformed as an F6F Hellcat squadron on April 18, 1944, at N.A.S. Alameda with Lt. Cdr. Marshall Beebe as Commanding Officer. They served with distinction on the U.S.S. *Hornet* from February 1, 1945, to June 19, 1945.

Rear Admiral J. J. Ballantine is shown with four of the thirteen aces of "Blackburn's Irregulars." L – R: Lt. Harry March, (5 victories); Lt. Cdr. Roger Hedrick (9 victories); Adm. Ballantine, now Chief of Staff, Air Force, Pacific Fleet; Lt. Cdr. J.T. Blackburn, (11 victories) and the No. 1 U.S. Navy ace (at that time), Lt. (jg) Ira C. Kepford, (16 victories). *Courtesy Robert Lawson Photograph Collection, National Museum of Naval Aviation / U.S. Navy photo.*

Three of the squadron's leading aces pose by a Corsair fighter after their unit left the combat zone, March 22, 1944. L – R: Roger Hedrick (9 victories), Tom Blackburn (11 victories), and "Ike" Kepford (16 victories). *Courtesy Robert Lawson Photograph Collection, National Museum of Naval Aviation / U.S. Navy photo.*

After serving with Fighting 17 Roger Hedrick became commanding officer of VF-84. *Courtesy U.S. Navy photo via the Diteman Family.*

L – R: Lt. Cdr. Roger Hedrick, Skipper of VF-84 (first left), and Cdr. George M. "Bunky" Ottinger (3rd left), Commander Air Group 84, with the Skippers of VT-84 and VB-84. *Courtesy U.S. Navy photo via the Diteman Family.*

VF-84 squadron photo. *Courtesy U.S. Navy photo via the Diteman Family.*

VF-84 was based at N.A.A.S. Twenty-Nine Palms for rocket practice in the summer and fall of 1944. *Courtesy the Matthews Family.*

SB2Cs at N.A.A.S. Twenty-Nine Palms. *Courtesy the Matthews Family.*

Corsairs landing at N.A.A.S. Twenty-Nine Palms and kicking up dust as a result. *Courtesy the Matthews Family.*

Corsairs in the desert at N.A.A.S. Twenty-Nine Palms. *Courtesy the Matthews Family.*

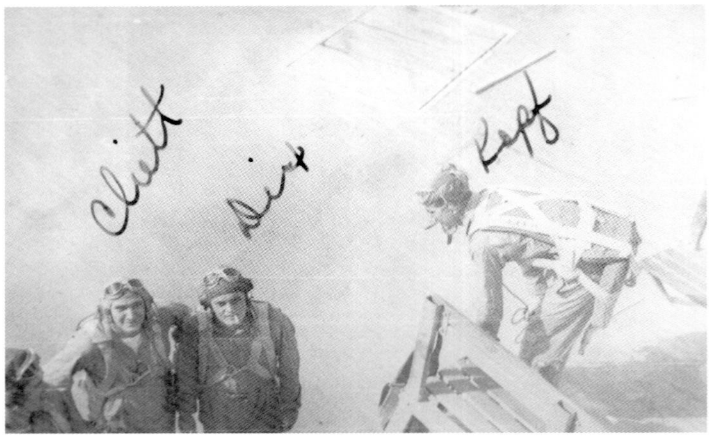

Fighting 84 pilots at N.A.A.S. Twenty-Nine Palms. Jimmy Dixon with cigarette third from left. Dixon reported to VF-84 after serving with Fighting 17. *Courtesy the Matthews Family.*

Hellcats and a lone Corsair at N.A.A.S. Twenty-Nine Palms. *Courtesy the Matthews Family.*

VF-84 pilots at N.A.A.S. Twenty-Nine Palms: Terrio, Dixon and Laney. Dixon was one of a number of ex-Fighting 17 pilots to serve with VF-84. *Courtesy the Matthews Family.*

VF-84 personnel at N.A.A.S. Twenty-Nine Palms. George in the picture is Crew Chief George Mauhar, who served with Fighting 17 and then was head-hunted by Roger Hedrick for VF-84. Dixon also served with Fighting 17. *Courtesy the Matthews Family.*

VF-84 pilots after a practice strike at N.A.A.S. Twenty-Nine Palms. *Courtesy the Matthews Family.*

Pilots of VF-84 in a jeep at N.A.A.S. Twenty-Nine Palms. 2nd from left Jimmy Dixon and 3rd from left Harvey "Matty" Matthews, who both served with Fighting 17 in the Solomon Islands before reporting to VF-84. *Courtesy the Matthews Family.*

Pilots of VF-84 at N.A.A.S. Twenty-Nine Palms. L-R: Unknown, 2nd from left Jimmy Dixon, and 3rd from left Harvey "Matty" Matthews, who both served with Fighting 17 in the Solomon Islands. *Courtesy the Matthews Family.*

Jack Diteman at N.A.A.S. Twenty-Nine Palms. Diteman served with Fighting 17 in the Solomon Islands before reporting to VF-84. *Courtesy the Matthews Family.*

Jack Diteman and "Dick" Einar at N.A.A.S. Twenty-Nine Palms. Both served with Fighting 17 in the Solomon Islands before reporting to VF-84. *Courtesy the Matthews Family.*

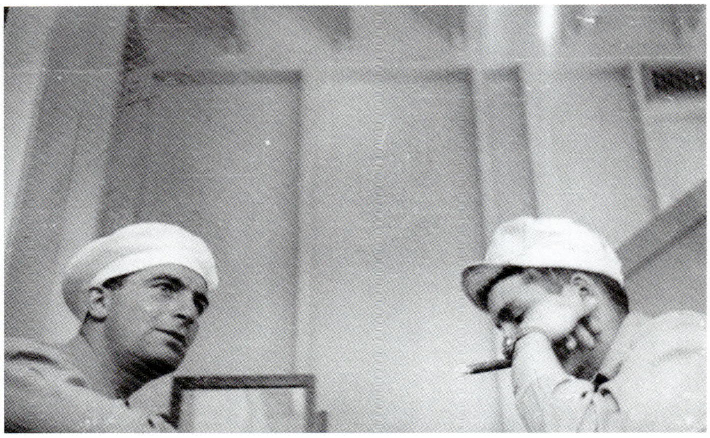

"Ike" Kepford and Jimmy Dixon (with cigar) at N.A.A.S. Twenty-Nine Palms. "Ike" was Fighting 17's top ace with sixteen victories; Dixon also served with Fighting 17. *Courtesy the Matthews Family.*

Jimmy Dixon at N.A.A.S. Twenty-Nine Palms. Dixon was credited with a shared victory and a probable with Fighting 17 before reporting to VF-84. *Courtesy the Matthews Family.*

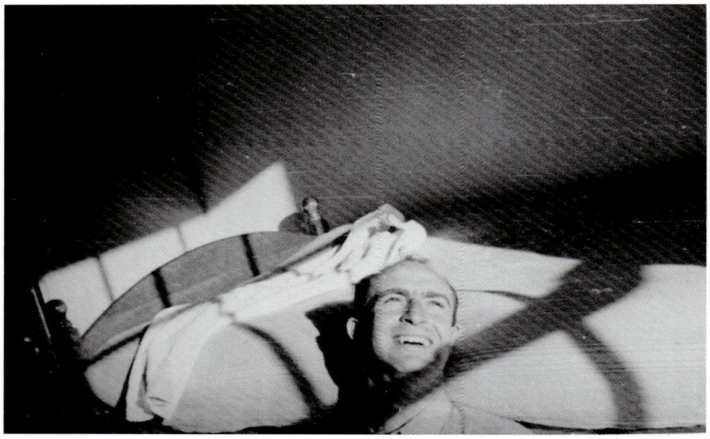

"Ike" Kepford at N.A.A.S. Twenty-Nine Palms. Kepford was one of many Fighting 17 combat veterans who formed the nucleus of VF-84. *Courtesy the Matthews Family.*

A Corsair at N.A.A.S. Twenty-Nine Palms in October 1944. *Courtesy U.S. Navy photo via Rick and Cathy Einar.*

Survivors of VF-84, by the scoreboard, after the kamikaze attack on the U.S.S. *Bunker Hill* on May 11, 1945. *Courtesy U.S. Navy photo via the Diteman Family.*

VF-84 pilots in front of a Corsair on the U.S.S. *Bunker Hill*. *Courtesy U.S. Navy photo via the Diteman Family.*

Another photo of VF-84 pilots on the U.S.S. *Bunker Hill. Courtesy U.S. Navy photo via the Diteman Family.*

Ground crew in front of a Corsair on the U.S.S. *Bunker Hill.* 7th from left back row is George Mauhar, who served with Fighting 17 as Crew Chief and was then chosen by Roger Hedrick to do the same with VF-84. *Courtesy U.S. Navy photo via the Matthews Family.*

VF-84 pilots in the ready room of the U.S.S. *Bunker Hill. Courtesy U.S. Navy photo via the Diteman Family.*

Another view of VF-84 pilots in the ready room of the U.S.S. *Bunker Hill. Courtesy U.S. Navy photo via the Diteman Family.*

Another view of VF-84 pilots in the ready room of the U.S.S. *Bunker Hill. Courtesy U.S. Navy photo via the Diteman Family.*

Another view of VF-84 pilots in the ready room of the U.S.S. *Bunker Hill. Courtesy U.S. Navy photo via the Diteman Family.*

SB2C-4 of Bombing Squadron 84 (VB-84) pictured on the flight deck of U.S.S. *Bunker Hill* (CV-17). Note the arrow tail symbol. VB-84 operated from *Bunker Hill* during the period February to May 1945, participating in the raid against the Japanese battleship Yamato and her escorts on April 7, 1945. The squadron lost twenty-one men and fifteen aircraft during the kamikaze attack against *Bunker Hill* on May 11, 1945. *Courtesy Robert Lawson Collection, National Museum of Naval Aviation.*

Flight deck personnel work on an SB2C-4 of Bombing Squadron 84 (VB-84) on board U.S.S. *Bunker Hill. Courtesy Robert Lawson Collection, National Museum of Naval Aviation.*

SB2C-4 of Bombing Squadron 84 (VB-84) pictured just prior to launch from U.S.S. *Bunker Hill* (CV-17). Note the enlarged side number and unconventional painted cowling. *Courtesy Robert Lawson Collection, National Museum of Naval Aviation.*

Flight deck personnel maneuver an SB2C-1 of Bombing Squadron Seventeen (VB-17) on the flight deck of U.S.S. *Bunker Hill* (CV-17). *Courtesy Robert Lawson Collection, National Museum of Naval Aviation.*

SB2C- of Bombing Squadron Seventeen (VB-17) pictured just prior to take off from U.S.S. *Bunker Hill* (CV-17). *Courtesy Robert Lawson Collection, National Museum of Naval Aviation.*

SB2C-4s of Bombing Squadron 83 (VB-83) pictured with other aircraft of Air Group 83 on the flight deck of U.S.S. *Essex* (CV-9) during operations off Okinawa. The burning carrier in the background is U.S.S. *Bunker Hill* (CV-17), which suffered two kamikaze hits. VB-83 operated from the U.S.S. *Essex* during the period March-September 1945. *Courtesy Robert Lawson Collection, National Museum of Naval Aviation.*

Training flight at N.A.A.S. Green Cove Springs, Florida. Earl May back row 3rd from left; "Andy" Jagger front row 3rd from left. May and Jagger and a number of other Fighting 17 pilots served as instructors at N.A.A.S. Green Cove Springs after returning from combat with Fighting 17. *Courtesy Del and Pat May Collection.*

Air Group 10 pilots before boarding the U.S.S. *Intrepid*. Earl May is in 2nd row 9th from right. To the right of Earl are Paul Cordray and Dan Cunningham. *Courtesy U.S. Navy Photo via Del and Pat May Collection / Maureen Schub.*

"Timmy" Gile served as Executive Officer of VF/VBF-10 after his combat tour with Fighting 17. *Courtesy the Gile Family.*

VBF-10 pilots Paul Cordray (top bunk) and Earl May (bottom bunk) on board the U.S.S. *Intrepid*. *Courtesy Del and Pat May Collection.*

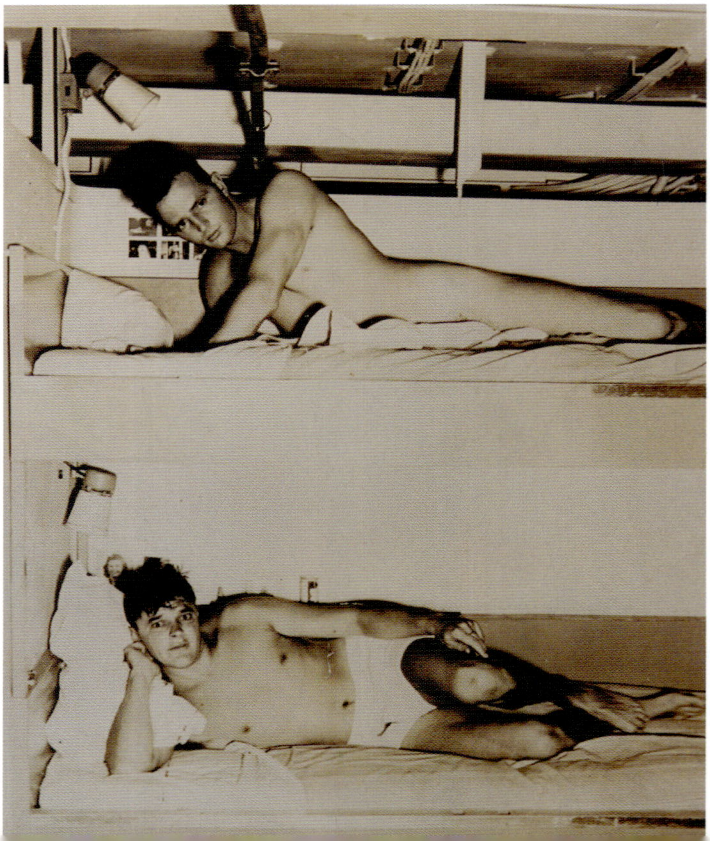

Lt. Cdr. James Alex Halford, Jr., as a flight instructor in 1944. *Courtesy James. A. Halford Collection.*

Another view of Lt. Cdr. James Alex Halford, Jr., as a flight instructor in 1944. *Courtesy James. A. Halford Collection.*

Jack Chasnoff (back row 4th from left) as a flight instructor at N.A.S. Melbourne, Florida, in the summer of 1944. *Courtesy the Chasnoff Family.*

Alice and Jack Chasnoff in Melbourne, Florida, in June 1944, where Jack was based as a flight instructor. *Courtesy the Chasnoff Family.*

Another photo of Jack Chasnoff (back row first left) as a flight instructor at N.A.S. Melbourne, Florida. *Courtesy the Chasnoff Family.*

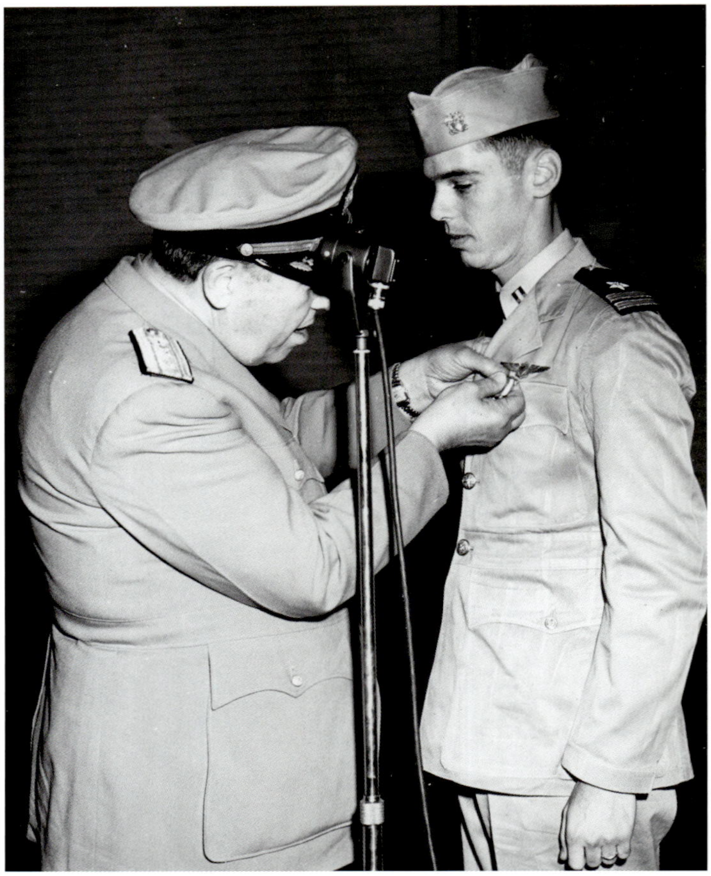

Jack Chasnoff receiving his Air Medal for service with Fighting 17, presented on board U.S.S. *Boxer* on May 19, 1945. *Courtesy the Chasnoff Family.*

Hal Jackson, "Big Jim" Streig and "Hap" Bowers in May 1944 after their return from combat with Fighting 17. *Courtesy Alexandra Bowers.*

"Hap" Bowers in the summer of 1944 when he was based at N.A.A.S. Green Cove Springs, Florida. *Courtesy Alexandra Bowers.*

"Hap" Bowers (back row 2nd left) with his flight as a flight instructor at N.A.A.S. Green Cove Springs. *Courtesy Alexandra Bowers.*

"Hap" Bowers receiving an award at N.A.A.S. Green Cove Springs. *Courtesy Alexandra Bowers.*

Lt. (jg) Earle Carpenter "Pete" Peterson, Jr. After his service with Fighting 17 Peterson became a flight instructor. *Courtesy Earle Carpenter Peterson, Jr. Collection.*

Lt. Earle Carpenter "Pete" Peterson, Jr., in 1945. *Courtesy Earle Carpenter Peterson, Jr. Collection.*

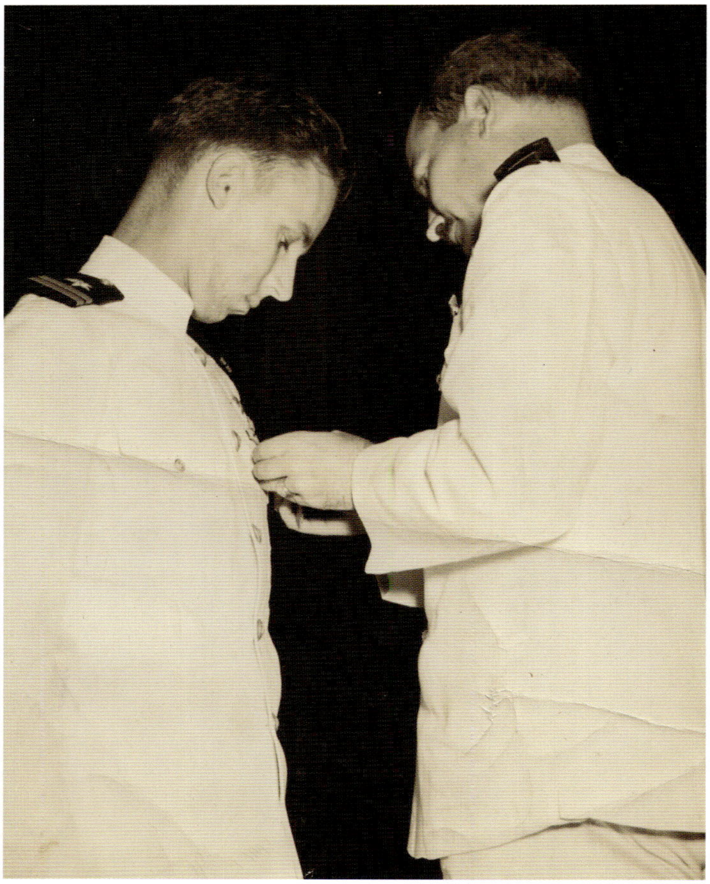

Lt. Earle Carpenter "Pete" Peterson, Jr., receiving an award. *Courtesy Earle Carpenter Peterson, Jr. Collection.*

Ed Beeler in the cockpit of his Corsair. After serving with Fighting 17 Beeler was test pilot for a repair squadron at Guadalcanal in 1944. *Courtesy Edward E. Beeler Collection.*

Ed Beeler with inspection crew and test pilots. Front row L – R: 4th from left Ed Beeler. *Courtesy Edward E. Beeler Collection.*

Ed Beeler with test and repair crew. Standing 3rd from left is Ed Beeler. *Courtesy Edward E. Beeler Collection.*

Chow time for the repair crew at Guadalcanal. *Courtesy Edward E. Beeler Collection.*

Another view of chow time for the repair crew at Guadalcanal. *Courtesy Edward E. Beeler Collection.*

2nd from left is Ward Cole, 4th from left is George Keller, and 6th from left Ed Beeler. All of these pilots served with Fighting 17. *Courtesy Edward E. Beeler Collection.*

Ed Beeler (back row 3rd from left) relaxing with his crew. *Courtesy Edward E. Beeler Collection.*

Ed Beeler in the cockpit of his Corsair. *Courtesy Edward E. Beeler Collection.*

Getting a boat ready for a fishing trip on Guadalcanal. *Courtesy Edward E. Beeler Collection.*

Ed Beeler and his test and inspection crew on a fishing trip in October 1944. Ed Beeler is first from left with fishing rod. *Courtesy Edward E. Beeler Collection.*

Another view of Ed Beeler and his test and inspection crew on a fishing trip in October 1944. Ed Beeler 2nd from left front row. *Courtesy Edward E. Beeler Collection.*

Ed Beeler (first left) with two friends; 3rd from left is his assistant. Many happy moments were spent in this flying boat, exploring neighboring islands near Guadalcanal. *Courtesy Edward E. Beeler Collection.*

Ed Beeler's flying boat moored while he and his crew are on one of the islands. *Courtesy Edward E. Beeler Collection.*

"The old duck just wallowed contentedly and didn't give a damn if we ever got back," recalled Ed Beeler. *Courtesy Edward E. Beeler Collection.*

Typical view from one of the Pacific islands. *Courtesy Edward E. Beeler Collection.*

Another view from one of the Pacific islands. *Courtesy Edward E. Beeler Collection.*

Another view from one of the Pacific islands. *Courtesy Edward E. Beeler Collection.*

Japanese ship beached at Guadalcanal. *Courtesy Edward E. Beeler Collection.*

Native hut on Guadalcanal. *Courtesy Edward E. Beeler Collection.*

Native village on Guadalcanal. *Courtesy Edward E. Beeler Collection.*

Another view of a native village on Guadalcanal. *Courtesy Edward E. Beeler Collection.*

A native boy climbing for coconuts for Ed Beeler and his crew to quench their thirst. *Courtesy Edward E. Beeler Collection.*

One of the local population on Guadalcanal. *Courtesy Edward E. Beeler Collection.*

One of the local population on Guadalcanal with his child. *Courtesy Edward E. Beeler Collection.*

Some of the local population on Guadalcanal. *Courtesy Edward E. Beeler Collection.*

Collecting fish from the beach on Guadalcanal. *Courtesy Edward E. Beeler Collection.*

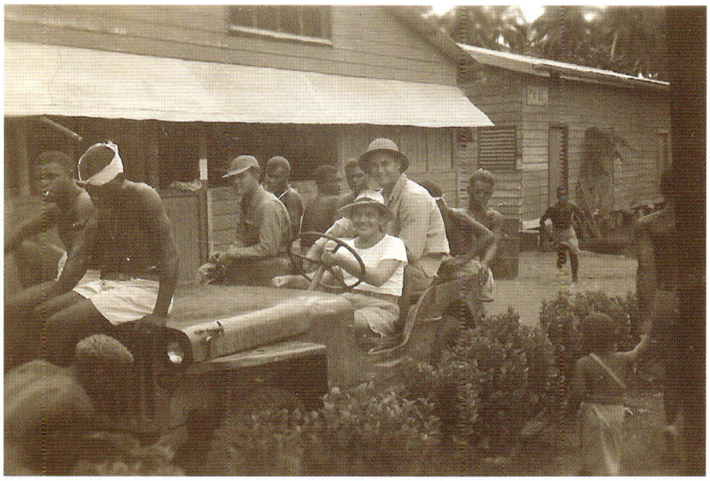

Ed Beeler (behind driver of jeep) and crew meeting the local people on Guadalcanal. *Courtesy Edward E. Beeler Collection.*

Stranded on an island just after an unsuccessful attempt to summon the attention of a passing plane with distress signals. Ed Beeler cigarette in hand, sitting watching a plane disappear into the distance. *Courtesy Edward E. Beeler Collection.*

Ed Beeler in the middle of the picture looking at the camera, stranded on an island waiting for help. *Courtesy Edward E. Beeler Collection.*

This picture was taken on a small island where Ed Beeler and his crew were stranded. The entire population of the island came to see Ed and his crew. *Courtesy Edward E. Beeler Collection.*

Our high ranking officer meets their high ranking officer. L-R: Humpal AMM1/c-Plane Captain, Lt. Cdr. Bowers-Executive Officer, Lt. (jg) Beeler Pilot, Reverend Rene, Native Chief and priest, Native child. *Courtesy Edward E. Beeler Collection.*

Meeting together are U.S. Navy and local inhabitants. Everybody seems to appreciate the gravity of the situation. Questions brought up in the discussion include such things as canoe making, airplanes and coconut trees. *Courtesy Edward E. Beeler Collection.*

"Andy" Anderson at Yosemite in 1944, following his rehabilitation from injuries sustained from being shot down in November 1943. He was based at the Naval Hospital at Alameda, California, and then to the Ahwahnee Hotel in Yosemite National Park, California, to recuperate. *Courtesy the Anderson Family.*

"Dick" Einar receiving an award. *Courtesy Rick and Cathy Einar.*

Otis Field in August 1945. Tom Blackburn Air Group Commander VBF-74. *Courtesy the Anderson Family.*

Lou Fitzgerald with flight gear on U.S.S. *Shangri-La*, in December 1944. *Courtesy the Fitzgerald Family.*

Lou Fitzgerald with his car, a LaSalle coupe, on leave in 1944, between Solomon Islands and U.S.S. *Shangri-La* assignments. *Courtesy the Fitzgerald Family.*

Lou Fitzgerald (on far right) on carrier with Corsair, thought to be the U.S.S. *Shangri-La*, in 1944 or 1945. *Courtesy the Fitzgerald Family.*

Lou Fitzgerald receiving an award or citation. *Courtesy the Fitzgerald Family.*

Lou Fitzgerald in dress whites, on leave in 1944, between Solomon Islands and U.S.S. *Shangri-La* assignments. *Courtesy the Fitzgerald Family.*

Ward Cole and Brother Russ in July 1944 while on leave. *Courtesy the Cole Family.*

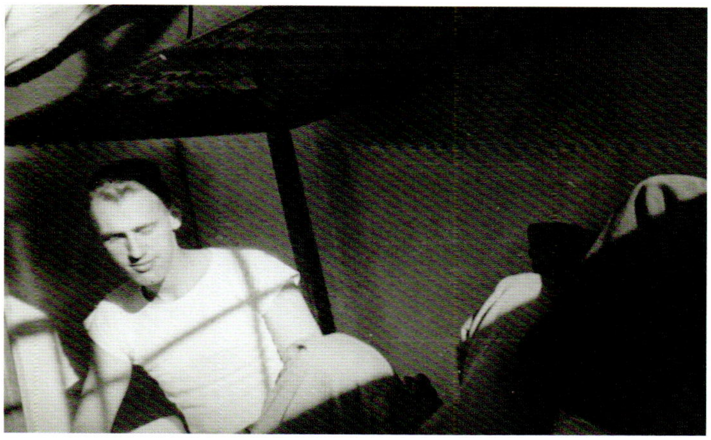

John M. Smith while serving with VF-84 at N.A.A.S. Twenty-Nine Palms in the fall of 1944. *Courtesy the Matthews Family.*

Lt. (jg) Louis M. Kelley in 1944 with his daughter, Patricia Ann, on his lap, and his brother, Richard, holding the cane. The chief of a band of head hunters carved the cane for Lt. (jg) Kelley when he spent two nights on a Pacific Island after his float plane was stuck on a reef. *Courtesy Sarah Bradshaw Lewis.*

L - R. #1 "Win" Rowley, #2 John M. Smith (Smitty), #3 "Heck" Kramer, and #4 James C. Dixon (Jimmy). Harvey Matthews is on the bottom. *Courtesy the Matthews Family.*

Lt. Louis M. Kelley with wife, Mary Helen, and daughter, Patricia Ann, in 1945. Lt. Kelley's last assignment was with VF-50 on the U.S.S. *Cowpens*, which was the first American carrier to enter the waters of Tokyo Bay. *Courtesy Sarah Bradshaw Lewis.*

Lt. (jg) John Cantrell in 1944. *Courtesy U.S. Navy photo via the Cantrell Family.*

John Cantrell on the U.S.S. Wasp whilst serving with VF-14 in 1944. *Courtesy U.S. Navy photo via the Cantrell Family.*

John Cantrell front row 4th from left with his training flight at N.A.S. Melbourne, Florida in February 1945. *Courtesy U.S. Navy photo via the Cantrell Family.*

14

Life After Combat

One of the most striking things about the men of Fighting 17 is how successful many of them became after the war in service and in business careers. The achievements they set in the Pacific paved the way for success in the Navy, business, and public life. One of the things not discussed much was how many of the pilots suffered with health issues after the war due to alcohol, cigarettes, and the stresses of combat flying, which took its toll on the men and in many cases for the rest of their lives.

Fighting 17 was given a big party by Chance Vought when they returned to the States from the Solomon Islands, and it was almost forty years before they got together for a reunion at Oceana in 1983. Following this reunion they got together regularly ever since, with the last big reunion in 1997 in San Diego.

To describe what it was like for Mills Schanuel after returning from combat his son Phil explains:

"Although Fighting 17 inflicted heavy casualties on the Japanese, the damage continued following the return of these men and continues all these decades later. They were expected to pack up their gear and resume normal life. No one had ever heard of post traumatic stress in those days. No one understood G forces and the affect on the human body. The men of Fighting 17 also flew ground attack missions. They saw first hand the effect of six .50 caliber machine guns on a person's body. The pilot's internal organs were pulled down into their bodies when they pulled out of a steep, high speed dive. Many had to undergo painful surgery following the war to repair this damage. Their children had to learn to expect the unexpected; the mood changes, the lack of attachment and what is now referred to as the 'thousand yard stare.' Mills has tried for over sixty years to forget the waste of lives that he witnessed firsthand. He doesn t see glory in his actions, but instead remembers the loss, fear and horror. He was just doing what men of his generation had to do, that's all."

"Andy" and Joy Anderson in 1942. *Courtesy the Anderson Family.*

Newlyweds Joy and "Andy" Anderson. *Courtesy the Anderson Family.*

Robert Sidney "Andy" Anderson

After he was shot down in November 1943 "Andy" was taken to the Naval Hospital at Alameda, California, and then to the Ahwanee Hotel in Yosemite National Park, California, to recuperate. After recuperation he was ordered to the Philadelphia Naval District for one year. He wanted to return to a Fighter Squadron, but it would take him a year to be given his desire, and he was sent to Cape

Lt. and Mrs. R. Temme, "Andy" and Joy Anderson, and Alice and Jack Chasnoff at the Chase Park Plaza, St. Louis, in October 1945. *Courtesy the Chasnoff Family.*

Cod, Massachusetts, to a new squadron with former Fighting 17 Skipper Tom Blackburn as Air Group Commander. However, on August 14, 1945, the Japanese surrendered and the war was over.

He had met Joy Williams in St. Louis, and they were married in 1942 and had three children – a girl named Sidney, and two boys, Scott and Ross.

He moved back to St. Louis, Missouri, where he attended Aircraft and Engine School, and while there was able to buy out a parts company and became a businessman until he retired in 1968 at age 50. He had by - pass surgery in 1971 and for many years suffered from Paget's Disease (a painful bone disease), and died one year after attending his first reunion in Illinois in 1984. He died on his forty-third wedding anniversary during his second by - pass surgery on May 14, 1985. Joy now lives near to her family in Texas.

Shelton Ray Beacham

At Dare County Regional Airport there is a display and a model of an F4U Corsair in honor of Ray Beacham from Kitty Hawk, who is credited with 2.5 victories. Beacham was credited with Fighting 17's first victory.

Ray Beacham retired after twenty-two years in the Navy and then taught Math at Northside Junior High School, Norfolk, for seventeen years. He died on January 11, 1997, after a long illness.

Edward Ellsworth Beeler

After serving with Fighting 17 Ed Beeler eventually became the test pilot for a Navy Aviation Repair Unit at Guadalcanal. He returned to civilian life after the war and became an entrepreneur, and later flew spam-cans (Cessna single engines) and then became a homebuilder. He died in August 1979 in Bowie, Maryland. His two sons Ned and Jack continue in the building business to this day.

Lt. Ray Beacham at Bougainville in 1944. *Courtesy National Archives.*

Ed Beeler in October 1944. *Courtesy Edward E. Beeler Collection.*

Harold James "Bitz" Bitzegaio

After his service with Fighting 17 "Bitz" was assigned to VF-10 on the U.S.S. *Intrepid*. He saw action against the Japanese and was awarded the Distinguished Flying Cross to add to the one he was awarded with Fighting 17. He was also wounded in action on April 16, 1945, and awarded the Purple Heart. After his distinguished WWII service he decided on the legal profession as a career.

In 1948 "Bitz" Bitzegaio married Betty Jean Law and they had five children, one boy and four girls. He received his Bachelor's degree from Indiana State University, his *juris* Doctorate from Indiana University, and also graduated from Indiana Judicial College. He passed the Bar examination in 1953, served with the U.S. District Court in 1953, and with the U.S. Court of Appeals in 1956. "Bitz" was Judge of Superior Court District 1 in Vigo County from 1959 to 1980.

He was Counsel for the Anderson & Nichols Law Office and was part of the Terre Haute Mayor's Commission on Civil Rights and Indiana Advisory Commission on Civil Rights.

His memberships included the American Bar Association, Indiana State Bar Association, Terre Haute Bar Association, Indiana Judges Association and the Indiana Law Alumni Association. He practiced Law until retiring in 1988 and was a regular at Fighting 17 reunions.

His wife Betty died in May 2000 and "Bitz" died on October 5, 2005, of lung cancer.

John T. "Tom" Blackburn

After his distinguished service with Fighting 17 Tom Blackburn was recognized as one of the finest Skippers of a fighter squadron in the Navy. He was awarded two Navy Crosses, two DFCs, and three Air Medals with Fighting 17. In May 1945 Blackburn was made CAG (Commander Air Group-74) of U.S.S *Midway* and served there until September 1946. He had various assignments with the Bureau of Aeronautics and as Executive Officer of U.S.S. *Saipan*, and was promoted to Captain on July 1, 1952. He studied at the Naval War College and was on the Joint Strategic Plans Group. His most challenging assignment was as Commanding Officer of the carrier U.S.S. *Midway* (CVA-14) from May 1958 to May 1959.

His last duty assignment was as Commanding Officer U.S. Naval and Marine Corps Reserve Training Center, Alameda, CA. He retired after an illustrious career with active service of 33 years 1 month and 15 days on July 31, 1962.

Harold J. "Bitz" Bitzegaio in 1990. *Courtesy Harold J. Bitzegaio.*

Lt. Cdr. Tom Blackburn discusses the successful operations of his unit, Fighting 17 in the Central Solomons during the November 1943 to February 1944 period. "Blackburn's Irregulars" were credited with shooting down 154 Japanese aircraft. Photo taken after Blackburn's return to the U.S. *Courtesy National Archives.*

Tom Blackburn and Jolly Rogers Commander J. S. Daughtry, Jr., at the Fighting 17 reunion in 1983. *Courtesy the Chasnoff Family and Andy Jagger.*

The famous Corsair test pilot Boone Guyton had this to say about Tom Blackburn:

"The chemistry between us was always good, and our friendship lasted for fifty three years. I should add, that as Tom later acknowledged, after his retirement from the Navy as Captain, he was out of touch with many of us for some twenty years. He became a patron of the drinking class, had a divorce and several short marriages and spent much time off the beaten path, raising grapes for a winery in California.

When he finally married - to a lovely Navy widow who brought him around properly - our old relationship returned and we visited each other and kept in contact.

Tom Blackburn was an exemplary military person from a family of Naval officers. I need not comment on his war record. It was one of the finest in the Navy's war in the Pacific."

Tom married Jamie in 1983, as Jamie had known Tom for years before that and both attended squadron reunions until his death on March 21, 1994, aged 81. He is interred in the Arlington National Cemetery.

"Hap" and Alice Bowers on their wedding day on October 12, 1944, in St. Augustine, Florida. *Courtesy Alexandra Bowers.*

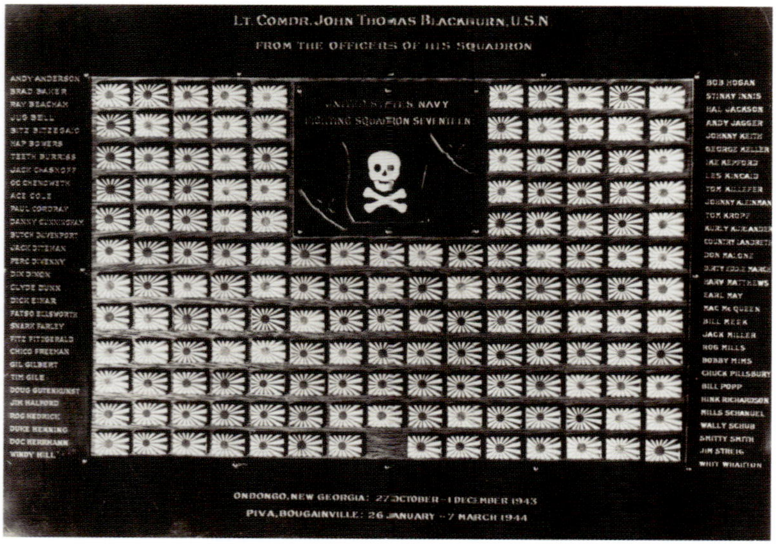

This scoreboard was presented to Tom Blackburn by his officers. *Courtesy the Richardson Family.*

George Franklin "Hap" Bowers

For his service with Fighting 17 "Hap" Bowers was awarded the Distinguished Flying Cross.

"Hap" and Alice Foster corresponded all through the war while he was overseas and serving away from her. They married in St. Augustine, Florida, in October 1944 while "Hap" was serving as a flight instructor at N.A.A.S. Green Cove Springs, Florida. He was then transferred to N.A.S. Miami in January 1945 and then assigned to VBF-74 based in Cape Cod, Massachusetts, on July 26, 1945.

After the war they went to Milwaukee, and jobs were scarce. "Hap" ended up taking a job as a travelling salesman for the Trackson Company, which had the Caterpiller Tractor franchise for a huge territory. "Hap" and Alice had a daughter Alexandra in 1947.

In the early '50s "Hap's" father died from cancer, and he took over his father's company, Industrial Heating & Engineering. It provided heating, piping and air conditioning for large commercial buildings, and he ran the company until about 1976, when he sold it to another company. "Hap" stayed on doing desk work, which he hated, until he retired aged 62 in 1981.

He and Alice moved to Virginia, Alice's home state, where they had a happy time, and where "Hap" could indulge his great passion for sailing. He was on sailboats before he could walk and sailed his whole life. He was Commodore of the Milwaukee Yacht Club in 1973 and 1974, as was his father exactly 60 years earlier.

"Hap" and Alice attended the Oshkosh reunion in 1994 and Alice died in 1995. "Hap" then moved to be near his daughter Alexandra in Savannah, Georgia, where he died in May 2000.

Another view of "Hap" Bowers and daughter Alexandra. *Courtesy Alexandra Bowers.*

Alice and "Hap" Bowers. *Courtesy Alexandra Bowers.*

"Hap" Bowers and daughter Alexandra. *Courtesy Alexandra Bowers.*

John Hailey Cantrell

John Cantrell served with Fighting 17 from early 1943 until August 1943 during their training period before being assigned to VF-14 on the U.S.S. *Wasp* (CV-18) in August 1943.

He was awarded the Distinguished Flying Cross for his actions against a heavy Japanese Cruiser on October 25, 1944, during the Battle of Leyte Gulf.

He served in the Naval Reserve after his active duty, and his other assignments included service with VBF-81 and VF-713 until he retired from the Naval Reserve in 1953 as a Lt. Cdr.

He taught flying lessons for several years and was also a high school teacher of biology until his retirement.

He died on July 14, 1992, in Portales, New Mexico, and was survived by his wife Lois and two daughters, Barbara and Gail.

Lt. John Cantrell in 1945. *Courtesy U.S. Navy photo via the Cantrell Family.*

Melbourne, Florida, home of Jack and Alice Chasnoff while he was based there as a flight instructor. *Courtesy the Chasnoff Family.*

John Cantrell in the cockpit of a Grumman F8F Bearcat. *Courtesy U.S. Navy photo via the Cantrell Family.*

Another view of John Cantrell in an F8F Bearcat. *Courtesy U.S. Navy photo via the Cantrell Family.*

Jack M. Chasnoff

After leaving Fighting 17 in January 1944, Jack Chasnoff was awarded the Distinguished Flying Cross and two Air Medals. He became a flight instructor for operational training at Melbourne, Florida, and then applied for a transfer to fighter director school. Upon completion of his training he was assigned as fighter director to the new Essex class aircraft carrier U.S.S. *Boxer*, then under construction at the Portsmouth Navy Yard. Until August 1945 he served on the *Boxer*, going on her shakedown cruise to Guantanamo Bay, Cuba, refitting in Norfolk, and eventually going to sea, taking her through the Panama Canal and up the west coast to San Francisco. While making final preparations there to join the Pacific fleet the war against Japan ended, and within a few days he was detached and sent back to St. Louis for a month before being discharged in September 1945. Jack entered Law School and completed his studies in two calendar years by attending classes on a year - round basis. He passed the Bar examination late in 1947 and began to practice law early in 1948 with a partner in the firm of Tucker and Chasnoff. After several decades Mr. Tucker retired and Jack practiced on his own. During those years he was

Jack and Alice Chasnoff at the Fighting 17 reunion in San Diego 1997. *Courtesy Lee Cook.*

"Of Council" with the firm created by his father and others, but retained his independence.

Jack married Alice Wides in October 1942 and had three children: John, Judith Ann and Joseph. Jack and Alice were regulars at Fighting 17 reunions and organized the 1996 reunion in St. Louis. Jack died on October 19, 2007, and Alice in September 2009.

Oscar Ivan "Oc" Chenoweth, Jr.

When Fighting 17 returned from the Pacific, Lt. Chenoweth was awarded the Silver Star and Distinguished Flying Cross for his actions. He reported to N.A.S. Miami in November 1944 and served until October 1945 as a Flight Instructor. He was promoted to Lt. Cdr. on October 3, 1945. His other assignments included Flight Deck Officer and Assistant Air Officer on the U.S S. *Midway*, Executive Officer of VF-42, Commanding Officer of VA-44, and he was later in the second graduating class of test pilots from the Naval Air Test Center at Patuxent River, Maryland.

He then served as Assistant Operations Officer on the Staff of Commander Second Fleet and Executive Officer of VC-9. He left the service with the rank of Commander on April 1, 1954.

After his service career Chenoweth worked for his grandfather, Robert Shelley, in self levelling dispensers, and then went to Dallas to work for Chance Vought in government sales. He then worked as a sales rep in service equipment sales and also helped various companies increase their business. He had just started working with John Andrews, who developed a salt water ice machine, when he died of a heart attack on May 19, 1968.

He left a wife Ruth and three children, Janet, Gayle and Oscar III.

Mervin Ward "Ace" Cole

Ward Cole served with Headquarters Squadron Five upon his return from the Pacific and received the Distinguished Flying Cross and three Air Medals for his service with Fighting 17. After the war, while stationed in Virginia Beach, he met Mary on a blind date

"Oc" Chenoweth at Bougainville in February or March 1944. *Courtesy U.S. Naval Historical Center / M.W. "Butch" Davenport Collection.*

Lt. (jg) Ward Cole after his return from the Pacific. *Courtesy the Cole Family.*

Another view of Lt. (jg) Ward Cole. *Courtesy the Cole Family.*

Mary Payne Jett Cole and Mervin Ward Cole on their wedding day, September 7, 1946. *Courtesy the Cole Family.*

Another view of Mervin Ward Cole and Mary Payne Jett Cole on their wedding day, September 7, 1946. *Courtesy the Cole Family.*

Ward and Mary Cole by a lake. *Courtesy the Cole Family.*

Another view of Ward and Mary Cole by a lake. *Courtesy the Cole Family.*

that his wingman insisted he go on. After getting married he went to the University of North Carolina at Chapel Hill on the GI Bill. Then he worked for his father-in-law, had three children, became a successful stock broker after selling his father-in-law's business, and in general, as his daughter Katie said, lived "a charmed life." This was until his beloved wife Mary died and he lost a son to alcohol and drug addiction. He went to the Oshkosh reunion in 1994, just a few months after Mary died, and he enjoyed it so much he wore the Fighting 17 cap he received there until the day he died on September 19, 2006.

Paul Cordray

Paul returned to the States in May 1944 an ace and a hero. He was asked to speak on numerous occasions. He said "*I just ask for their questions.*"

While on leave after a whirlwind courtship Paul married Mary Lou Cain and was then assigned to VBF 10 flying F4U-1Ds from the U.S.S. *Intrepid.* During his next combat tour he was credited with one more victory when he destroyed a Zeke on April 16, 1945, near Kikai Airfield, Japan. He was awarded the Distinguished Flying Cross with three Gold Stars and Air medal with five Gold Stars for his service with Fighting 17 and VBF-10.

After the war Cordray left the service and joined his old school buddy, Ed Gibson, to become manufacturers representatives.

Paul had a heart attack on October 20, 1963, when he was only 44 years old. He left a wife Mary Lou and four children, Paul Jr., Mark, Gary and Gayle.

Daniel Gerald Cunningham

For his four victories on his February 19, 1944, mission with Fighting 17 Dan Cunningham was awarded the Navy Cross. He ended his tour an ace with seven confirmed Japanese aircraft to his credit.

Dan then served with VBF-10 in the Pacific and on September 1945 returned to civilian life. He married Irene during the war and they had a son Danny Jr. and daughter Irene. They were divorced, and in September 1954 he married Dolores May Brettman in Pensacola, Florida. They met while both were working at Equitable Life Assurance. They eloped, as her father didn't approve of Danny. They lived in Evanston, where their daughter Kimberley was born on May 8, 1956.

At Equitable Life he was a member of the million dollar round table. (An honor for those who sold that much insurance in a one year period.) He later acquired a seat on the Mercantile Exchange and traded in the futures market.

After around twenty-two years together Dan and Dolores were divorced and he married Ruthie, and was with her until he died on February 24, 2006.

Paul Cordray with his brother Don, sister Sue, twin Pauline, Paul Cordray, brother John, and his mother in 1961. *Courtesy John Cordray.*

Fighting 17 aces Roger Hedrick, Dan Cunningham, and "Big Jim" Streig at Oshkosh in 1994. *Courtesy Lee Cook.*

"Ike" Kepford and "Butch" Davenport in 1985. *Courtesy Kraeg Kepford.*

Merl William "Butch" Davenport
"Butch" Davenport finished his tour with Fighting 17 as an ace with 6.25 victories and was awarded the Distinguished Flying Cross.

After the war Davenport stayed in the Navy and later became a test pilot at N.A.S. Patuxent River. On November 20, 1946, at Wright Patterson Air Force Base in Cleveland, Ohio, an F8F Grumman Bearcat with Lt. Cdr. Davenport as pilot took off in a distance of 115 feet from a standing start and climbed to 10,000 feet in 94 seconds. "Butch" held this record for some time. "Butch" was also one of the first naval officers to attend the Empire Test Pilot School in England. Davenport amassed 7,500 flight hours during his six years in the Navy. He continued to fly after leaving the Navy in 1949. He flew his Piper Comanche around the country well into the 1980s, visiting many of his squadron colleagues. "*The aircraft has navigation and flight equipment that I would have traded my soul for in WW II.*" Said Davenport.

On hearing that he had contracted cancer "Butch" tracked down every possible lead for a cure to treat it. He died of cancer in Dexter, Michigan, on September 19, 1989.

Raymond Patrick DeLeva
Ray DeLeva was a Field Service Technician for the original Chance Vought Aircraft Co. for 40 years. Among his assignments was a nine month period in action with the Marines and Navy in the South Pacific - including Pappy Boyington's "*Black Sheep Squadron*" in Bougainville and Fighting 17 in the Solomons. In 1950 he was promoted to supervisor of the Field Service Technical Group and held this position for fifteen years based in Dallas. He then asked to work in the field again, and his assignments included serving on the U.S.S. *John F. Kennedy* (CV-67) aircraft carrier. He retired in 1973 and attended Fighting 17 reunions.

He died on July 9, 1995, after a brief illness. He was married to his beloved wife Milly for 61 years.

Jack Evans Diteman
In my book *The Skull and Crossbones Squadron - VF-17 in World War II* the name I had for Jack was quoted as James; I have since found this to be incorrect. His correct name was Jack Evans Diteman.

Ray DeLeva at the Fighting 17 reunion in Denton, Texas, in 1993. *Courtesy Milly DeLeva.*

Lt. (jg) Jack Diteman presented with his second Distinguished Flying Cross and second, third, and fourth Air Medals by Capt. H. L. Young in late 1945. *Courtesy U.S. Navy photo via the Diteman Family.*

After Fighting 17 Jack Diteman served with VF-84 and was credited with one Frank on May 4, 1945, and five aircraft on the ground. He was awarded the Distinguished Flying Cross and six Air Medals for his service with VF-84.

Jack ranched for a few years after the war, and with two others started an aluminium extrusion business. He married Irene and had a son Drake in 1947.

In the 1950s he got interested in skiing, and after his divorce from his first wife Irene went to Sun Valley, Idaho, where he became a ski patrolman and ski instructor. He married Joanie in the fall of 1958. He and Joanie went to Europe to find a sailboat to sail back to the States. Despite neither having sailed before they bought a 50 year old 47 foot sailboat in Norway, refitted it, and made the crossing. They went back to Sun Valley, where Jack built a few houses and was a popular cabinet maker.

He hiked, skied, rode his mountain bike, and did one or more almost every day of his life. When he was in his 80s he finally gave up the bike and downhill skiing, but cross country skied and walked 12 miles every day. He walked up until a day or two before he died.

His wife Joanie said "*He never did anything he didn't want to do and he did everything he wanted to do.*" He died on April 24, 2007.

Charles E. Dixon

Charlie Dixon left the Navy after 4½ years service. On leaving he found that life in post-war America was hard, made even harder by his leaving school early. However, with the help of his uncle he joined the railway, and for the next forty years served as a brakeman and conductor in Alabama and Kentucky. When he was cut off of railroad work at various times he worked as a truck driver. Charlie finally retired in 1987 and lives in Kentucky.

James Cass Dixon

After leaving Fighting 17 Jimmy Dixon was assigned to VF-84 and served with ex-Fighting 17 Executive Officer Roger Hedrick as his C.O. He was credited with three confirmed victories whilst

Jimmy Dixon (center) at N.A.A.S. Twenty-Nine Palms in 1944. *Courtesy the Matthews Family.*

serving with VF-84, and on April 16, 1945, Jimmy was reported missing in action. He became a prisoner of war and ended up in the same camp as "Country" Landreth. They were both held at the Kempei Tai jail adjacent to the Imperial Palace in Tokyo. They were moved to a local jail just prior to the firebombing of May 25 to 26, 1945, wherein over 65 aviators were locked in their cells and were burned to death in the raid. Jimmy was moved to Ofuna in late July or the first week of August. Upon his release in September 1945 he was admitted to U.S. Naval Hospital, Norman, Oklahoma, for treatment. In January 1946 he was discharged from hospital and was released from active duty on August 29, 1946. He was awarded the Distinguished Flying Cross and seven Air Medals for his service with VF-84.

After the war Jimmy Dixon was a feed salesman for Ralston Purina Co. for twelve years. In 1958 he left Purina, purchased a large grain elevator, and started to move into the commercial hen laying business. In 1966 he purchased a shell egg processing plant from Ralston Purina and continued to expand the laying hens. His son Chris then took over the business. Jim and his wife Jan were regular attendees at Fighting 17 reunions.

Charlie Dixon worked on the railroad as a brakeman and conductor for 40 years before retiring in 1987. *Courtesy Charles E. Dixon.*

Jan and Jim Dixon at the Fighting 17 reunion in San Diego in 1997. *Courtesy Lee Cook.*

Fighting 17 reunion in 1984. "Red" Edmisten and "Hap" Harlow, buddies from WWII, Korea, and civilian life. *Courtesy Hap Harlow.*

Jimmy Dixon died peacefully during the night of December 15, 2005, after a long period under dialysis treatment.

Lennard "Red" Edmisten

In May 1950, whilst in the Navy Reserve, "Red" was called up for duty in the Korean War. Although he worked on lots of different aircraft, he was back with a Corsair squadron aboard the U.S.S. *Bon Homme Richard.*

"Red" worked for North American Aircraft on guidance systems for aircraft, missiles and submarines. He retired after thirty-three years with the company and lived for many years in California. He regularly attended Fighting 17 reunions, which he enjoyed immensely. He moved to Heber City in Utah and passed away in a hospital in Provo, Utah, on June 23, 2006.

Richard Martin "Dick" Einar, Jr.

In my book *The Skull and Crossbones Squadron - VF-17 in World War II* the name I had for Richard was quoted as Robert; I have since found this to be incorrect. His correct name was Richard Martin Einar, Jr. and he was known as "Dick."

After returning home with Fighting 17, "Dick" Einar served with VF-84 from April 1944 to December 1944. He was then assigned to VBF-1 and served on the U.S.S *Bennington* and took part in strikes against the Japanese home islands. For his service with VBF-1 he was awarded the Distinguished Flying Cross with one Gold Star and Air Medal with four Gold Stars. He also served as Primary Flight Instructor at N.A.A.S. Rodd Field, Corpus Christi, Texas, from June 1946 to August 1946 and stayed in the reserves until 1961.

While at N.A.S. Corpus Christi "Dick" married Emily Jane Kellogg, who travelled from Washington State to Corpus Christi, Texas, for the wedding.

"Dick" had a younger brother, Ensign Robert K. Einar, who was killed in the South Pacific theatre during WWII. No one knew the details of how he died on June 21, 1945.

"Dick" Einar in 1981 with two king salmon he caught from Puget Sound, Washington State, near the home of his youth. "Dick" Einar was an avid steelhead fisherman. *Courtesy Rick and Cathy Einar.*

After leaving the service "Dick" went into banking. In 1957 he was transferred to Leavenworth, WA, to be a Branch Manager of Seattle 1st National Bank. He liked the small town of Leavenworth, and preferred staying there over a promotion elsewhere. Years later, when faced with another transfer, he left the bank, taking an administrative job in the forest products industry. "Dick" was an avid golfer, and one of the highlights of his life was winning the Edelweiss Golf Tournament; he also liked to bowl. He volunteered much of his time to community service and he served as a hospital commissioner for many years. He "was a true gentleman" and tried to live a quiet, peaceful life. "Dick" and Emily had a son Rick and an adopted daughter Christine who preceded "Dick" in death.

"Dick" had a long ordeal with Supra-Nuclear Palsy, and before he died had to move to assisted living and then to a nursing home. He died on April 20, 2007.

"Dick" and Emily Einar on their 50th wedding anniversary. *Courtesy Rick and Cathy Einar.*

Ray Ferguson retired as a Commander from the Navy Reserve in 1963. *Courtesy U.S. Navy Photo via the Ferguson Family.*

Raymond Webster Ferguson

Ray Ferguson, after leaving Fighting 17, became a production test pilot working on some of the problems of the early models of the Corsair which needed changing.

Despite an ongoing eye problem which curtailed his combat flying, Ray continued with the Navy as a career during and after WWII. In 1953 he left active service and continued in the Naval Reserves, from which he retired as a Commander in 1963.

He was later in business for Resource Services Inc., serving as president of this company. Ray attended the Fighting 17 San Diego reunion in 1997 and died on January 2, 2008.

Louis Allen Fitzgerald

Following his service with Fighting 17 Louis Fitzgerald returned to the States for a short leave and was then assigned to Air Group 85, serving on the U.S.S. *Shangri La*. He was discharged from active duty in November 1945.

He returned to school at Augustana College, Rock Island, Illinois, and completed his Bachelor's Degree in May 1946. Louis then began graduate school at the University of Iowa, Iowa City, in June 1946. He married Jeanne Anne Kloster in Iowa City, Iowa, on September 12, 1948. In September 1949 he became a fifth grade teacher in Macon City, Iowa, and returned to graduate studies at the University of Iowa in May 1951.

Louis stayed in the Navy reserves after WWII, and his reserve squadron was activated for the Korean War. He was assigned as a special weapons instructor at Moffett Field, Sunnyvale, California, in April 1953. After the Korean War he returned to doctoral studies at the University of Iowa and then became Instructor of Psychology at Emporia State Teacher's College, Emporia, Kansas, in August 1954.

In October 1957 Louis became Education Consultant to the Brazilian Government. He returned to the States to continue his doctoral dissertation in October 1959 and was awarded his PhD in Special Education in August 1960.

In September 1960 he was appointed as Assistant Professor of Elementary Education, Psychology and Reading at the University of Cincinnati, and then Associate Professor of Education and Director of the Reading Clinic at Purdue University, West Lafayette, Indiana, in September 1961.

In July 1965 Louis became Director of Communication Skills, Board of Education, Pittsburgh Public Schools, Pittsburgh, Pennsylvania, and Adjunct Professor at the University of Pittsburgh.

Louis Fitzgerald's Augustana College graduation photo in the spring of 1946. *Courtesy the Fitzgerald Family.*

Lou and Jeanne Anne Fitzgerald on their wedding day September 12, 1948. *Courtesy the Fitzgerald Family.*

The Fitzgerald family: Ray, Jeanne Anne, Kevin Yatidi, and Lou Fitzgerald in front of their Pittsburgh home in 1974. *Courtesy the Fitzgerald Family.*

Lou Fitzgerald leaving an Altoona, Iowa, school with a balloon, which was part of a celebration of reading in September 1979, the last picture the family has of him. *Courtesy the Fitzgerald Family*

In September 1977 he was appointed Reading Consultant, State of Iowa, Department of Public Instruction, Des Moines, Iowa.

Louis Fitzgerald died on October 31, 1979, of a heart attack and was survived by his wife Jeanne Anne and children Raymond, Kevin and Yatidi.

Carl Wilson Gilbert, Jr.

In my book *The Skull and Crossbones Squadron - VF-17 in World War II* the information I had available about Carl at the time I have since found to be incorrect; the correct information is as follows:

Carl Wilson Gilbert, Jr. was born in Worland, Wyoming, on April 24, 1918, and not in St Louis as I had noted. He stayed in the Navy after World War II, served in the Korean War, and retired as a Lt. Cdr. on October 14, 1954.

After the Navy he worked for the Atlantic Oil Corporation until his retirement due to a bad heart. He died on May 9, 1974, in Riverside, California.

Clement Dexter "Timmy" Gile

"Timmy" Gile returned home an ace with eight victories after his service with Fighting 17. After a period of leave he served as a flight instructor at N.A.A.S. Green Cove Springs from May to July 1944. He was then assigned to VF/VBF-10 as Executive Officer from August 1944 to September 1945. He was awarded three Distinguished Flying Crosses, three Air Medals, and a Purple Heart for wounds received on March 18, 1945.

"Timmy" Gile met and married Jean (June) Hill Tyner on January 18, 1945, in New York. They only had about six dates before they were engaged.

After the war he was the Vice President of a seaplane and helicopter commuter airline and spent three years in Lima, Peru, for Panagra. He then went to work at Morgan Guarantee Trust Company and was a Vice President at the time he took early retirement in 1976 because of health problems. He had four children: Anne (Toni), Shelley, Jean (Robin), and Susan.

"Tim" spent every Summer with his family in Chatham, Massachusetts, where he played golf and loved to fish for the "*wily Bass*." He built a speed boat and used it for waterskiing, trips to the North Beach, and all around the waters of Cape Cod.

Flying was always his great passion, and he maintained his instrument rating and flew a twin - engined aircraft N5888S that he co-owned until 1977, flying out of Westchester and the Chatham Airports. He was a great do-it-yourselfer and an expert at carpentry. He also played tennis and loved bridge and classical music. Although he was a smoker all his life he was very fit and ran every morning, and generally took very good care of himself.

Carl Gilbert retired from the Navy in 1954 as a Lt. Cdr. *Courtesy U.S. Navy Photo.*

Newlyweds "Tim" and June Gile. They were married on January 18, 1945, in New York City. *Courtesy the Gile Family.*

"Tim" and June Gile pictured in 1946. *Courtesy the Gile Family.*

"Tim" Gile and daughter Toni in 1947. *Courtesy the Gile Family.*

"Tim" and June Gile in Antigua in 1947, where his father had a house. *Courtesy the Gile Family.*

June, Toni and "Tim" Gile at Toni's "coming out" party at the Westchester Cotillion in 1964. *Courtesy the Gile Family.*

On October 13, 1985, a Corsair FG-1D identical to the one that he flew was dedicated on the deck of the *Yorktown* to "Tim" Gile. It was also dedicated to "Chuck" Pillsbury, who died while serving with Fighting 17. *Courtesy the Gile Family.*

He enjoyed almost perfect health until two years before he died. In those two years he had triple heart by - pass surgery and prostate cancer, followed by lung cancer. "Tim" Gile died on November 21, 1978.

On October 13, 1985, a Corsair FG-1 was dedicated on the deck of the U.S.S. *Yorktown* in the colors of Lt. "Timmy" Gile and squadron-mate "Chuck" Pillsbury. The Corsair is still on the *Yorktown* at Patriots Point Museum in Charleston, South Carolina, but has been moved below decks on permanent display.

Boone Guyton

Boone Guyton's association with Tom Blackburn began in 1938 when Lt. (jg) Blackburn reported to dive bombing squadron VB-5 at San Diego Naval Air Station.

Although not a member of Fighting 17, the famous Chance Vought Corsair test pilot was aboard during their shakedown cruise in July 1943. He helped his close friend Tom Blackburn train his pilots for combat with the Corsair.

A family portrait of Boone Guyton. *Courtesy Peter S. Guyton.*

Guyton worked for Vought for twelve years until 1951, when he worked for Hamilton Standard, and eventually he ran his own company. He acted as a manufacturer's representative for a number of companies, including Sargent Industries (who made emergency slide rafts for airliners and corporate jets) and a number of companies that made aircraft industry related components (hinges and valves that went into jet engines).

As part of one deal he had to go on the Faberge (cologne perfume) Lear Jet when they were trying to sell them emergency flotation devices. He had to adjust his schedule because they had to leave to collect Elizabeth Taylor.

He also spoke frequently at conferences about his test pilot experiences and participated in a reunion at Stratford airport in 1976 where many of his war - time colleagues, such as engineers, pilots and office people, gathered.

During his retirement years Guyton lectured on the Corsair and V-173 and continued to write. His third and last book, *Whistling Death – the Test Pilot's Story of the F4U Corsair*, was published in 1990 by Schiffer

Boone Guyton died from cancer on April 4, 1996, at the age of 82. He is buried in Woodbridge, Connecticut, where he spent the last 40 years of his life. He was married to Doris Marie Boies, known as "Susie," and they had five children.

He is best remembered as the chief experimental test pilot for the F4U Corsair.

James Alexander Halford, Jr.

Jim Halford continued in the Navy and reserves after WWII and retired as a Lt. Cdr. He married Janis Madeline Boone during the war and had two children. Jim served with distinction at some of the great battles of the Pacific: Midway, Guadalcanal, and Rabaul. He was awarded the Distinguished Flying Cross with one Gold Star for his actions at Midway and Guadalcanal.

Jim Halford married Janis Boone on November 24, 1942, and was married to her for the rest of his life. *Courtesy the James A. Halford Collection.*

Jim Halford in 1955. *Courtesy the James A. Halford Collection.*

After his service he returned to the family farm in California, where his family had farmed in the area for approximately 100 years. There was a small dairy and the farming of many crops, such as cotton, alfalfa, grain, and stone fruit, including many different types of plums and nectarines, table and wine grapes, pomegranates, and oranges. The farm currently has a nursery for orange trees and supplies many farms in California's Central Valley.

Jim died on June 7, 1987, and Janis in 1997.

Glenn Franklin Hall

Following his service with Fighting 17 as Assistant Operations Officer, Glenn Hall served in the Navy until October 6, 1945, when he returned to civilian life after WWII. He died in Corpus Christi, Texas, on December 23, 1987.

Harry S. "Hap" Harlow, Jr.

"Hap" was originally assigned to Fighting 17 as a Plane Captain as part of the ground crew. When Fighting 17 was detached from the U.S.S. *Bunker Hill*, "Hap" was not one of the men who went with them. He served on the *Bunker Hill* in every combat engagement in the Pacific until late December 1944, when the *Bunker Hill* went back to Bremerton for overhaul. He was then transferred to N.A.S. Whidbey Island, then to Aviation Engine School in Chicago. He graduated at the time the war ended and then went back to N.A.S. Whidbey Island and later to N.A.S. Adak, Alaska, then to N.A.S. Corpus Christi, Texas, until January 1950. "Hap" then got out, going to college on the GI Bill. He joined the Naval Reserve to supplement his meagre income, and was in another F4U Squadron - VF-783, which was activated when the Korean conflict broke out. He served on the U.S.S. *Bon Homme Richard* (CV-31). Once this was over he was released to inactive duty and received his third honourable discharge in January 1954.

"Hap" ran a sales territory for 22½ years in the desert area of Southern California, retiring in 1998. His wife June died of cancer in May 2001 and he married Marje in 2002. They live in Yucca Valley, California.

Glenn Franklin Hall in October 1943. *Courtesy the Anderson Family.*

"Hap" Harlow and Hal Jackson at the Fighting 17 reunion in San Francisco in 1988. *Courtesy Hap Harlow.*

Roger Richards Hedrick

Roger Hedrick returned from the Pacific as an ace with nine victories and enhanced his already considerable reputation as an aerial marksman. Roger was then assigned as Commanding Officer of VF-84. He scored another three victories and one on the ground and took over as Air Group Commander in March 1945 until the U.S.S. *Bunker Hill* was put out of action by a kamikaze on May 11, 1945. Included in his awards were the Silver Star, Distinguished Flying Cross with three Gold Stars, and Air Medal with two Gold Stars.

Roger Hedrick continued in the Navy after WWII. In July 1945 he assumed command of Experimental Fighting Squadron 200, and from October 1945 until May 1946 had command of Fighter Squadron 200 of Composite Air Group, Operational Development Force, and of the Composite Air Group, Operational Development Group. He was a student at the Naval School, General Line, Newport, Rhode Island, the next year, and in June 1947 reported to Naval Air Station, Jacksonville, Florida, for duty as Officer in Charge of the Instructors Aviation Training Unit. From November 1948 to July 1949 he had similar duty at the Naval Air Station, Corpus Christi, Texas.

Completing the course at the Naval War College, Newport, Rhode Island, in June 1950, he became Executive Officer of the Fleet All Weather Training Unit, Pacific, at Barbers Point, Hawaii, training night attack and night fighter pilots for the Korean hostilities. On September 19, 1952, he reported to the Naval Air Station, Whidbey Island, Washington, as Executive Officer. When

Roger Hedrick and his three children taken on a small power boat while on vacation at Lake Tahoe in September 1955. L – R: Alida, Roger, Barbara and Rick. *Courtesy the Hedrick Family.*

Roger Hedrick walking down the line on the U.S.S. *Boxer* (CVA-21) on October 2, 1954. *Courtesy U.S. Navy photo via the Hedrick Family.*

Roger Hedrick whilst serving with VX-4 at Pt. Mugu age 42 on November 24, 1956. *Courtesy the Hedrick Family.*

detached in June 1954 he had a brief period at the Naval Schools Command, U.S. Naval Station, Treasure Island, San Francisco, California, and the same month reported on board the U.S.S. *Boxer* (CVA-21). He served as Executive Officer of the *Boxer* until September 1955.

Hedrick's next deployment was as Commanding Officer of Air Development Squadron Four, the F7U-3M Cutlass squadron which first deployed the Sparrow 111 air-to-air missile, until July 1957.

In August 1957 he reported for a tour of duty in the Bureau of Ordnance, Navy Department, Washington, D.C., where he served as Deputy Director, Plans and Programs Division for development of the Polaris ballistic missile submarine weapons system.

In October 1958, after a distinguished twenty-two year Naval career, he retired from the service at the ripe old age of 44! Roger went to work for his brother as Director of Planning for a construction company that built and managed apartment buildings and settled in Arcadia, CA. He retired from the company in 1975 at the age of sixty-two and bought a home overlooking the beach and Catalina Island in Orange County, CA. After the death of his wife Barbara after 53 years of marriage he decided in 1998 to move to a retirement community. After a bad fall in his apartment he moved to a smaller sheltered community that had 6 residents.

Roger Hedrick died on January 10, 2006, aged 91 with his children Barbara, Rick, and Alida with him when he died.

Basil Duke Henning

For forty-three years between 1935 and his retirement in 1978, Duke Henning's life was devoted to Yale University, and the BA student in 1933 rose to become Professor of History.

This was only interrupted by the war years and his service in the Navy, and particularly Fighting 17, where he was Air Combat Information Officer.

For 29 years, from 1946 to 1975, Duke Henning was Master of Saybrook College, a record for the longest Mastership. The plaque under Duke's portrait in the Saybrook Dining Hall describes him as "*the archetypal Master, truly without term.*"

Duke Henning relaxing with his guitar and a beer. *Courtesy the Henning Family.*

Duke Henning with buddies probably in Hawaii during World War II. *Courtesy the Henning Family.*

Saybrook College under Duke and his wife Alison won the Gimbel Cup for the highest standing in scholarship more times than any other college did. He was presented the William Clyde DeVane Medal for distinguished scholarship and teaching in Yale College.

After his retirement from Yale he worked full time in England on the completion of his book *The History of Parliament: the Commons, 1660-1690*, and was in London every summer for ten years. He appeared in Who's Who and the Directory of American scholars.

Duke Henning died on January 15, 1990, and his wife Alison in July 2008. They are survived by sons Cameron, William, and daughter Morgan.

Duke Henning with his Gibson guitar. Duke Henning started playing the guitar when he was a boy in Kentucky. *Courtesy the Henning Family.*

Lyle Franklyn Herrmann

Lyle Herrmann was the Flight Surgeon with Fighting 17. He served several years on the aircraft carrier U.S.S. *Leyte* (CV-32) as Flight Surgeon and later as Senior Medical Officer.

His other assignments included serving as Senior Medical Officer at N.A.S. Anacostia, D.C., and Senior Medical Officer on the U.S.S. *Franklin D. Roosevelt* (CVB-42) and at N.A.S. Patuxent River, Maryland. He served fourteen years, plus seven years in the Navy Reserve, and retired with the rank of Captain.

After the Navy he practiced medicine in the Atlanta, Georgia, area until he retired around 1985. He attended Fighting 17 reunions and enjoyed the time doing so. His son Lyle Herrmann, Jr. remembered:

"*He was reluctant to talk about his Navy days and he was a quiet man who was reluctant to talk about any of his past. Even*

Lt. Lyle F. Herrmann, Fighting 17 Flight Surgeon at Bougainville in 1944. *Courtesy National Archives.*

though - I could tell he truly enjoyed his Navy time and was proud to serve his country with such a fine group of people."

Lyle Herrmann died on October 12, 1994, in Seminole County, Florida.

Robert Hugh "Windy" Hill, Jr.

Following his return from the Pacific with Fighting 17, "Windy" Hill served with VBF-10 and was awarded the Distinguished Flying Cross with two Gold Stars, Air Medal with one Silver, and two Bronze stars and a Purple Heart for his war service.

Immediately following World War II he served in China and Korea. On December 14, 1945, he married Evelyn Barker in Beaufort, North Carolina.

"Beads" Popp, "Pete" Peterson, "Windy" Hill, "Hap" Bowers, Jack Chasnoff and Wally Schub at a Fighting 17 reunion in the 1980s. *Courtesy Alexandra Bowers.*

During 1949 "Windy" served on the U.S.S. *Coral Sea*, and in 1952 was assigned to VF-22 flying F2H Banshees aboard the U.S.S. *Tarawa* (CV-40). He qualified as a helicopter pilot while stationed at N.A.S. Pensacola, Florida. His last active duty assignment was in charge of the Navy's Survival, Escape, and Evasion School at N.A.S. North Island, California.

"Windy" left the service in 1958 and was employed by the Lockheed - Georgia Company as a military sales representative before retiring in 1975. He then worked in county government for DeKalb County, Georgia, until his retirement in 1985. "Windy" Hill died on January 24, 2003, in Atlanta, Georgia.

Robert Hal Jackson

Hal married Barbara Hancock on November 14, 1942, in the St. Andrew Presbyterian Church in Denton, Texas. After serving with Fighting 17, Hal went back to the Pacific with VBF-10 and received the Silver Star for his actions in the sinking of the Japanese battleship *Yamato* on April 7, 1945. In addition to the Silver Star he was also awarded two DFCs and eight Air Medals.

After the war he served two terms as Representative in the Texas Legislature, and finished his Law education at Baylor University and Southern Methodist University, receiving his Law license in 1952. He was an active trial lawyer until his retirement in 2003. Hal was a member of the Denton County Bar Association, the Denton County Criminal Defense Lawyers Association, and a founding member of the Texas Criminal Defense Lawyers Association.

Hal and Barbara regularly attended Fighting 17 reunions and organized the 1993 reunion in Denton, Texas. Hal died on January 19, 2008. Barbara still lives in Denton.

Frank Andrew "Andy" Jagger

"Andy" Jagger was never known as Gump and it really annoyed him. "*No one ever called me That. Another mistake is quoting me as Frederick instead of Frank*," he stated.

Following his service with Fighting 17 "Andy" Jagger returned to the States in April 1944 and served as an instructor at N.A.A.S Green Cove Springs. He was awarded the Distinguished Flying Cross and eight Air Medals.

After the war "Andy" went back to Grumman Aircraft in Bethpage, Long Island, where he had worked before the war. "*I told them what a good airplane the Corsair was.*" To keep his hand in he joined the Navy Reserve and flew F6F Hellcats from N.A.S. Floyd Bennett Field in Brooklyn. He also qualified on jets in the FH Phantom.

"Andy" and Betty Jagger's 63rd wedding anniversary on April 19, 2007, in Virginia Beach, VA. *Courtesy Andy and Betty Jagger.*

Hal Jackson at the 1993 Fighting 17 reunion in Denton, Texas. *Courtesy Hal and Barbara Jackson.*

"Andy" was recalled to active duty during Korea. He went to Pensacola for a second stint at instructing, this time in SNJs, until joining the Admiral's staff as Safety Officer.

"Andy" returned to Grumman in 1957 and to New York Naval Reserve flying S2F-1s. He assumed command of Fleet Air Service Squadron (FASRon) 831 and made his last Navy flight in December 1961. He was with Grumman for 25 years, eventually heading the company's safety branch, and then moved to Virginia Beach.

"Andy" had married Elizabeth "Betty" Lundgren in Burlington, Iowa, on Easter Day of 1944.

They had a son, Bob, and daughter, Mary.

"Andy" was a founder for the city's Meals on Wheels program and a member of the board of directors. "Andy" was also a regular at Fighting 17 reunions. "Andy" died on December 26, 2009, after a long illness.

George Monteith Keller, Jr.

George Keller followed his father, Cdr. George Keller, Sr., into the Navy after graduating from Princeton with an Economics degree.

After serving with Fighting 17 he was assigned to Fleet Air Wing Five and then VF-95. After finishing his active service in 1945, George Keller stayed in the Navy reserves until resigning in 1955.

George Keller returned to civilian life after WWII and a business career. He is listed in *"Who's Who in Finance and Industry. 18th edition, 1974-1975."*

He died in September 1993 in Chicago and is buried at Arlington National Cemetery.

Louis Marsden Kelley

Louis Marsden Kelley graduated from Classen High School in Oklahoma City in 1939 and Oklahoma City Junior College in 1941. Upon graduation he applied to the United States Navy. In 1942 he graduated, got his wings and his commission as an Ensign, and

Ensign Louis M. Kelley in October 1943. *Courtesy the Anderson Family.*

Mary Helen and Louis Kelley with daughters Patricia Ann and Karen Sue in a family portrait in 1949. *Courtesy Sarah Bradshaw Lewis.*

Ens. George. M. Keller, Jr., at Bougainville in 1944. *Courtesy National Archives.*

Louis Kelley with daughters Karen Sue and Patricia Ann in December 1951. *Courtesy Sarah Bradshaw Lewis.*

Louis with granddaughter Sarah in May 1987. *Courtesy Sarah Bradshaw Lewis.*

Louis Kelley in Mexico in 1991. *Courtesy Sarah Bradshaw Lewis.*

married his hometown sweetheart, Mary Helen Gentry, in the same weekend, November 9, 1942.

Louis and Mary Helen had two daughters, Patricia Anne and Karen Sue.

After his service with Fighting 17 Louis Kelley served with VF-33, VF-38, and his last assignment was with VF-50 on the U.S.S. *Cowpens* (CVL-25), "*The Mighty Moo*," which was the first American carrier to enter Tokyo Bay. He was awarded the Air Medal for his service with VF-50.

Louis returned to his family in Oklahoma City and got his Bachelor's Degree in Accounting from Oklahoma City University. He applied for the Federal Bureau of Investigation on the urging of a relative employed with the Bureau. He started as a Clerk while still in school, and was promoted to the position of Special Agent upon receiving his degree. His area of focus was bank robberies and embezzlement. His area of expertise became setting up security systems for FBI field offices. Of the many important cases to which Louis was assigned, the integration of Central High School in Little Rock, Arkansas, in 1957, and the assassination of President John F. Kennedy in 1963 are the most notable. He retired from the Bureau in 1973, following which he freelanced as a locksmith for numerous banks in Oklahoma City.

As a retiree, Louis and his wife, Mary Helen, travelled all over North America, finally leading tours into Mexico. They were often on the road seven to nine months out of the year. After losing Mary Helen to complications following a stroke in 1999 Louis moved to Ft. Worth, Texas, where he lived until he passed away on May 7, 2006.

Norman Dale Kellogg

Norman Kellogg was assigned to Fighting 17 during their training period in early 1943 until August 1943.

He then reported to VF-14 on the U.S.S. *Wasp* (CV-18), where he saw action in the Philippine Islands and was awarded the Distinguished Flying Cross on June 20, 1944, in combat action against a Japanese Task Force.

Norman Dale Kellogg served with Fighting 17 and "The Iron Angels" VF-14 during WWII. *Courtesy U.S. Navy photo.*

He was also awarded Four Air Medals and finished his active service in October 1945.

He died on November 14, 2000, in California.

Ira Cassius "Ike" Kepford

"Ike" Kepford returned to the States in April 1944 as the top ace of the U.S. Navy and a hero's welcome. His awards included the Navy Cross with Gold Star, the Silver Star and Distinguished Flying Cross.

He spent a lot of time in public relations tours for the Navy all around the country and many speaking engagements. He was then assigned to VF-84, and then on to the staff of Commander Fleet Air West Coast.

"Ike" and Esther Kraegel were married at the chapel of the roses in Chula Vista, California, while they were both stationed at San Diego, North Island. Kraeg was a W.A.V.E. (Women Accepted for Volunteer Emergency Service) and met "Ike" on a blind date.

Following the war, Kepford worked his way through the ranks to become President of Liggett and later retired as President of Liggett - Rexall Drug Co. "Ike" then became President of a metropolitan tobacco business, but he was not happy with them and resigned. He dabbled in the plastics and the gravel business,

Portrait of "Ike" Kepford when he became President of Liggett-Rexall Drug Company in 1957. *Courtesy Kraeg Kepford.*

Fishing was one of "Ike" Kepford's great passions. *Courtesy Kraeg Kepford.*

but decided to retire and moved to Harbor Springs in 1971. He retired early at fifty-one, as he "*had lived a hard life*" and was ready to retire at that time despite offers from other companies.

In his retirement he was very much an outdoors man. More than anything he loved to fish, and until Lake Michigan froze over he would stop every day and drop a line or cast in Little Traverse Bay where he lived. He also gardened and liked to hunt and collected Kentucky Rifles. He was woodcarving in his workshop during the last of his years.

"Ike" Kepford died in Michigan on January 19, 1987. Kraeg still lives in Harbor Springs.

"Ike" Kepford fishing at Diamond Lake in August 1982. *Courtesy Kraeg Kepford.*

"Ike" Kepford and a buddy pheasant hunting in Nebraska in November 1961. *Courtesy Kraeg Kepford.*

"Ike" Kepford gardening. *Courtesy Kraeg Kepford.*

Robert Wayne Kieffer

Following World War II, Bob Kieffer graduated with a degree in Aeronautical Engineering from the Naval Postgraduate School in Annapolis, MD. He completed his training at the Navy Test Pilot School in Patuxent River, Md.

His service included assignments on the U.S.S. *Bunker Hill*, U.S.S. *Wasp*, U.S.S. *Princeton*, and the U.S.S. *Siboney*. His awards for service in WWII and Korea included three Distinguished Flying Crosses, eight Air Medals and Purple Heart. His last assignment before retirement in 1967 was officer in charge of the Fleet Air Control and Surveillance Facility at North Island Naval Air Station.

When he retired from the Navy he worked for twenty years as a programmer and analyst for Computer Science Corporation of San Diego.

Bob was a man active in the Christian faith, was married to Patricia for nearly 60 years, and had a son and two daughters.

Cdr. Kieffer passed away on April 13, 2003, in Coronado at the age of eighty-one.

Tom Killefer

After Fighting 17 Tom Killefer ran a school for instructors of fighter tactics in Jacksonville, FL, then went to the R.A.F. Central Flying School and then to form a fighter squadron, VBF-74, on the *Midway*, with Tom Blackburn as Commander Air Group.

He then finished Law school at Harvard and went to Oxford for two years, where on USNR duty he got to fly Spitfire 21s, with the counter rotating propellers and Griffon engine.

He was awarded the Distinguished Flying Cross, Air Medal and Purple Heart among his decorations with Fighting 17.

After the war Tom practiced law with Lillick, Geary, Wheat, Adams & Charles in San Francisco and Washington, D.C., from 1947 to 1959. He was appointed to the staff of the U.S. High

Robert Wayne Kieffer on the U.S.S. *Princeton* (CV-37) on October 28, 1952. *Courtesy the Kieffer Family.*

Commission for Germany in 1951 and 1952 and was Executive Director of the Committee of American Steamship Lines in 1959 and 1960. From 1959 until 1962 he was First Vice President, Vice Chairman and a Director of the Export - Import Bank of the United States. From 1962 until 1966 he was Executive Director of the Inter - American Development Bank and was Special Assistant to the Secretary of the Treasury. He became General Counsel and Chief Financial Officer for the Chrysler Corporation in 1966, and was made Executive Vice President in 1975. He served as representative of the Maritime Law Association of the United States at the U.N. Conference on the Law of the Sea at Geneva in 1958, and was senior adviser and member of the U.S. delegation to meetings of the Interamerican Economic and Social Council of the United Nations from 1962 to 1966. In 1971 he became a member of Stanford University's Board of Trustees, serving until 1981.

In 1976 he became Chairman, President and Chief Executive Officer of the trust and investment managers U.S. Trust Company of New York, and he served as Chairman until he retired in 1982. Tom also served as a Director of the Pullman Corp., Northrop Corp., and American Natural Resources. In 1976 he became Chairman of the board of directors of the Detroit branch of the Federal Reserve Bank of Chicago and of Henry Ford Hospital in Detroit.

Tom Killefer was honoured many times for his post-war achievements, including the Order of Merit for Distinguished Service from the Government of Peru, the National Award of Honor from the American Association of College Baseball Coaches in 1974, and the Distinguished Achievement Medal of the Stanford University Athletic Board in 1977. Among his many gifts to Stanford was the endowment of the Killefer dissertation fellowship for doctoral students in English. Tom and Carolyn had four children: Wade, Caroline, Gail, and Anne. He died suddenly on Sunday, June 16, 1996, at his Portola Valley home. He collapsed while dressing for a Father's Day dinner and after having played 18 holes of golf. He was seventy-nine years of age

Lester Raymond Kincaid

Ensign Lester R. Kincaid served with Fighting 17 as Assistant Gunnery Officer from February 15, 1944, until March 15, 1944.

After the war he married (Clara) Louise Kimberly of Tyler, Texas. At the end of the war they left the service together and she actually out-ranked Les by one pay grade! They moved back home to Plevna, MO, and ran a grocery store for several years. Kincaid joined the Masonic Lodge and the Veterans of Foreign Wars at that time and was awarded a 50 year pin from each shortly before he died. After the grocery burned down Kincaid sold insurance for American Family Ins. for a few years. He left American Family and started selling industrial John Deere equipment. Once he became comfortable selling tractors he bought into the John Deere

Ens. Lester R. Kincaid, Assistant Gunnery Officer at Bougainville in 1944. *Courtesy National Archives.*

Tom Killefer as Chairman of the Board and Chief Executive Officer of U.S. Trust Company. *Courtesy the Killefer Family.*

agricultural dealership in Edina, MO. As a partner with Dudley Gillespie, he ran the dealership until 1981, when they closed the doors. He then invested the proceeds from the sale into land, on which he farmed and raised Charlais cattle until his death. Les and Louise raised two children: John (Hubba) Raymond and Nancy Lou. Louise died in 1998 and Les remarried to Margaret Shemp, who still survives. He died in Knox, Missouri, at the age of eighty on April 3, 2001.

Melvin Monroe "Kurly" Kurlander

After Fighting 17 "Kurly" went to N.A.A.S. Green Cove Springs, Florida, as an instructor. He was awarded the Distinguished Flying Cross and five Air Medals for his service with Fighting 17.

After the war "Kurly" went to work with his father in a womens wear company, selling suits and coats for four to five years in Chicago. Due to the economic situation he went on the road as a salesman for the same company and had a territory saved for him. After his father died the company went into other hands and he went into the life insurance business, with the main company being American General, which was later taken over by AIG. He was the best salesman in the country for one month and stayed in the insurance business until he retired at 65, when he then "*played golf, tennis and ran around with girls*."

He was married three times and had four children, three boys and one girl.

"Kurly" still lives in Chicago where he has all his life after his family moved there when he was a few months old.

William Lee "Country" Landreth

William "Country" Landreth was the youngest original pilot in Fighting 17 and went on to serve with VF/VBF-10 before being captured by the Japanese in March 1945 and incarcerated for six months as a prisoner of war until repatriation. His son William Lee Landreth, Jr., was born as "Country" was being liberated from the prison camp. "Ginger" didn't know he was alive until about August 24 or 25, 1945. As the family story goes, "Ginger" (who had been told her husband was missing, presumed dead) had almost died due to a breech birth and was recuperating in the hospital when she got a telegram from the Red Cross saying that "Country" had been found. The good news travelled from floor to floor, marked by sounds of cheering. "Ginger" was not surprised...she knew in her heart he was alive. "Country" was one of the lucky ones who survived as a prisoner of the Japanese.

"Country" was awarded the Distinguished Flying Cross with Gold Star, Air Medal with four Gold Stars and Purple Heart among his many decorations.

"Country" served in the Navy for 27 years in various assignments, including as Commanding Officer of VS-37, a carrier-based anti-submarine squadron. He then went on the staff of Commander Carrier Division 17 and then to the Naval Research Lab, then became the Naval Air Station Pt. Mugu Liaison Officer to Vandenberg Air Force Base.

He was the founding director of a degree - granting program at Naval Air Station Pt. Mugu, California, and helped to start degree - granting programs on two other military bases.

He received a Bachelor Degree at the age of 47 from Chapman College in Orange, California, just before retiring as a Commander in 1969.

After retiring, "Country" spent five years in further education and received his Master of Arts Degree in Education in 1975, and a Master of Science Degree in Counselling in 1976, both from Cal - Lutheran University in Thousand Oaks, California.

Mel Kurlander at the Washington Navy Yard Museum, where there is an exhibit to which he donated several items. *Courtesy Mel Kurlander.*

William Lee "Country" Landreth. "Country" spent 27 years in the Navy before retiring as a Commander. *Courtesy Landreth Family Collection.*

"Country" and "Ginger" Landreth in Hawaii in 1984. *Courtesy Landreth Family Collection.*

"Country" was self - employed in a specialized form of insurance for financial institutions for the last twenty years or so of his working life.

In 1994 "Country" and "Ginger" celebrated their Golden Wedding anniversary and were regulars at Fighting 17 reunions.

His good friend Ray Ferguson had this to say about "Country" Landreth in 1995:

"Bill is a marvellous gentleman as well as a warrior. My wife and I think he is the model of a Naval Officer and citizen."

Bill's wife "Ginger" died after a long illness in 1999. Bill still lives in Camarillo, California They had a son, Bill, Jr., a Vietnam veteran who was seriously wounded and medically retired who died at 41 from a sudden heart attack, and a daughter Linda.

Harvey "Matty" Matthews

The Navy ran in the Matthews family. His father Fern Paul Matthews was aboard the U.S.S. *Charleston* from 1905 to 1908 in the South China Sea, and his Uncle, Commander Roy Matthews, was a submarine commander in the 1940s and 1950s. His grandson is currently deployed on the U.S.S. *Michigan* nuclear submarine as a Lieutenant.

After finishing his service with Fighting 17, "Matty" Matthews was assigned to VF-84, along with many other Fighting 17 pilots. He served with distinction until the U.S.S. *Bunker Hill* was put out of the war by a kamikaze. He was awarded the Distinguished Flying Cross with one Gold Star and Air Medal with 3 Gold Stars.

"Matty" would wake up with nightmares right up until 2001 as a result of the kamikaze attack that he had survived on the U.S.S. *Bunker Hill*. He had been on the flight deck when he saw the two kamikazes diving in to attack

"Matty" married Geraldine on January 31, 1951, and they were lifelong residents of Texarkana, Arkansas. His wife was previously married and had two sons. One was killed along with her husband in an automobile crash in 1947. The surviving son, James Stacks,

Ens. Harvey "Matty" Matthews at Bougainville in 1944. *Courtesy National Archives.*

still lives in Texarkana. "Matty" and Geraldine had a son Paul who also lives in Texarkana.

"Matty" was a home builder until his retirement. He probably built over 200 homes; with a small team they would build one home at a time. He was also an avid duck hunter and fisherman.

Geraldine passed away on December 25, 1989, and "Matty" died in Texarkana, Arkansas, on May 22, 2005.

George Mauhar

After Fighting 17 George Mauhar was requested by Roger Hedrick to join VF-84 as a Crew Chief.

George served in the Navy for twenty-two years, with VF-84 being his last fighter squadron, as he then moved to multi-engined aircraft. He retired from the service whist in Guam and returned to the U.S., where he worked in the Civil Service doing supervision

Harvey Matthews at the Fighting 17 reunion in 1983. *Courtesy the Matthews Family.*

George Mauhar at the Fighting 17 reunion in Denton, Texas, in May 1993. *Courtesy George and Laurie Mauhar.*

Don and Janet McQueen on their wedding day on March 16, 1952. *Courtesy the McQueen Family.*

Just married. Don and Janet McQueen on their wedding day on March 16, 1952. *Courtesy the McQueen Family.*

and engineering type work, and retired there after seventeen years. He initially retired to Missouri and then moved to Coronado.

George ran into "Andy" Jagger at a reunion and has attended the reunions ever since.

George's beloved wife Laurie died in an automobile accident whilst out driving with George in 2002. George still lives in Coronado.

Donald Roy McQueen

Don McQueen was awarded the Distinguished Flying Cross and four Air Medals with Fighting 17, and served in various assignments until the end of WWII.

After the war ended Don was offered a position with Trans World Airlines; however, Don thought it would be boring to sit in a cockpit with no action.

After flying he wanted to do financial analysis at U.S. Gypsum, then went into sales and marketing and then became a Sales Rep., Branch Manager, then Regional Manager and National Marketing Manager and retired aged 65.

The McQueens were residents of Marietta, Georgia, from 1971 until 1999, when his wife Janet died. In his retirement Don enjoyed playing golf and travelling all over the world.

Don and Janet McQueen with daughter Donna. *Courtesy the McQueen Family.*

Don McQueen and daughter Donna. *Courtesy the McQueen Family.*

Don McQueen went into sales and marketing after WWII. *Courtesy the McQueen Family.*

He has daughters Donna and Sharon and a son Steve, and lives in Texas.

His daughter Donna has this to say about her father:

"There is no question in my mind that he is probably the most amazing person I have ever met. At 90, blind and widowed, he is still one of the most positive, optimistic people that I have ever met. He is happy to be alive every day, exercises like a 30 year old, always sees the good in people, except he would never buy a Japanese car. Still a ladies' man even at 90. The women love him."

Don McQueen in July 2005. *Courtesy the McQueen Family.*

Lionel Thiel "Mac" McQuiston

In my book *The Skull and Crossbones Squadron - VF-17 in World War II* the name I had for Lionel was quoted as Louis; I have since found this to be incorrect. His correct name was Lionel Thiel McQuiston, and he was known as "Mac."

"Mac" was a graduate of the Naval Academy Annapolis, Maryland, in 1938, and after the war he continued in the service until June 30, 1962 when he retired from the Navy.

Inspection of enlisted personnel of VPMS-4 in August 1947 by Cdr. Lionel T. McQuiston at N.A.S. Coco Solo. *Courtesy U.S. Navy Photo via Della McQuiston.*

Group shot of officers of VPMS-4 in August 1947, Commanded by Cdr. Lionel T. McQuiston. *Courtesy U.S. Navy Photo via Della McQuiston.*

A Martin PBM5 Mariner. The PBM-5 was fitted out for "Jet (rocket) assisted take-off" (JATO / RATO). Cdr. Lionel T. McQuiston was Commanding Officer of VPMS-4 flying these patrol seaplanes. *Courtesy U.S. Navy Photo via Della McQuiston.*

"Mac" enjoyed his life after the Navy; he retired to golfing, gardening, reading and working around the house. He married his second wife in 1983 and travelled, renewing old military friendships and attending military ceremonies.

He lost the use of his legs in 1999 and spent his last three years in a care home facility. He studied religion in depth and was a donor to numerous charities.

"Mac" McQuiston died on September 9, 2002.

Robert "Bobby" Mims

Bobby Mims was awarded the Distinguished Flying Cross with Fighting 17 and finished his active service on November 5, 1945, after serving on the U.S.S. *Hancock* (CV-19). He continued in the reserves, and Lt. Cdr. Mims was placed on the retired list of the Naval Reserve on March 1, 1953.

After the war he married Doris Elaine Crockett, who was a distant relative of Davy Crockett. They had two girls, Betsy and Susan. They divorced in the late 1950s when the girls were six and seven and then had little contact with him after then.

Bobby went into the oil business after the war and was very successful, a big "Wheeler Dealer" who put deals together to drill for oil and in the leasing business. He made $300,000 in one particular deal.

Unfortunately Bobby had an alcohol addiction. He didn't go to the war with an alcohol problem but came back with one. He was known as a "hell raising kind of a guy" by the squadron.

Bobby was married several times after Doris, but continued to have problems with alcohol addiction and was a hard drinking man who had a very short fuse and temper.

Another view of a Martin PBM5 Mariner. The PBM-5 was fitted out for "Jet (rocket) assisted take-off" (JATO / RATO). Cdr. Lionel T. McQuiston was Commanding Officer of VPMS-4 flying these patrol seaplanes. *Courtesy U.S. Navy Photo via Della McQuiston.*

Captain Lionel T. McQuiston retired from the Navy in 1962. *Courtesy U.S. Navy Photo via Della McQuiston.*

Bobby and Doris Mims on their wedding day. *Courtesy Betsy Bryant and Susan Ritter.*

Lt. Cdr. Marvin Russell "Russ" Novak in 1961. *Courtesy U.S. Navy photo.*

On April 9, 1963, Robert Mims was convicted of a felony. On April 15, 1963, he was sentenced to fifteen years and a fine of $10,000. On December 13, 1964, the sentence was reduced to five years and the fine suspended. Apparently he boarded a plane quite drunk, and in the middle of the flight tried to attempt to take over the plane and had an altercation with the pilot. He was sent to the Federal Correctional Institution in Seagoville, Texas, and died of a heart attack in prison on September 19, 1966; he is buried at Restlands Cemetery, Dallas, Texas.

Bobby was the love of Doris' life and a superb fighter pilot and ace with six victories.

Marvin Russell "Russ" Novak

"Russ" Novak served with Fighting 17 from January 1943 until August 1943 all through the training period. He was assigned to VF-14 on the U.S.S. *Wasp* (CV-18) in August 1943, where he served with distinction and became an ace with five confirmed victories.

He continued in the Navy after WWII and was in combat during the Korean conflict serving aboard the U.S.S. *Boxer*. He retired from the Navy in 1963 as a Lt. Cdr. and lives in San Diego.

Earle Carpenter "Pete" Peterson, Jr.

"Pete" was the son of Earle C. Peterson, Sr., who was one of the earliest Naval aviators. For his service with Fighting 17 "Pete" was authorized to wear among his awards the Air Medal and Purple Heart.

He went back to Columbus, Ohio, after the war to work for his wife's family's paper distribution business, but his love continued to be with the Navy and flying.

A few years after the end of the war he left active duty as a Lt. Commander, but stayed in the Naval Air Reserves and was eventually promoted to Captain before retiring in 1981. He served as President of the Navy League of Ohio as well.

After his service he was engaged in aircraft sales and real estate. He was a member of the athletic club, Columbus Country Club, and Columbus Beach Club of Indian River, Michigan, and Chairman of Aviation Committee of Columbus Area Chamber of Commerce.

He occasionally tried to relive his fighter pilot days when he would fly twenty feet over the lake near his summer cottage in his Beech Bonanza.

"Pete" Peterson, Jr., married Marilyn Miller Peterson in 1944 and was married for forty-one years until his death from a heart attack on February 12, 1985, in Columbus, Ohio. His ashes are interred at Arlington National Cemetery, in Arlington, VA. They had three children: Earle III, Robert and Marilyn.

"Pete" Peterson standing next to a Catalina PBY flying boat. *Courtesy Earle C. Peterson, Jr. Collection.*

"Pete" Peterson, 5th from left front row with his reserve squadron after WWII. *Courtesy Earle C. Peterson, Jr. Collection.*

Bottom left: "Pete" Peterson in his Navy uniform. A few years after the end of the war he left active duty as a Lt. Cdr., but stayed in the Naval Air Reserves and was eventually promoted to Captain before retiring in 1981. *Courtesy Earle C. Peterson, Jr. Collection.*

Below: "Pete" Peterson was engaged in aircraft sales and real estate in his career after the Navy. *Courtesy Earle C. Peterson, Jr. Collection.*

"Beads" Popp and Lee Cook at the Fighting 17 reunion at Oshkosh in 1994. *Courtesy Bill and Jean Popp.*

Wilbert Peter "Beads" Popp

After combat tours with Fighting 17 and VF-84 Bill was awarded three Distinguished Flying Crosses and seven Air Medals. He was assigned shore duty at Los Alamitos, California, for ten days, then from June to September 1945 was a type instructor in Corsairs for pilots preparing to go to the fleet at Thermal Naval Air Facility in California.

After the war he completed his education at the University of Washington in Seattle, graduating in June 1947 with a BA in Business Administration and an Insurance Major. He then became an Insurance Agent. Bill married Jean Constance Page in May 1950 and had three daughters and made their home in Oregon.

Photography and fishing for steelhead and salmon were his great loves, along with travelling.

Bill and Jean were regulars at Fighting 17 reunions, and he was known for his excellent memory. He completed his book called *The Survival of a WWII Navy Fighter Pilot* shortly before he died on February 25, 2006. His devoted wife Jean still lives in Oregon.

Harmond Becker "Hink" Richardson, Jr.

In my book *The Skull and Crossbones Squadron - VF-17 in World War II* the name I had for Harmond was quoted as Harold; I have since found this to be incorrect. His correct name is Harmond Becker Richardson, Jr., and he was known as "Hink."

"Hink" married Adele Alberta Paskins of Cleveland on August 16, 1943, shortly before going overseas. They had four children: Howard, Harmond B. III, Pamela, and Thomas. He returned to the States after serving with Fighting 17, and after leave reported to Air Force Atlantic Fleet, Norfolk, Virginia, in April 1944.

He reported to Headquarters Squadron 51 at Elizabeth City, North Carolina, on May 9, 1944, and from there was assigned to Headquarters Squadron 52, Fleet Air Wing Five, in January 1945. On April 24, 1945, he reported to VBF-74 and was released from active duty in September 1945. "Hink" remained in the Navy Reserve until 1957.

Harmond "Hink" Richardson (Left) in flight gear with a couple of buddies. *Courtesy U.S. Navy photo via the Richardson Family.*

After leaving the service "Hink" worked for the Armstrong Cork Co. in Cincinnati, Ohio, from 1945 to 1949 as Construction Superintendent, and then for the International Mineral and Chemical Co. in Lockland, Ohio, in general plant and maintenance work in 1950.

He then worked for the General Electric Co. in Evendale, Ohio (Jet Engine Manufacturer), as a specifications specialist from June 1953 to 1955.

He started work for the Zirconium Corp of America, Solon, Ohio, as a Plant Operator in June 1956 and worked there for many years.

"Hink" was an avid reader and historian, a baseball and Cleveland Browns football fan, and his love of aviation continued as he made and competed with model aircraft. He died on October 16, 1977, at U.H.H.S. (University Hospitals Health System), Geauga Regional Hospital at the age of fifty-five from acute Lymphatic Leukaemia.

Mills Schanuel

Mills had never set out to become a Naval Aviator. He went from the St. Louis Post Dispatch to the Navy recruiting office and asked to be a Navy journalist. Following a series of tests they assigned him to flight training. After the war he was employed by Wilbur Willis Brokerage as an Import - Export Commodities Broker.

He achieved his Commercial Pilot's License in June 1946 and in 1947 married Marilee, whom he met on one of his regular trips through San Francisco. They had four children, two boys and two girls. He spent a few years travelling, in the U.S. and abroad, building up his business with the main office in Chicago. Well into his 50s Mills retained his skill as an excellent shot, knocking 25 of 25 clay targets out of the air with uncanny ease.

Mills spent four years fighting cancer with multiple surgeries and won this battle. He is now into his nineties and lives quietly with Marilee in Missouri.

Mills Schanuel with the Navy Colt .45 he carried during his years in the Pacific. *Courtesy Phil Schanuel.*

Mills and Marilee Schanuel on their 62nd wedding anniversary on September 28, 2008. *Courtesy Phil Schanuel.*

Walter John "Wally" Schub

Following his deployment with Fighting 17 "Wally" served from December 1944 until December 1946 with VF-10 as Flight Officer. He was on the U.S.S. *Intrepid* during the Okinawa campaign and in Japan until November 1945. He was awarded five Distinguished Flying Crosses and twelve Air Medals for his service during the war and scored 4.25 victories in air to air combat.

Returning to the U.S. in January 1946 to 1948 he was at N.A.S. Corpus Christi as Squadron Commander of V12-C. From February to August 1948 he served with U.S.S. *Taconic* as Flight Officer with Tactical Air Control Squadron Two.

"Wally" was assigned from February 1949 until August 1950 as Operations Officer, Tactical Air Control Squadron Two. From August 1950 until January 1952 he was Administrative Officer, Naval Technical Training Unit at N.A.S. Glenview, Illinois, and from January until December 1952 was at General Line School.

In January 1953 "Wally" became Commanding Officer of VF-33 and in July was promoted to the rank of Commander.

He served on the U.S.S. *Midway* and on the U.S.S. *Saratoga* as Air Operations Officer, and from 1961 to 1963 "Wally" was Executive Officer at N.A.S. Jacksonville and was Acting C.O. at Jacksonville during the Cuban missile crisis in 1962.

Cdr. Walter Schub in his last assignment as Executive Officer at N.A.S. Jacksonville in 1962. *Courtesy U.S. Navy via Maureen Schub.*

Wally Schub, Lee Cook and Hal Jackson at the Fighting 17 reunion in St. Louis in 1996. *Courtesy Hal and Barbara Jackson.*

"Wally" retired as a Commander on June 30, 1963. He was a regular at Fighting 17 reunions along with his beloved wife Maureen.

He died on September 16, 2000, in Jacksonville, Florida, and is buried at Arlington National Cemetery.

John Malcolm "Smitty" Smith

After his successful combat duty with Fighting 17 John became the joint top ace of VF-84 and the fourth ranked Navy Corsair ace of WWII with ten confirmed victories. He was awarded the Silver Star, five Distinguished Flying Crosses and four Air Medals.

Following his service John enrolled at St. Mary's College in Winona, Minnesota, under the GI Bill in 1946. He attended St. Mary's for three years, and then went to Creighton University in Omaha, Nebraska, for his L.L.B., which he obtained in 1950. After passing the bar he was employed by the Mutual Service Insurance Company. In 1950 he was admitted to the Nebraska and Minnesota bars.

He met Therese Frances Martin whilst at college and they were married on July 29, 1950, in Emmetsburg, Iowa. They had seven children: sons Bernard, Steve, Robert; and daughters Anne, Molly, Tracy, and Kasey. John was a devoted family man.

John was a practicing attorney in his home town of Owatonna, Minnesota, since 1954, and in 1958 was elected Steele County Attorney. He served one four-year term. He was a member of the Minnesota Trial Lawyers Association and the Association of Trial Lawyers of America.

John continued flying in the reserves after the war and was recalled to active duty during the Korean War. He served as a legal officer for the Twin Cities Naval Air Station until the end of 1954, when he returned to the reserves. In 1957, the reserve unit he commanded won the Noel Davis Trophy awarded annually by the Navy Department for the most efficient aviation division of the U.S. Naval Reserve. He retired in 1972 with the rank of Captain.

He was a fundamental part of life in Owatonna, from director of the Owatonna Civil Defense in 1955, to member of the Owatonna Chamber of Commerce Board of Directors 1969 to 1971. He was a member and contributor to numerous community associations and in 1965 was honored as Boss of the Year in Owatonna.

He was a member of the Marian High School Building Commission in 1956, and served as a member of the St. Mary's - Marian Catholic School Board of Education 1966 to 1971, and as its Chairman from 1969 to 1971. He was treasurer of the Catholic Education Memorial Fund and a member of Knight of Columbus Council, serving as Grand Knight in 1959 to 1960. He was a member of the St. Joseph Church finance committee and the Christian Board of Education for Dodge and Steele counties.

Politically active and a lifelong Democrat, John served on the Executive Committee of the Steele County Democratic-Farmer-Labor Party, and was active in a number of campaigns, including those for fellow Navy veterans John F. Kennedy and Eugene McCarthy. He was a delegate to the First Congressional District and State Conventions from 1960 through 1966, and was an alternate delegate to the national Democratic convention in 1964.

An avid outdoorsman, hunter, and fisherman who loved golf, boating, and snowmobiling, John Malcolm Smith died suddenly while jogging on June 9, 1981, of a heart condition.

John M. Smith continued flying in the Navy Reserve. In 1957, the reserve unit he commanded won the Noel Davis Trophy awarded annually by the Navy Department for the most efficient aviation division of the U.S. Naval Reserve. *Courtesy John M. Smith Collection.*

Frederick James "Big Jim" Streig

"Big Jim" arrived home after his combat with Fighting 17 an ace with 5.5 confirmed victories and was awarded the Distinguished Flying Cross with two Gold Stars and Air Medal with six Gold Stars. He served from May 1944 until December 1945 at N.A.A.S. Green Cove Springs as Operational Flight Instructor and Aviation Equipment Officer. After the war "Big Jim" married Vera Mae Dodge and had four sons: James, Richard, Frederick and Eric.

From March 1946 until December 1947 he was V-2/V-4 Division Officer and Senior Watch Officer on the U.S.S. *Antietam*, and from January 1948 until June 1950 was at N.A.S. Alameda as Flight Operations and Assistant Operations Officer.

From July 1950 until August 1952 "Big Jim" was with VR-5 as Transport Pilot and Assistant Operations Officer, and from September 1952 until June 1953 at the R.O.T.C. Unit of the University of California, Berkeley. In July 1953 "Big Jim" attended General Line School at Monterey, California, until February 1954, when he reported to C.I.C. Officer School, Glenview until July 1954. In September 1954 until April 1956 he was Air Operations; Acting Navigator; Communications Officer; Nuclear Weapons Employment Officer on U.S.S. *Shangri La* (CVA-38).

"Big Jim" was promoted to Commander in July 1956 whilst he was serving with VW-12 as Personnel Officer; A.E.W. Aircraft Commander. From January 1959 until March 1961 he served as Aircraft Maintenance Officer at N.A A.S. Saufley Field, Pensacola.

Cdr. F. J. "Big Jim" Streig in 1968. *Courtesy U.S. Navy.*

L – R: "Country" Landreth, Hal Jackson, Roger Hedrick, "Andy" Jagger and Jim Streig at the Fighting 17 reunion in San Francisco in 1988. *Courtesy Hal and Barbara Jackson.*

In March 1961 until January 1962 he was assigned to CNABATRA Staff Pensacola as Staff Aircraft Maintenance and Material Officer, and was there during the April 1961 Bay of Pigs crisis and in "*Lock Down*" with President Kennedy at the critical time of the crisis.

From February 1962 until July 1965 "Big Jim" served at CINCLANT Nuclear Operations, and from August 1965 to June 1969 at COMWESTSEAFRON on Staff in Logistics Plans and Programs.

Commander Streig retired from the Navy on June 30, 1969, after a distinguished career.

After retiring from the Navy he went back and completed his degree in History, and taught as a substitute teacher at high school and did a lot of work for the 4H Organization. He retired from this in 1975.

He attended the Fighting 17 reunion at E.A.A. Oshkosh in 1994 and died following a long illness on August 31, 1995, in Alameda, CA. He is buried in Golden Gate National Cemetery.

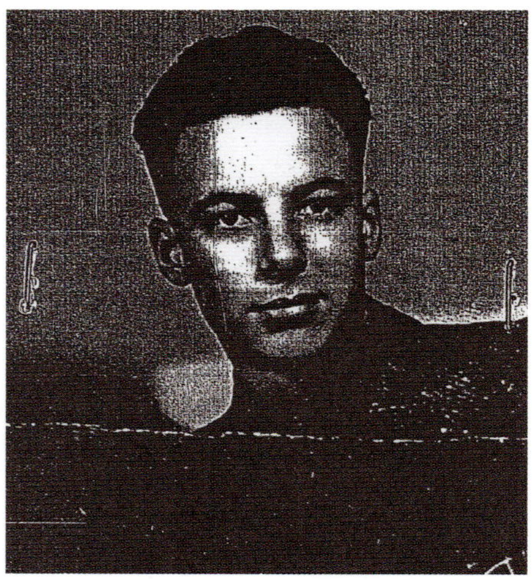

Jack Raby Travers. *Courtesy U.S. Navy.*

Jack Raby Travers

After his brief service with Fighting 17 Jack was transferred to VF-40 along with his friend Kenneth Babkirk, who was listed missing in action on January 17, 1944.

Whilst serving with VBF-5 in February 1946, Jack requested a commission in the regular Navy. However he later withdrew this request and returned to civilian life.

He died on April 23, 2005, in Fort Worth, Texas.

Edward Bennett Turner

Edward Turner served with Fighting 17 for five months from March to August 1943, and was then assigned to VF-14 on the U.S.S. *Wasp* (CV-18).

On October 18, 1944, he shot down five enemy aircraft in one aerial battle over Clark Field Manila, in the Philippine Islands. For his heroism in this engagement he was awarded the Navy Cross. He finished his distinguished WWII service as an ace with seven confirmed victories.

After the war he was a member of the Warbirds aerobatic exhibition team and owned La Grange Airport in Georgia, where he operated a flight instruction school.

He died on February 21, 1998.

Lt. Edward Bennett Turner with his Hellcat on the U.S.S. Wasp in 1944. *Courtesy U.S. Navy photo via the Edward Bennett Turner Family.*

Whit Wharton (third from left) and buddies after serving with Fighting 17. *Courtesy Joyce Wharton.*

Whitfield Carlisle Wharton, Jr.

Following his deployment with Fighting 17 Whit flew as wingman to Wally Schub with VF-10. He served on the U.S.S. *Intrepid* in attacks on the Japanese home islands and during the Okinawa campaign, and was awarded the Distinguished Flying Cross and four Air Medals for his WWII service.

Whit stayed in the Navy on active service until June 1947, then remained in the Navy reserves and retired in October 1956.

Whit thought Fighting 17 was the very best. He attended the May 1983 reunion and said, "*It was like old times.*" He died only four months later of a heart attack in September 1983. He was 62 years old.

15

Fighting 17 in Color

A selection of color photos featuring Fighting 17, F4U Corsairs, aviation art and reunions.

Three new F4U Corsairs in flight. *Courtesy Vought.*

In flight, a bomb - carrying F4U-1D. *Courtesy Vought*

The Fighter Factory's FG-1D Corsair was purchased in 1999. In 2001 an extensive restoration program was undertaken. It was repainted in 2002 in the markings of Lt. Ray Beacham, who was assigned to Fighting 17. Ray Beacham, "the Kitty Hawk Kid," was credited with Fighting 17's first kill. *Courtesy Paul Bowen, www.airtoair.net.*

Another view of the Fighter Factory's Fighting 17 marked FG-1D Corsair. *Courtesy Paul Bowen, www.airtoair.net.*

Another view of the Fighter Factory's Fighting 17 marked FG-1D Corsair. *Courtesy Paul Bowen, www.airtoair.net.*

Another view of the Fighter Factory's Fighting 17 marked FG-1D Corsair. *Courtesy Paul Bowen, www.airtoair.net.*

This Corsair used to be operated by the Old Flying Machine Company and flew in the colors of Tom Blackburn's "Big Hog" at Duxford, England. *Courtesy Howard Cook.*

FG-1D painted up to represent #29 of Fighting17 flown by Lt. (jg) Ira Cassius "Ike" Kepford. Kepford was the U.S. Navy's top Corsair ace with sixteen confirmed victories. Vintage Fighters owned by Charles Osborn and managed by Brad Hood restored this plane, which won an E.A.A. Grand Champion award. *Courtesy Paul Bowen, www.airtoair.net.*

Another view of Vintage Fighters' FG-1D in Fighting 17 colors. *Courtesy Paul Bowen, www.airtoair.net.*

"Crucible Rabaul" by Steven Heyen.
Ensign Frederick J. Streig's F4U-1A of VF-17 on a head-on attack with Zekes over Rabaul's Simpson Harbour. *Courtesy Steven Heyen,* www.stevenheyenart.com.

Another view of Vintage Fighters' FG-1D in Fighting 17 colors. *Courtesy Paul Bowen, www.airtoair.net.*

"Fighting 17" by Wade Meyers.
This painting depicts VF-17 *Jolly Rogers* commanding officer Lt. Cdr. Tommy Blackburn in his "Big Hog" F4U Corsair, circa late November 1943. Sporting beards in many cases, and known for their aggressiveness, "Blackburn's Irregulars," as the pilots of VF-17 were known in certain quarters, actually played a large role during their own training period in preparing the Corsair for fleet-wide use. Eliminating the F4U's tendency to "bounce" during carrier landings and taming the plane's nasty stall characteristics were two important VF-17 technical innovations. They didn't do so bad once they entered combat, either, scoring a record 152 victories in only 76 days of combat during the Solomons campaign. *Juried into the American Society of Aviation Artists 2008 International Aerospace Art Exhibition, The Museum of Flight, Seattle, WA. Courtesy Wade Meyers, www.wademeyersart.com.*

"Chasing the Sun" by Sam Lyons.
Here's a dramatic scene out of WWII. A pair of F4U Corsairs are pursuing a Japanese Zero with golden sunlight giving the clouds a brilliant glow. The careful observer will know the time frame is around 1943 because of the Corsair markings. The plane in the foreground has red markings. Those were changed to blue that year to avoid confusion with red markings on enemy aircraft. You can see the plane in the background has been switched to blue markings. Jim Streig is the pilot in the number 3 plane, and Tommy Blackburn sits in the cockpit of number 1. Both men were members of the Jolly Rogers, Fighting Squadron 17. *Courtesy Sam Lyons, www.LyonsStudio.com. 1-800-544-4992*

"Short Stop" - Ira Kepford in his F4U Corsair off Carrier Bunker Hill. *Signed by Tim Kepford - Son of Ira Kepford*
Ira Cassius Kepford is well known as the US Navy's most successful Corsair pilot with a total of 16 confirmed air to air victories. He is depicted here at the beginning of his illustrious career in The Battle of the Solomon Sea. In this battle he shot down a Japanese "Kate" torpedo bomber a mere 1000 yards from the carrier *Bunker Hill* just fractions of a second before the enemy bomber could release its deadly load. Simultaneously a Japanese Zero was attempting to remove Ira from action, but was eliminated by a Navy Hellcat. Although low on fuel Ira continued through the intense anti-aircraft fire from the *Bunker Hill* and its escorts and went on to shoot down 3 more Japanese aircraft within minutes before running out of ammunition. For this day's actions he was awarded the Navy Cross. Ira Kepford is shown here in the VF17 – "Jolly Rogers" Colors flying his Vaught F4U Corsair. This rendition truly captures the intense action of the event in stunning detail. Action Art Publishing, 4215 29th Ave., Edmonton, Alberta, Canada T6L 5K3. *Email: len@actionart.ca or lenkrenzler@yahoo.com. Courtesy Len Krenzler*

"Salute to the Jolly Rogers" by Domenic DeNardo. Having shot down 152 Japanese aircraft in 76 days of combat, the "Jolly Rogers" became one of the most famous fighter squadrons in the US Navy. Signed by the artist. *Courtesy Domenic DeNardo.*

FG-1D "VF-17 Remembered" painted to represent #17 of Fighting 17 flown by Lt. Cdr Roger Hedrick. Vintage Fighters, owned by Charles Osborn and managed by Brad Hood, restored this plane, which won an E.A.A. Grand Champion award. *Courtesy Brad Hood Director / Chief Pilot - Vintage Fighters.*

Another view of FG-1D "VF-17 Remembered" painted up to represent #17 of Fighting 17 flown by Lt. Cdr. Roger Hedrick. *Courtesy Brad Hood Director / Chief Pilot - Vintage Fighters.*

FG-1D "VF-17 Remembered" painted as #17 flown by Lt. Cdr. Roger Hedrick. This aircraft appeared at Oshkosh in 1994 for the Fighting 17 reunion before it was fully restored in Hedrick's colors. *Courtesy Brad Hood Director / Chief Pilot - Vintage Fighters.*

FG-1D "VF-17 Remembered" painted up to represent #17 of Fighting 17 flown by Lt. Cdr. Roger Hedrick. This aircraft was beautifully restored by Vintage Fighters and is one of the finest examples of a Corsair flying today. *Courtesy Brad Hood Director / Chief Pilot - Vintage Fighters.*

FG-1D "VF-17 Remembered" painted up to represent #17 of Fighting17 flown by Lt. Cdr. Roger Hedrick. This aircraft was owned at the time by Paul Morgan. Paul was tragically killed in a flying accident in 2001. *Courtesy Howard Cook.*

FG-1D "VF-17 Remembered" painted up to represent #17 flown by Lt. Cdr. Roger Hedrick. Vintage Fighters restored this Corsair. The plane was eventually purchased by Paul Morgan and transported to England. Paul was tragically killed in a flying accident in 2001. The photos were taken at the Imperial War Museum, Duxford, England. *Courtesy Howard Cook.*

FG-1D "VF-17 Remembered" #17 in the colors of Lt. Cdr. Roger Hedrick. This photo was taken at the Imperial War Museum, Duxford, England. *Courtesy Howard Cook.*

FG-1D "VF-17 Remembered" was a regular on the air show circuit where it proudly displayed Lt. Cdr. Roger Hedrick's markings. This photo was taken at the Imperial War Museum, Duxford, England. *Courtesy Howard Cook.*

The Fighter Collections FG-1 Corsair in "Ike" Kepford's markings flying at an airshow in England prior to a change of color scheme. *Courtesy Howard Cook.*

An F4U Corsair in "Ike" Kepfords markings flying at an airshow in England prior to a change of color scheme. *Courtesy Howard Cook.*

An F4U Corsair in "Ike" Kepford's markings flying at an airshow in England prior to a change of color scheme. *Courtesy Howard Cook.*

An F4U Corsair "Big Hog" that was operated by the Old Flying Machine Company in England in the colors of Tom Blackburn before it was repainted. *Courtesy Howard Cook.*

Fighting 17 reunion 1983, Oceana. Back Row L – R."Pete" Peterson, "Matty" Matthews, Jack Chasnoff, Ward Cole, "Country" Landreth, Lou Antonnaci, Lyle Herrmann, Tom Blackburn (in front of Herrmann), Dan Cunningham, "Beads" Popp, "Ike" Kepford, and "Butch" Davenport. Front Row L – R: "Bitz" Bitzegaio, Whit Wharton, "Andy" Jagger, Hal Jackson, "Hap" Bowers, and Mel Kurlander. *Courtesy U.S. Navy photo / the Chasnoff Family / "Andy" Jagger.*

Fighting 17 reunion 1983, Oceana. Back Row L – R: "Pete" Peterson, "Matty" Matthews, Jack Chasnoff, Ward Cole, "Country" Landreth, Lou Antonnaci, Lyle Herrmann, Tom Blackburn, "Beads" Popp, Dan Cunningham, "Ike" Kepford and "Butch" Davenport. Front Row L – R: "Bitz" Bitzegaio, Whit Wharton, "Andy" Jagger, Hal Jackson, "Hap" Bowers and Mel Kurlander. *Courtesy U.S. Navy photo / the Chasnoff Family / "Andy" Jagger.*

"Ike" Kepford and Bill Popp at 1983 reunion at Oceana. *Courtesy U.S. Navy photo / the Chasnoff Family / "Andy" Jagger.*

"Big Jim" Streig, "Red" Edmisten, "Hap" Harlow, "Country" Landreth and Mel Kurlander on May 28th at the 1934 reunion departing at the Hilton Hotel. *Courtesy Hap Harlow / Red Edmisten.*

"Hap" Harlow, "Red" Edmisten, and Tom Blackburn at the Fighting 17 reunion in San Diego on June 5, 1986. *Courtesy Hap Harlow.*

"Hap" Harlow, Roger Hedrick, Lennard Edmisten, and George Cantrell. *Courtesy Hap Harlow.*

Fighting 17 reunion in San Francisco in 1988. *Courtesy Hap Harlow.*

Another view of the Fighting 17 reunion in San Francisco in 1988. *Courtesy the Chasnoff Family.*

Fighting 17 reunion in 1993 in Denton, Texas. *Courtesy the Chasnoff Family.*

Fighting 17 were honoured by the E.A.A. at Oshkosh in 1994. *Courtesy Hal and Barbara Jackson.*

Oshkosh reunion 1994. Jack Chasnoff, Dan Cunningham, Roger Hedrick, "Andy" Jagger and Ward Cole. *Courtesy Lee Cook.*

George Mauhar, Lee Cook (Author) and Lennard Edmisten at the San Diego reunion in 1997. *Courtesy Hal and Barbara Jackson.*

San Diego Reunion 1997. Back row L-R: Hal Jackson, Lennard Edmisten, George Mauhar, Jack Chasnoff, Ray Ferguson, "Country" Landreth and Mel Kurlander. Front Row L-R: Wally Schub, Lee Cook (Author), and Bill Popp. *Courtesy Hal and Barbara Jackson.*

Aviation Artist Nicholas Trudgian and Lee Cook at the Imperial War Museum, Duxford, England, in 1998. *Courtesy Howard Cook.*

16

The Skull and Crossbones Lives On

After World War II the Skull and Crossbones insignia continued in various squadrons, such as VF-5B, VF-61, VA-86, VF-84, and VF-103.

The current Skull and Crossbones Squadron are VFA-103.

The Skull and Crossbones lives on in its 21st Century incarnation VFA - 103 Jolly Rogers flying the FA - 1&F Super Hornet. A selection of photos of VFA-103 taken in the North Arabian Sea in the summer of 2009 while the squadron was aboard the U.S.S. *Dwight D. Eisenhower* (CVN-69). *Courtesy U.S. Navy Photo / Brian M Garrison Commanding Officer Fighting 103.*

201

VFA-103
NAVY
200

200

200
AG
E
200
NAVY
166620

205
VFA-103
205
AG
NAVY

203
VFA-103

203
AG
NAVY

AG
VFA-103
200

211
AG
VFA-103
211

206
VFA-103
206

205
VFA-103
205
NAVY

VFA-103
211

201

204
AG
E
VFA-103
204

211
AG
E
VFA-103
211

Appendix

Appendix A: Fighting 17 Victory Credits (Olynyk)

110143	0745-0800	2 Zeke	Lt. Cdr. John Thomas Blackburn	6-30S, 155-10E
110143	0745-0800	2 Zeke dam.	Lt. Cdr. John Thomas Blackburn	6-30S, 155-10E
110143	0745-0800	Zeke	Lt. Shelton Ray Beacham	6-30S, 155-10E
110143	0745-0800	Zeke	Ens. Frederick James Streig (0.5) Lt. (jg) Tom Killefer (0.5)	6-30S, 155-10E
110143	0745-0800	Zeke	Lt. (jg) Tom Killefer	6-30S, 155-10E
110143	0745-0800	Zeke dam.	Lt. Thaddeus Richard Bell	6-30S, 155-10E
110143	0745-0800	Val dam.	Lt. (jg) Douglas H. C. Gutenkunst	6-30S, 155-10E
110143	1330	Zeke	Lt. Cdr. Roger Richards Hedrick	6-30S, 155-10E
110143	1330	Zeke dam.	Lt. Clement Dexter Gile (0.5) Lt. (jg) Daniel Gerald Cunningham (0.5)	6-30S, 155-10E
110143	1330	Val dam.	Lt. (jg) Mills Schanuel	6-30S, 155-10E
110643	1040	Betty	Lt. Merl William Davenport (0.25) Lt. Walter John Schub (0.25) Lt. (jg) Robert Hal Jackson (0.25) Ens. Robert Roy Hogan (0.25)	15 m SW of Cape Moltke, Bougainville
110843	0710	Ruth	Lt. Cdr. John Thomas Blackburn Lt. Harry Andrew March, Jr. (0.0)	Buka Airfield
110843	1100	3 Zeke dam.	Lt. Cdr. Roger Richards Hedrick	W coast of Bougainville
110843	1100	Zeke	Lt. (jg) Mills Schanuel	W coast of Bougainville
110843	1100	Hamp	Lt. (jg) Robert Sidney Anderson	W coast of Bougainville
110843	1100	Zeke dam.	Lt. (jg) Robert Sidney Anderson	W coast of Bougainville
110843	1100	Zeke	Lt. (jg) Daniel Gerald Cunningham	W coast of Bougainville
110843	1100	Zeke dam.	Lt. (jg) Daniel Gerald Cunningham (0.0) Lt. (jg) Paul Cordray	W coast of Bougainville
111143	1315-1415	Tony	Lt. Cdr. John Thomas Blackburn	Approx. 6-30S, 153-30E
111143	1315-1415	Zeke dam.	Lt. Cdr. John Thomas Blackburn	Approx. 6-30S, 153-30E
111143	1315-1415	Zeke	Lt. Cdr. Roger Richards Hedrick	Approx. 6-30S, 153-30E
111143	1315-1415	Zeke	Lt. (jg) Robert Hal Jackson	Approx. 6-30S, 153-30E
111143	1315-1415	Zeke dam.	Lt. (jg) Paul Cordray	Approx. 6-30S, 153-30E
111143	1315-1415	Tony	Ens. Frederick James Streig	Approx. 6-30S, 153-30E
111143	1315-1415	Zeke	Ens. Frederick James Streig	Approx. 6-30S, 153-30E
111143	1315-1415	Zeke dam.	Ens. Frederick James Streig	Approx. 6-30S, 153-30E
111143	1315-1415	Hamp dam.	Ens. Frederick James Streig	Approx. 6-30S, 153-30E
111143	1315-1415	Kate	Lt. Clement Dexter Gile	Approx. 6-30S, 153-30E
111143	1315-1415	Zeke dam.	Lt. (jg) Jack M. Chasnoff (0.5) Lt. (jg) Robert Sidney Anderson (0.5)	Approx. 6-30S, 153-30E
111143	1315-1415	Kate	Lt. John Milton Kleinman	Approx. 6-30S, 153-30E
111143	1315-1415	Kate dam.	Lt. John Milton Kleinman	Approx. 6-30S, 153-30E
111143	1315-1415	Val	Lt. Thaddeus Richard Bell	Approx. 6-30S, 153-30E
111143	1315-1415	Val	Lt. Thaddeus Richard Bell	Approx. 6-30S, 153-30E
111143	1315-1415	3 Val	Ens. Ira Cassius Kepford	Approx. 6-30S, 153-30E
111143	1315-1415	Kate	Ens. Ira Cassius Kepford	Approx. 6-30S, 153-30E
111143	1315-1415	Val dam.	Ens. Ira Cassius Kepford	Approx. 6-30S, 153-30E
111143	1315-1415	Zeke	Ens. Robert Roy Hogan	Approx. 6-30S, 153-30E
111143	1315-1415	Zeke	Ens. Bradford Warren Baker	Approx. 6-30S, 153-30E
111143	1315-1415	Kate	Ens. Robert Hugh Hill	Approx. 6-30S, 153-30E

111143	1315-1415	Kate	Lt. (jg) Howard McClain Burriss	Approx. 6-30S, 153-30E
111143	1400	0.5 Kate	Lt. (jg) Howard McClain Burriss (0.5)	Approx. 6-30S, 153-30E (VF-33: 154-15E)
111143	1400	Betty	Lt. (jg) Howard McClain Burriss	Approx. 6-30S, 153-30E
111743	0800	Kate	Lt. (jg) Paul Cordray	Empress Augusta Bay
111743	0800-0815	Zeke	Lt. Cdr. Roger Richards Hedrick	Empress Augusta Bay
111743	0800-0815	2 Zeke	Lt. (jg) Jack M. Chasnoff	Empress Augusta Bay
111743	0800-0815	Zeke	Lt. (jg) Mills Schanuel	Empress Augusta Bay
111743	0800-0815	3 Zeke	Lt. Clement Dexter Gile	Empress Augusta Bay
111743	0815	2 Tony	Lt. (jg) Paul Cordray	over Empress Augusta Bay
112143	0535	2 Zeke	Lt. Merl William Davenport	Empress Augusta Bay
112143	0535	Zeke	Lt. Shelton Ray Beacham	Empress Augusta Bay
112143	0535	2 Zeke	Lt. (jg) Doris Clyde Freeman	Empress Augusta Bay
112143	0535	Zeke	Ens. Frank Andrew Jagger	Empress Augusta Bay
012644	1215-1230	Zeke	Lt. Cdr. John Thomas Blackburn	Rabaul Area
012644	1215-1230	2 Zeke	Lt. (jg) Douglas H. C. Gutenkunst	Rabaul Area
012644	1215-1230	Zeke	Lt. Cdr. Roger Richards Hedrick	Rabaul Area
012644	1215-1230	Zeke	Lt. (jg) James Miller	Rabaul Area
012644	1215-1230	Zeke	Lt. (jg) Paul Cordray	Rabaul Area
012644	1215-1230	Zeke dam.	Lt. (jg) Paul Cordray	Rabaul Area
012644	1215-1230	Zeke	Lt. (jg) Tom Killefer	Rabaul Area
012644	1215-1230	Zeke	Lt. Clement Dexter Gile	Rabaul Area
012644	1215-1230	Zeke prob.	Lt. (jg) William Lee Landreth (0.5)	Rabaul Area
			Ens. Clyde Howard Dunn (0.5)	
012744	0900	2 Zeke	Lt. (jg) Daniel Gerald Cunningham	Rabaul Area
012744	0900	2 Zeke	Lt. (jg) Frederick James Streig	Rabaul Area
012744	0900	Zeke	Lt. (jg) Frederick James Streig (0.5)	Rabaul Area
			Lt. (jg) Robert Mims (0.5)	
012744	0900	Zeke	Lt. (jg) Robert Mims	Rabaul Area
012744	0900	u/i A/C	Lt. (jg) Robert Mims	Rabaul Area
012744	0900	Zeke	Lt. Oscar Ivan Chenoweth, Jr.	Rabaul Area
012744	0900	Zeke	Lt. (jg) Harold James Bitzegaio	Rabaul Area
012744	0900	2 Hamp prob.	Lt. (jg) Harold James Bitzegaio	Rabaul Area
012744	0900	Zeke	Lt. (jg) Carl Wilson Gilbert	Rabaul Area
012744	0900	Zeke	Lt. (jg) Howard McClain Burriss	Rabaul Area
012744	0900	Zeke	Lt. (jg) Earl May	Rabaul Area
012744	0900	2 Zeke	Lt. (jg) Ira Cassius Kepford	Rabaul Area
012744	0900	Zeke prob.	Lt. (jg) Ira Cassius Kepford	Rabaul Area
012744	0900	Zeke	Ens. Donald Roy McQueen	Rabaul Area
012744	0900	Zeke prob.	Lt. Walter John Schub	Rabaul Area
012744	0900	Zeke	Ens. Frank Andrew Jagger	Rabaul Area
012844	0900	2 Zeke	Lt. Harry Andrew March, Jr.	over Tobera A/F
012844	0900	0.5 Zeke	Lt. (jg) Robert Mims (0.5)	over Tobera A/F
012844	0900	Zeke prob.	Lt. (jg) Robert Mims	over Tobera A/F
012844	0900	2 Zeke	Lt. (jg) Douglas H. C. Gutenkunst	over Tobera A/F
012844	0900	2 Zeke	Ens. Percy Eugene Divenney	over Tobera A/F
012844	0900	2 Zeke	Lt. (jg) Tom Killefer	over Tobera A/F
012844	0900	Zeke	Ens. William Preston Meek	over Tobera A/F
012844	0900	Zeke	Lt. Cdr. Roger Richards Hedrick	over Tobera A/F
012844	0900	2 Zeke	Lt. (jg) Paul Cordray	over Tobera A/F
012844	0900	Zeke prob.	Lt. (jg) James Miller	over Tobera A/F
012844	0900	Zeke	Lt. (jg) James Miller	over Tobera A/F
012844	0900	Zeke	Lt. (jg) Robert Hal Jackson	over Tobera A/F
012844	0900	Zeke prob.	Ens. John Orrin Ellsworth	over Tobera A/F
012844	0900	Zeke prob.	Lt. (jg) Carl Wilson Gilbert	over Tobera A/F

012944	1105-1115	4 Zeke	Lt. (jg) Ira Cassius Kepford	over Cape Gazelle area
012944	1105-1115	4 Zeke	Lt. (jg) Howard McClain Burriss	over Cape Gazelle area
012944	1105-1115	Zeke	Lt. Clement Dexter Gile	over Cape Gazelle area
012944	1105-1115	Zeke	Lt. (jg) Earl May	over Cape Gazelle area
012944	1105-1115	Zeke prob.	Ens. John Malcolm Smith	over Cape Gazelle area
012944	1105-1115	Zeke prob.	Lt. Oscar Ivan Chenoweth, Jr.	over Cape Gazelle area
012944	1105-1115	Zeke prob.	Ens. James Cass Dixon	over Cape Gazelle area
013044	1120	Zeke	Lt. Cdr. Roger Richards Hedrick	over Rabaul area
013044	1120	Zeke	Ens. John Orrin Ellsworth	over Rabaul area
013044	1120	Zeke prob.	Lt. (jg) James Miller	over Rabaul area
013044	1120	Zeke prob.	Ens. John Malcolm Smith	over Rabaul area
013044	1120	Zeke prob.	Ens. George M. Keller, Jr.	over Rabaul area
013044	1120	Zeke prob.	Lt. (jg) G. F. Bowers	over Rabaul area
013044	1740	Tony	Lt. (jg) Ira Cassius Kepford	over Simpson Harbor
013044	1740	Zeke	Lt. (jg) Ira Cassius Kepford	over Simpson Harbor
013044	1740	2 Zeke	Lt. Merl William Davenport	over Simpson Harbor
013044	1740	Zeke	Lt. (jg) Mills Schanuel	over Simpson Harbor
013044	1740	2 Zeke	Lt. Oscar Ivan Chenoweth, Jr.	over Simpson Harbor
013044	1740	Zeke	Lt. Oscar Ivan Chenoweth, Jr. (0.5) Ens. James Cass Dixon (0.5)	over Simpson Harbor
013044	1740	2 Zeke	Lt. Cdr. John Thomas Blackburn	over Simpson Harbor
013044	1740	3 Zeke prob.	Lt. Cdr. John Thomas Blackburn	over Simpson Harbor
020344	1350	Zeke	Lt. (jg) Ira Cassius Kepford	Cape Tawui, New Britain
020344	1350	Zeke prob.	Lt. Oscar Ivan Chenoweth, Jr.	Cape Tawui, New Britain
020444	1130	Zeke	Lt. (jg) Earl May (0.0) Ens. Wilbert Peter Popp	over Tobera area
020544	1100-1105	Zeke	Lt. Merl William Davenport	over Lakunai off Cape Gazelle
020544	1100-1105	Zeke	Lt. Walter John Schub	over Lakunai off Cape Gazelle
020544	1100-1105	Zeke	Lt. (jg) William Lee Landreth	over Lakunai off Cape Gazelle
020644	1105	Tojo	Lt. (jg) Robert Mims	Rabaul area
020644	1115-1145	Zeke	Lt. Walter John Schub	Rabaul area
020644	1115-1145	Hamp	Lt. (jg) Harold James Bitzegaio	Rabaul area
020644	1115-1145	3 Zeke	Lt. Cdr. John Thomas Blackburn	Rabaul area
020644	1115-1145	Hamp	Lt. Cdr. John Thomas Blackburn	Rabaul area
020644	1115-1145	2 Zeke prob.	Lt. Cdr. John Thomas Blackburn	Rabaul area
020644	1115-1145	2 Zeke	Lt. (jg) Robert Mims	Rabaul area
020644	1115-1145	2 Zeke prob.	Lt. (jg) Robert Mims	Rabaul area
020744	1030-1100	Zeke	Lt. (jg) William Lee Landreth	Rabaul area
020744	1030-1100	Hamp	Lt. (jg) William Lee Landreth	Rabaul area
020744	1030-1100	Zeke	Lt. (jg) Earle Carpenter Peterson, Jr.	Rabaul area
020744	1030-1100	Zeke dam.	Ens. Clyde Howard Dunn	Rabaul area
020744	1030-1100	2 Zeke prob.	Ens. Clyde Howard Dunn	Rabaul area
020744	1030-1100	Zeke prob.	Lt. (jg) Doris Clyde Freeman	Rabaul area
020744	1030-1100	Hamp prob.	Lt. (jg) Doris Clyde Freeman	Rabaul area
020944	1230	Zeke	Lt. Oscar Ivan Chenoweth, Jr.	Vunakanau area
020944	1230	Zeke	Lt. (jg) Earl May	Vunakanau area
020944	1230	Hamp dam.	Lt. (jg) Mills Schanuel	Vunakanau area
021044	1235	Zeke prob.	Lt. (jg) Harold James Bitzegaio (0.5) Ens. Frank Andrew Jagger (0.5)	Vunakanau A/F
021044	1245	Zeke	Lt. Merl William Davenport	Tobera area
021044	1245	Zeke	Ens. John Orrin Ellsworth	Tobera area
021344	1050	Zeke dam.	Lt. (jg) Daniel Gerald Cunningham	over Vunakanau
021744	0900	Zeke	Ens. Clyde Howard Dunn	over Cape Gazelle
021744	0900	Zeke	Ens. John Malcolm Smith	over Cape Gazelle

021744	0900	Zeke dam.	Ens. John Malcolm Smith	over Cape Gazelle
021744	0900	Oscar prob.	Ens. John Malcolm Smith	over Cape Gazelle
021844	1050-1110	3 Zeke	Lt. Cdr. Roger Richards Hedrick	over Cape Gazelle
021844	1050-1110	Zeke	Lt. Clement Dexter Gile	over Cape Gazelle
021844	1050-1110	2 Zeke	Lt. (jg) Earl May	over Cape Gazelle
021844	1050-1110	Zeke	Ens. John Malcolm Smith	over Cape Gazelle
021844	1050-1110	Zeke prob.	Lt. (jg) Paul Cordray	over Cape Gazelle
021944	0945	Rufe	Lt. (jg) Ira Cassius Kepford	Cape Siar, New Ireland
021944	0945	2 Zeke	Lt. (jg) Ira Cassius Kepford	Cape Siar, New Ireland
021944	1010-1025	4 Zeke	Lt. (jg) Daniel Gerald Cunningham	Rabaul area
021944	1010-1025	2 Zeke	Lt. Oscar Ivan Chenoweth, Jr.	Rabaul area
021944	1010-1025	Tojo	Lt. Oscar Ivan Chenoweth, Jr.	Rabaul area
021944	1010-1025	3 Zeke	Lt. (jg) Earl May	Rabaul area
021944	1010-1025	Zeke	Ens. Wilbert Peter Popp	Rabaul area
021944	1010-1025	Tojo	Ens. John Malcolm Smith	Rabaul area
021944	1010-1025	Zeke	Lt. Clement Dexter Gile	Rabaul area

	Rank	Name	Confirmed	Probable	Damaged
1	Lt. (jg)	Ira C. Kepford	16	1	1
2	Lt. Cdr.	John T. Blackburn	11	5	3
3	Lt. Cdr.	Roger R. Hedrick	9		3
4	Lt.	Oscar I. Chenoweth, Jr.	8.5 (1)	2	
5	Lt.	Clement D. Gile	8		0.5
6	Lt. (jg)	Earl May, Jr.	8		
7	Lt. (jg)	Howard M. Burriss	7.5		
8	Lt. (jg)	Daniel G. Cunningham	7		1.5
9	Lt.	Merl W. Davenport	6.25		
10	Lt. (jg)	Paul Cordray	6	1	3
11	Lt. (jg)	Robert Mims	6	3	
12	Lt. (jg)	Frederick J. Streig	5.5		2
13	Lt.	Harry A. March, Jr.	5 (2)		
14	Lt. (jg)	Tom Killefer	4		
15	Lt. (jg)	Doug H. C. Gutenkunst	4		1
16	Lt.	James A. Halford, Jr.	(3.5)		
17	Lt. (jg)	William L. Landreth	3	0.5	
18	Lt. (jg)	Mills Schanuel	3		2
19	Lt. (jg)	John M. Smith	3	3	1
20	Lt. (jg)	Robert H. Jackson	2.25		
21	Lt.	Walter J. Schub	2.25	1	
22	Lt.	Shelton R. Beacham	2		
23	Lt.	Thaddeus R. Bell	2		1
24	Lt. (jg)	Harold J. Bitzegaio	2	2.5	
25	Lt. (jg)	Jack M. Chasnoff	2		0.5
26	Ens.	Percy E. Divenney	2		
27	Ens.	John O. Ellsworth	2	1	
28	Lt. (jg)	Doris C. Freeman	2	2	
29	Ens.	Frank A. Jagger	2	0.5	
30	Lt.	John M. Kleinman	2 (1)	(1)	1
31	Lt. (jg)	James Miller	2	2	
32	Ens.	Wilbert P. Popp	2		
33	Ens.	Robert R. Hogan	1.25		
34	Lt. (jg)	Robert S. Anderson	1		1.5
35	Ens.	Bradford W. Baker	1		
36	Ens.	Clyde H. Dunn	1	2.5	1
37	Lt. (jg)	Carl W. Gilbert	1	1	

38	Ens.	Robert H. Hill	1		
39	Lt.	Donald A. Innis	(1)		
40	Ens.	Donald R. McQueen	1		
41	Ens.	William P. Meek	1		
42	Lt. (jg)	Earle C. Peterson, Jr.	1		
43	Ens.	James C. Dixon	0.5	1	
44	Lt. (jg)	George F. Bowers		1	
45	Ens.	George M. Keller, Jr.		1	
Totals			152	31	23

Notes

In brackets is the score of pilots' previous kills before reporting to Fighting 17, not included in totals.

Official lists count 152 confirmed victory credits, not 154 as stated in the war diary.

An interesting example of a conflict between citations and squadron records.

Citations for awards to Blackburn and March appear to give them both credit for the Ruth shot down on November 8, 1943. The VF-17 war diary gives full credit to Blackburn, while the aircraft action report would appear to share the credit. March was therefore given an assist in the victory, as being the accreditation closest to the contemporary reports. The citation for March's first Air Medal gives him credit for one bomber on this date. In the above totals this credit is counted as one for Blackburn.

Streig had two shared victories: one with Killefer and one with Mims. The aircraft action report indicates the victory with Killefer is shared, while the war diary says that Streig got full credit.

The war diary and official lists have conflicting information on November 8, 1943.

The official lists and the aircraft action reports have the same information. However, the war diary has Anderson given full credit for a Zeke instead of a damaged. Cordray was also given full credit for a Zeke on this date. Marine Air Intelligence reports on this date have found their way into the VF-17 war diary with conflicting information, with two more full victory credits added to the total.

Appendix B:
Fighting Squadron 17 War Diary

OCTOBER

Enemy airplanes destroyed	None.
Enemy ships destroyed	2 AK 5 Landing barges

Note: As ships were destroyed as the result of strafing by entire flights, pilot's names are not given.

Losses	
Pilots	None
Airplanes	None

NOVEMBER

Enemy surface vessels destroyed	2 AK, 11 Barges.

Note: As ships were destroyed as the result of strafing by entire flights, pilots' names are not given.

Enemy aircraft destroyed in the air:	47 28 Zekes 4 Tonys 1 Hamp 5 Vals 6 Kates 2 Bettys 1 Ruth

Individual scores:	
Lt. Cdr. J. T. Blackburn	2 Zekes, 1 Ruth, 1 Tony.
Lt. Cdr. R. R. Hedrick	3 Zekes.
Lt. S. R. Beacham	2 Zekes.
Lt. T. R. Bell	2 Vals.
Lt. M. W. Davenport	2 Zekes.
Lt. C. D. Gile	3 Zekes, 1 Kate.
Lt. J. M. Kleinman	1 Kate.
Lt. (jg) R. S. Anderson	1 Zeke, 1 Hamp.
Lt. (jg) H. M. Burriss	1 Zeke, 1 Betty.
Lt. (jg) J. M. Chasnoff	2 Zekes.
Lt. (jg) P. Cordray	1 Zeke, 1 Kate, 2 Tonys.
Lt. (jg) D. G. Cunningham	1 Zeke.
Lt. (jg) D. C. Freeman	2 Zekes.
Lt. (jg) R. H. Jackson	1 Zeke.
Lt. (jg) T. Killefer	1 Zeke.
Lt. (jg) M. Schanuel	2 Zekes.
Ens. B. W. Baker	1 Kate.
Ens. R. H. Hill	1 Kate.
Ens. R. R. Hogan	1 Zeke, 1 Betty.
Ens. F. A. Jagger	1 Zeke.
Ens. I. C. Kepford	1 Kate, 3 Vals.
Ens. F. J. Streig	2 Zekes, 1 Tony.

Enemy aircraft destroyed on the ground: 2

Lt. L. D. Cooke Ens. W. P. Popp	)) 1 Betty.
Ens. J. O. Ellsworth	1 Betty.
Own losses:	3 Pilots:
Lt. (jg) J. H. Keith	by enemy A/A fire.
Ens. B. W. Baker	by enemy aircraft.
Lt. C. A. Pillsbury	probably by enemy A/A fire.

7 Planes:

2 shot down by enemy aircraft.

3 shot down by enemy A/A fire.

2 lost as the result of water landings due to gas shortage after prolonged cover and air combat over Task Force 50.3 on November 11, 1943.

DECEMBER

No enemy planes or surface craft were destroyed during the month of December.

One F4U-1 was lost after an accident during night flying operations.

JANUARY

Surface vessels destroyed:	None.
Enemy aircraft destroyed in the air:	60½ 58½ Zekes 1 Tony 1 unidentified aircraft

Individual scores:	
Lt. Cdr. J. T. Blackburn	3 Zekes
Lt. Cdr. R. R. Hedrick	3 Zekes
Lt. O. I. Chenoweth	3 Zekes

Lt. M. W. Davenport	2 Zekes
Lt. C. D. Gile	2 Zekes
Lt. H. A. March	2 Zekes
Lt. (jg) T. Killefer	3 Zekes
Lt. (jg) H. J. Bitzegaio	1 Zeke
Lt. (jg) R. H. Jackson	1 Zeke
Lt. (jg) J. Miller	2 Zekes
Lt. (jg) P. Cordray	3 Zekes
Lt. (jg) D. G. Cunningham	2 Zekes
Lt. (jg) C. W. Gilbert	1 Zeke
Lt. (jg) H. M. Burriss	5 Zekes
Lt. (jg) D. H. C. Gutenkunst	4 Zekes
Lt. (jg) R. Mims	2 Zekes, 1 unidentified aircraft
Lt. (jg) E. May	2 Zekes
Lt. (jg) M. Schanuel	1 Zeke
Lt. (jg) I. C. Kepford	7 Zekes, 1 Tony
Lt. (jg) F. J. Streig	2½ Zekes
Ens. F. A. Jagger	1 Zeke
Ens. J. O. Ellsworth	1 Zeke
Ens. D. R. McQueen	1 Zeke
Ens. P. E. Divenney	2 Zekes
Ens. J. C. Dixon	1 Zeke
Ens. W. P. Meek	1 Zeke

Losses: 5 pilots missing in action.

Lt. T. R. Bell	shot down by enemy aircraft
Lt. (jg) R. R. Hogan	shot down by enemy aircraft
Lt. (jg) J. W. Farley	shot down by enemy aircraft
Lt. (jg) T. F. Kropf	shot down by enemy aircraft
Lt. (jg) H. M. Burriss	shot down by enemy aircraft

1 pilot operational loss.

Lt. (jg) D. H. C. Gutenkunst killed in mid - air collision.

13 planes

5 shot down by enemy aircraft
1 destroyed in mid - air collision
3 destroyed in operational crash landings
4 destroyed in crash landings after serious damage had been inflicted by enemy aircraft

FEBRUARY

Surface vessels destroyed: 1 AK
1 Barge

Enemy aircraft destroyed in the air: 46
40 Zekes
3 Hamps
2 Tojos
1 Rufe

Individual score:

Lt. Cdr. J. T. Blackburn	3 Zekes, 1 Hamp
Lt. Cdr. R. R. Hedrick	3 Zekes
Lt. O. I. Chenoweth	3 Zekes, 1 Tojo
Lt. M. W. Davenport	2 Zekes
Lt. C. D. Gile	2 Zekes
Lt. W. J. Schub	2 Zekes
Lt. (jg) E. C. Peterson	1 Zeke
Lt. (jg) H. J. Bitzegaio	1 Hamp
Lt. (jg) D. G. Cunningham	4 Zekes
Lt. (jg) W. L. Landreth	2 Zekes, 1 Hamp
Lt. (jg) E. May	6 Zekes
Lt. (jg) R. Mims	2 Zekes, 1 Tojo
Lt. (jg) I. C. Kepford	3 Zekes, 1 Rufe
Ens. J. O. Ellsworth	1 Zeke
Ens. C. H. Dunn	1 Zeke
Ens. W. P. Popp	2 Zekes
Ens. J. M. Smith	3 Zekes

Losses:

Lt. (jg) J. Miller	shot down by enemy A/A fire
Lt. (jg) D. T. Malone	shot down by enemy aircraft
Ens. P. E. Divenney	shot down by enemy aircraft
Ens. C. H. Dunn	shot down by enemy aircraft

4 planes

1 shot down by enemy A/A fire
3 shot down by enemy aircraft

MARCH

Surface vessels destroyed: 2 Barges

Enemy aircraft destroyed: None

Losses: None

Note:
The VF-17 War Diary gives two more aircraft credited shot down than the official lists (see notes after VF-17 victory credits).

Combat Statistics
(From War Diary)

I. First Tour: based at Ondongo, New Georgia, from October through December 1, 1943.

1. Combat hours flown: 4,985.5
2. Combat sorties flown: 1,570
3. Average hours flown by regularly flying pilots: 132
4. Damage inflicted on enemy:
   a. Planes destroyed in the air: 47½
   b. Planes destroyed on the ground: 2
   c. AKs sunk: 4
   d. Barges sunk: 14
5. Own losses:
   a. Planes lost: 8

I. 2 shot down by enemy aircraft
II. 3 shot down by enemy anti-aircraft fire
III. 2 lost in water landings as the result of gas shortage after prolonged cover and air combat over Task Force 50.3 on 11 November, 1943.
IV. 1 lost in operational crash landing
   b. Pilots lost: 3
I. 1 shot down by enemy aircraft
II. 2 shot down by enemy anti - aircraft fire

II. Second Tour: based at Piva Yoke, Bougainville, B. S. I. from January through March 4, 1944.

1. Combat hours flown: 3,386.9
2. Combat sorties flown: 1099*
   a. Missions to Rabaul: 671
   b. Dumbo escorts: 50
   c. Combat air patrols: 44
   d. Scouting: 35
   e. Task Force covers: 60
   f. Green Island covers: 201
   g. Barge hunts: 38
3. Average hours flown by regularly flying pilots: 89.8**
4. Damage inflicted on the enemy:
   a. Planes destroyed in the air: 106½
   b. AKs sunk: 1
   c. Barges sunk: 3
5. Own losses:
   a. Planes lost: 16
I. Shot down by enemy aircraft: 8
II. Shot down by enemy anti - aircraft fire: 1
III. Crash or water landings due to injury in combat: 4
IV. Operational losses: 3
   b. Pilots lost: 10
I. Shot down by enemy aircraft: 8
II. Shot down by enemy anti - aircraft fire: 1
III. Lost in operational crash: 1

* This figure includes only missions actually completed. If a pilot was forced to return early his flight was not counted as a combat sortie.
** This figure represents the average time flown by 30 pilots. It does not include the time of missing pilots, or those who were grounded for more than a week because of injuries, or of those pilots who arrived after February 10, 1944.

III. Totals for two tours of combat duty (76 days)

1. Combat hours flown: 8,372.4
2. Combat sorties flown: 2,669
3. Average hours flown by regularly flying pilots:
a. First tour: 132.0
b. Second tour 89.8
4. Damage inflicted on the enemy:
a. Planes destroyed in the air: 154
b. Planes destroyed on the ground: 2
c. AKs sunk: 5
d. Barges sunk: 17
5. Own losses:
a. Planes: 24
I. Combat losses: 20
II. Operational losses: 4
b. Pilots: 13
I. Combat losses: 12
II. Operational losses: 1

IV. Individual records of pilots attached to Fighting Squadron Seventeen on February 21, 1944:

SECOND TOUR -- 4 weeks

	Previous Combat Hours	Combat Days Flown	Missions Sorties Completed	Combat to Rabaul	Planes Hours Flown	Shot Down
Lt. Cdr. J. T. Blackburn	168.3	21	26	17	81.8	11
Lt. Cdr. R. R. Hedrick	127.0	13	14	11	49.7	9
Lt. S. R. Beacham	123.0	7	9	7	27.7	2
Lt. O. I. Chenoweth	120.0	16	21	12	72.3	8
Lt. M. W. Davenport	163.0	16	18	12	57.4	6
Lt. C. D. Gile	152.0	16	19	13	59.8	8
Lt. H. A. March, Jr.	322.0	12	15	11	45.3	5
Lt. W. J. Schub	122.9	15	17	12	52.9	2
Lt. (jg) T. Killefer	327.1	19	20	15	65.9	4
Lt. (jg) H. J. Bitzegaio		16	18	11	49.4	2
Lt. (jg) R. H. Jackson	130.0	11	13	10	47.8	2
Lt. (jg) G. F. Bowers	148.7	15	16	14	61.0	
Lt. (jg) P. Cordray	149.0	13	15	12	46.1	7
Lt. (jg) D. G. Cunningham	148.0	16	19	12	64.6	7
Lt. (jg) D. C. Freeman	132.0	18	21	14	68.8	2
Lt. (jg) C. W. Gilbert	123.0	13	15	9	41.9	1
Lt. (jg) W. L. Landreth	126.9	14	17	11	49.3	3
Lt. (jg) E. May	143.9	18	21	16	75.4	8
Lt. (jg) R. Mims		17	20	13	68.8	6
Lt. (jg) M. Schanuel	130.0	10	12	9	38.9	3
Lt. (jg) I. C. Kepford	158.0	10	11	10	36.9	16
Lt. (jg) F. J. Streig	108.0	14	18	8	48.9	5½
Ens. R. H. Hill	123.0	12	14	9	43.8	1
Ens. F. A. Jagger	63.8	14	16	12	46.1	2
Ens. W. C. Wharton, Jr.	110.0	17	19	11	49.7	
Ens. J. O. Ellsworth	138.9	16	19	12	66.0	2
Ens. W. P. Meek	112.3	21	22	13	64.7	1
Ens. D. R. McQueen		10	12	6	39.2	1
Ens. W. P. Popp	47.8	14	18	12	58.4	2
Ens. J. M. Smith		18	20	15	63.0	3
Ens. M. W. Cole		11	15	9	48.0	
Ens. J. C. Dixon		14	19	11	65.3	1
Ens. G. M. Keller, Jr.		15	18	10	52.5	
Ens. H. B. Richardson, Jr.		16	17	11	56.1	
Ens. L. A. Fitzgerald		12	15	8	57.3	
Ens. M. M. Kurlander	143.5	17	20	11	60.5	
Ens. R. M. Einar		5	5	4	15.4	
Ens. J. E. Diteman		5	5	1	16.7	
Ens. H. Matthews		6	10	4	36.2	

Appendix C: Fighting 17 Tactical Organization

June 1943

A Flight		B Flight		C Flight		D Flight	
1 Blackburn	(Tom)	9 Kleinman	(Johnnie)	17 Hedrick	(Rog)	25 Halford	(Lucky)
2 Gutenkunst	(Gute)	10 Gilbert	(Gil)	18 Schanuel	(Mills)	26 Henderson	(Tuffy)
3 Streig	(Jim)	11 Bowers	(Hap)	19 Ferguson	(Fergy)	27 Keith	(John)
4 Mims	(Bobby)	12 Hill	(Windy)	20 Baker	(Brad)	28 Landreth	(Country)
5 Bell	(Jug)	13 Pillsbury	(Chuck)	21 Gile	(Tim)	29 Cooke	(Lem)
6 May	(Earl)	14 Schub	(Wally)	22 Cunningham	(Dan)	30 Burriss	(Teeth)
7 Beacham	(Beach)	15 Hogan	(Bob)	23 Cordray	(Paul)	31 Davenport	(Butch)
8 Anderson	(Andy)	16 Jackson	(Hal)	24 Freeman	(Chico)	32 Kepford	(Ike)

Relief Flight Leaders:
1. Pillsbury
2. Bell
3. Cooke

Relief Division Leaders
In order of preference:
1. Davenport
2. Streig
3. Beacham
4. Ferguson

Relief Section Leaders
In order of preference:
1. Anderson
2. Henderson
3. Jackson
4. Kepford

Relief Pilots - In order of preference:
1. Malone - #33 (Maloney)
2. Chasnoff - #34 (Jack)
3. Kurlander - #35 (Kurly)
4. Kropf - #36 (Kropf)
5. Wharton (Whit)
6. Kelley (Kelley)
7. Jagger (Jag)

Radio calls indicated in parentheses.

Shortly after this was issued Ray Ferguson had to leave Fighting 17 due to eye trouble and "Tuffy" Henderson was killed in a mid - air collision.

Bobby Mims is shown on this list but due to illness in October 1943, had to wait until December 1943 to join up with the squadron.

October 1943

A Flight		B Flight		C Flight		D Flight	
1 Blackburn	(Tom)	9 Kleinman	(Johnnie)	17 Hedrick	(Rog)	25 Halford	(Lucky)
2 Gutenkunst	(Gute)	10 Gilbert	(Gil)	18 Schanuel	(Mills)	26 Ellsworth	
3 Streig	(Jim)	11 Bowers	(Hap)	19 Anderson	(Andy)	27 Keith	(John)
4 Killefer		12 Hill	(Windy)	20 Chasnoff	(Jack)	28 Landreth	(Country)
5 Bell	(Jug)	13 Pillsbury	(Chuck)	21 Gile	(Tim)	29 Cooke	(Lem)
6 May	(Earl)	14 Schub	(Wally)	22 Cunningham	(Dan)	30 Burriss	(Teeth)
7 Beacham	(Beach)	15 Hogan	(Bob)	23 Cordray	(Paul)	31 Davenport	(Butch)
8 Malone	(Maloney)	16 Jackson	(Hal)	24 Baker	(Brad)	32 Kepford	(Ike)
						33 March	
						34 Freeman	
						35 Innis	
						36Wharton	

Relief Pilots:
Jagger
Kelley
Kropf
Kurlander
Meek
Popp
Dunn

Notes:
Lt. Cdr. Blackburn made the decision to assign the pilots their own aircraft, and in time aircraft associated with the pilots became as well known as they were. This was adhered to where possible, but combat damage and losses meant that pilots had to fly what was available in the two tours of combat.

Changes were also made when it was clear promotion to flight, division or section leader was warranted. Only Blackburn's division finished the tour the same as it started.

Beads Popp shared #31 with Ray Beacham on Fighting 17's first combat tour.

When Keith, Baker and Pillsbury were listed as missing in action and Anderson hospitalized this necessitated changes to the tactical situation.

As the first tour progressed Davenport was promoted to a division leader and flew #33. When Kepford was promoted to section leader he flew #7 and Wharton flew #32 his old aircraft.

March took over #29 from Lem Cooke as the first tour ended.

When Anderson was shot down Cordray #19 took his place, and Ellsworth #20 took Chasnoff's place.

Schub took over Kleinman's flight.

March took over Halford's flight.

Davenport took over a division.

Kepford moved up to section leader from #32 to #7.

Beacham went from #7 to #31.

Relief Pilots moved up to take the place of losses and changes.

January 1944

A Flight	B Flight	C Flight	D Flight
Blackburn	Davenport	Hedrick	Bell
Gutenkunst	Freeman	Ellsworth	Bitzegaio
Streig	Beacham	Cordray	May
Mims	Kurlander	Miller	Popp
Killefer	March	Gile	Kepford
Farley	Burriss	Smith	McQueen
Hogan	Jackson	Bowers	Cunningham
Jagger	Malone	Hill	Fitzgerald

Schub
Wharton
Landreth
Dunn

Relief Flight Leaders
Chenoweth, Schub, Gile, March.

Relief Division Leaders-
May, Cordray.

The tactical organization of Fighting 17 changed immediately after the losses of Hogan and Farley on the first mission on January 26, 1944.

Meek became Killefer's wingman after Farley was lost.

Schanuel and his wingman Kropf joined Kepford's division, and March had his own division with Gilbert his wingman. Cunningham and Fitzgerald joined Chenoweth's division and Keller flew as Bowers' wingman after Hill was hospitalized on January 26, 1944. Dixon flew as Chenoweth's wingman.

Schub's division stayed together through the second tour, although Dunn was lost flying with another division on February 17, 1944.

Innis became Squadron Duty Officer.

Relief Pilots from combat reports)	First Mission (According to pilot's listed
**Beeler	Rabaul January 27, 1944
**Cole	Rabaul February 4, 1944
**Divenney	Rabaul January 28, 1944
*Richardson	Rabaul January 27, 1944
***McQuiston	Rabaul January 31, 1944
****Peterson	Rabaul February 6, 1944
*****Diteman	Rabaul February 19, 1944
*****Einar	Rabaul February 17, 1944
*****Matthews	Rabaul February 17, 1944

*Reported January 3, 1944
**Reported January 11, 1944
***Reported January 18, 1944
****Reported January 22, 1944
*****Reported 13 February, 1944

Notes
For the first tour Blackburn had nine months to train the pilots and ensure they understood the tactics required for combat.

For the second tour Blackburn only had a few weeks to assess pilots and decide on tactical changes required for intense combat over Rabaul.

Changes had to be made in line with losses on this tour. Due to the amount of losses changes were made on a daily basis, which is why many of the pilots are pictured in different aircraft to the ones they started with. Due to the losses of aircraft and pilots, changes were necessary and the scheduling of missions became much more difficult due to the amount of aircraft still in flying condition. From the combat reports, war diary, official records, and interviews the above is, I believe, as accurate as I can determine. The aircraft numbers may have changed due to losses, but the flights and sections are as they started the second tour.

Appendix D:
Roster of the U.S.S. *Bunker Hill*

This Fighting 17 roster was from the U.S.S. *Bunker Hill* sailing from Norfolk, Virginia, on July 13, 1943, for the shakedown cruise to Trinidad.

Ens. R. S. Anderson
Ens. B. W. Baker
Lt. S. R. Beacham
Lt. (jg) T. R. Bell
Lt. Cdr. J. T. Blackburn
Ens. G. F. Bowers
Ens. H. M. Burriss
Ens. J. H. Cantrell*
Lt. L. D. Cooke
Ens. J. M. Chasnoff
Ens. P. Cordray
Ens. D. G. Cunningham
Lt. (jg) M. W. Davenport
Ens. J. O. Ellsworth
Ens. R. W. Ferguson*
Ens. D. C. Freeman
Ens. C. W. Gilbert, Jr.
Lt. (jg) C. D. Gile
Ens. D. H. C. Gutenkunst
Lt. (jg) J. A. Halford, Jr.
Ens. G. F. Hall
Lt. Cdr. R. R. Hedrick
Ens. F. D. Henderson, Jr.**
Lt. (jg) B. D. Henning
Ens. R. H. Hill, Jr.
Ens. R. R. Hogan
Lt. (jg) L. H. Howe*
Lt. (jg) R. H. Jackson
Ens. F. A. Jagger
Ens. J. H. Keith
Lt. (jg) N. D. Kellogg*
Ens. L. M. Kelley
Ens. I. C. Kepford
Ens. R. W. Kieffer*
Lt. (jg) J. M. Kleinman
Ens. T. F. Kropf
Ens. M. M. Kurlander
Ens. W. L. Landreth
Ens. W. E. Maher**
Ens. D. T. Malone
Ens. E. W. May, Jr.
Ens. R. Mims***
Ens. M. R. Novak*
Lt. P. A. Patton*
Lt. C. A. Pillsbury
Ens. M. Schanuel
Lt. (jg) W. J. Schub
Ens. F. J. Streig
Lt. E. B. Turner*
Ens. W. C. Wharton, Jr.

Notes:
* Officers detached from Fighting 17 prior to first combat in October 1943.
** Officers killed in flying accident.
*** Was detached due to illness shortly after the shakedown cruise and reported back to Fighting 17 on December 5, 1943.

Bibliography

Cook, Lee. *The Skull and Crossbones Squadron - VF-17 in World War II.* Schiffer Publishing Ltd. 1998.
Blackburn, Tom. *The Jolly Rogers.* New York: Orion, 1989.
Foster, Col. Frank, and Lawrence Borts. *U.S. Military Medals 1939 to 1994.* Fountain Inn, S.C.: M.O.A. Press, 1994.
Olynyk, Frank J. U.S.N. *Credits for the Destruction of Enemy Aircraft in Air-to-Air Combat in World War II.* Aurora, OH: Frank J. Olynyk, 1982.
Tillman, Barrett. *Corsair: The F4U in World War Two and Korea.* Annapolis: U.S. Naval Institute Press, 1979.
Popp, Wilbert P. "Beads." *The Survival of a WWII Navy Fighter Pilot.*
Kepchia, John B. *Missing in Action over Rabaul.* The Palace Printer, 1986.
Nason, Joseph G. *Horio, You Next Die!* Pacific Rim Press, Inc. 1987.
Sakaida, Henry. *The Siege of Rabaul.* Phalanx Publishing Co., Ltd. 1996.
Bowman, Martin. *Vought F4U Corsair.* The Crowood Press Ltd. 2002.
Dwiggins, Don. *The S. O. Bees.* The New American Library of Canada Ltd. 1963.

Documents
Archival Official Military Personnel Files:
Baker, Bell, Burriss, Dunn, Ellsworth, Freeman, Gutenkunst, Hogan, Innis, Keith, Kleinman, Kropf, Malone, March, Meek, Pillsbury, Babkirk, Divenney, Farley, Miller, Richardson, Travers, Ferguson, Henderson, Maher, Anderson and Kelley.

National Personnel Records Center, Military Personnel Records:

Blackburn, Bowers, Chasnoff, Cooke, Cordray, Cunningham, Davenport, Gilbert, Gile, Halford, Hedrick, Hill, Jackson, Jagger, Kelley, Kepford, Kurlander, Landreth. May, Schanuel, Schub, Streig, Wharton, Hall, Herrmann, Beeler, Bitzegaio, Chenoweth, Cole, Diteman, Dixon, Einar, Keller, Matthews, Mims, McQuiston, Peterson, C. L. Smith, J. M. Smith, Kellogg, Cantrell, Bennett and Novak.

VF-17 Action Reports and Combat Statistics:
VF-17 War Diary
VF-84 Squadron History and Action Reports
VF/VBF-10 Squadron History.

Recommended Reading
Abrams, Richard. *F4U Corsair at War*. New York: Scribners, 1981.
Green, William. *Famous Fighters of the Second World War*. New York: Doubleday, 1962.
Guyton, Boone. *Whistling Death*. Atglen, PA. Schiffer, 1994.
Johnson, Frederick A. and Watanabe, Rikyu. *F4U Corsair*. New York: Crown, 1983.
Maloney, Edward T. and Feist, Uwe. *Chance Vought Corsair*. Fallbrook, CA: Aero.
Musciano, Walter A. *Corsair Aces The Bent-Wing Bird Over The Pacific*. New York: Arco.
Styling, Mark. *Corsair Aces of World War Two*. London: Osprey, 1995.
Veronico, Nicholas A. and Campbell, John M. and Donna. *F4U Corsair*. Osceola, WI: 1994.
Gurney, Gene and Friedlander, Jr., Mark P. *Five Down and Glory*. G. P. Putnam's Sons. New York. 1958.

Videos
Fighting Seventeen, The Jolly Rogers. Kenwood Productions, Minneapolis, 1990.
VF-17 Remembered. RDR Video Productions. Northbrook, Illinois, 1984.
World War Two Pacific Heroes. U.S. News Video, 1991.
VF-17 at Oshkosh 1994. RAD Productions, Beverly Hills, 1995.
Dare County Regional Airport "Then and Now." Cable AD. Kill Devil Hills, N.C.